Searching for the Beaumont children

Australia's Most Famous Unsolved Mystery

Alan J Whiticker

WILEY

John Wiley & Sons Australia, Ltd

First published in 2006 by
John Wiley & Sons Australia, Ltd
42 McDougall Street, Milton Qld 4064

Offices also in Sydney and Melbourne

Typeset in 12/16 pt Adobe Garamond Light

© Alan J. Whiticker 2006

National Library of Australia
Cataloguing-in-Publication data

Whiticker, Alan.
Searching for the Beaumont children: Australia's most famous
unsolved mystery.

Includes index.
ISBN-13   978 1 740 31106 9.
ISBN-10   1 740 31106 X.

1. Beaumont, Jane. 2. Beaumont, Arnna. 3. Beaumont,
Grant. 4. Cold cases (Criminal investigation) — South
Australia — Glenelg. 5. Missing children — South
Australia — Glenelg — Case studies. 6. Abduction —
South Australia — Glenelg — Case studies. I. Title.

364.1540994231

Photographs on cover: (beach) Getty Images/The Image
Bank/Sean Justice; (boy sitting) © Banana Stock;
(standing girl) © Corbis Images

Cover design: Wiley Art Studio

10 9 8 7 6 5 4 3 2 1

Dedication

Non nobis solum

Contents

About the author

Alan J. Whiticker was born in 1958 in Penrith, New South Wales, and educated at St Dominic's College. Since attaining his Bachelor of Education in 1986, he has pursued the dual roles of teacher and freelance writer, emerging as a prolific writer of sporting history, biography and true crime. His books include *Jimmy Barnes: Say it Loud*; *Wanda: The Untold Story of the Wanda Beach Murders*; *A History of Rugby League Clubs*; his first children's book, *The Battle for Troy: An Adaptation of Homer's Iliad*; *12 Crimes That Shocked Australia*; and *Speeches That Shaped the Modern World*.

Searching for the Beaumont Children is Alan's seventeenth book.

In 1997 Alan completed his Master of Education Degree and is currently Assistant Principal of a western Sydney Catholic primary school. He lives in Penrith with his wife, Karen, and children Timothy and Melanie.

Acknowledgements

There are many people whom I would like to thank for their assistance in the writing and publishing of this book: Ronnie Gramazio at John Wiley & Sons for his faith and enthusiasm for this project; Cynthia Wardle for her painstaking work in editing this book; Stuart Mullins for his friendship, support and research work; Mike Smith, Vincent Ross and Sharon Polkinghorne at News Limited; Pat Plummer and members of the Swaine family in Adelaide; Ernie and Shirley Keech at Goolwa; Douglas Steele, Doug Easom and Leigh Bottrell; Russell Oxford in New South Wales and Peter Alexander of the Police Association of South Australia; Brian Swan and Peter Woite of the South Australia Police; Graham Archer at Channel Seven; the staff of the Brighton Historical Society; and lastly my wife, Karen, and my family for their patience and support.

Source acknowledgements

The author and publisher would like to thank the following copyright holders, organisations and individuals for their assistance and for permission to reproduce copyright material in this book.

Images

Title page: • © Corbis Images (girl with ring) • © Banana Stock (sitting boy)

Text

• Quotations from members of the Swaine family in chapter 7 reproduced by permission of Alexandra Kelly, Margaret Klecko, Patricia Plummer and Elizabeth Swaine • Extracts in chapter 7 from Stanley Swaine's diaries reproduced by permission of the Swaine family • Extracts in chapter 10 from 'The Beaumonts Keep Their Optimism', © News Limited, *The Advertiser*, 26 January 1967, by Ian Mackay • Article page 78 © News Limited, *The Sunday Mail*, Adelaide, 29 January 1996 • Extracts in chapter 3 from 'The Beaumont Disclosures' © News Limited, 21–22 February 1968, by Ken Anderson, Doug Easom and Brian Francis.

Every effort has been made to trace the ownership of copyright material. Information that will enable the publisher to rectify any error or omission in subsequent reprints will be welcome. In such cases, please contact the Permissions Section at John Wiley & Sons, who will arrange for the payment of the usual fee.

Introduction

On Wednesday 26 January 1966, Australia Day, the three children of Jim and Nancy Beaumont left their home in the Adelaide suburb of Somerton Park to spend the morning at the beach. The children went to Glenelg beach alone and were seen playing on a grass reserve with a tall, thin man. By the end of the day, the worst fears of every parent were realised when the three siblings — Jane, aged nine, her sister Arnna, aged seven, and their four-year-old brother, Grant — did not return home.

The Beaumont Case remains Australia's most famous unsolved mystery. More than any other crime, the disappearance of the three Beaumont children has become one of the defining events in the history of this country. It was the day Australia lost its national innocence. But because the police investigation revealed few known facts, and failed to identify a known suspect, the fate of the three children has also become an integral part of Australia's urban mythology.

Adelaide has been described over the years as a sleepy town, but for those of us of the Beaumont generation, no place was sleepy if you had imagination. There was only black and white television back then, and the channels only started transmission in time for the midday movie, but you didn't watch a lot of television anyway. There were the *Channel Niners* with Ian Fairweather, *Concentration*, *Jungle Jim* and a host of imported American shows, but when you did start to watch something your parents would tell you to turn the darn thing off and get outside in the fresh air.

That's where you spent the daylight hours — outside.

For people who grew up in Adelaide in the 1960s, there are so many things that remind them of childhood: Woodroofe and Mirinda lemonade, Balfours cakes, Amscol ice-cream, and liquorice blocks. South Australians pronounced pasties as *pahstees*; ate Fritz, not Devon; and green frog cakes were already a state treasure. Peter Stuyvesant may have been the passport to international smoking pleasure but your dad preferred Craven A, Capstan or Marlboro. Mum used Persil or Rinso washing detergent, and although Menthoids was spelled M.E.N.T.H.O.I.D.S., Bex was better.

In the 1960s, soccer was still struggling to make inroads into a children's world dominated by Aussie Rules, netball, cricket and surf lifesaving. Netball was the dominant girls' sport in winter with literally thousands of young girls wearing pleated skirts pounding the bitumen in the suburban grounds of Adelaide. Most children spent Saturday afternoons watching their Aussie Rules heroes playing for Glenelg, Port Adelaide and Sturt, which were the top clubs at the time. Glenelg had some great players back then: Neil Kerley, Fred and Wayne Phillis, Graham Cornes, Peter Marker, Harry Kernahan and Ken Eustice. John Tilbrook from Sturt could kick a ball further than anyone could remember, while Port Adelaide's Eric Freeman was gifted in both Aussie Rules and cricket. Victoria always beat South Australia in the interstate matches but South Australians still lived in hope.

On Saturdays, a whole horde of friends would pile into a Zephyr or Hillman Hunter (these were the days before seatbelts) and fly up to Glenelg Oval to watch the Tigers. Invariably, children saw little of the match, but spent their time collecting Coke and Fanta bottles for the refund, sliding down the grass slopes of the spectator hills on large pieces of cardboard, or playing their own game of footy behind the grandstands.

Cricket was the dominant school sport for boys in summer. Every Saturday morning schools from Darlington, Ascot Park, Dover Gardens, Seaview Downs, Brighton and Glenelg would fill the local parks and the air would be thick with the smell of Kiwi shoe-white. Everyone had their cricket heroes too: in South Australia it was hard to go past Ian and Greg Chappell, the grandsons of the great Test captain of the 1930s, Victor Richardson. But just as importantly, there were the backyard and driveway 'test matches' where the rules never changed: over the fence was 'six and out' (and you had to go and get the ball); you couldn't bowl after having a bat; and you had to catch the ball with only one hand if it rebounded off the house.

Life was worry free and children felt safe in Adelaide during the early 1960s. People were friendlier and life less rushed. You knew everyone in your street and everyone in the neighbourhood knew you. Kids would walk to school and home again, and there was no dropping children off at the school gates by parents in four-wheel drives. You bought your lunch from the canteen maybe once or twice a term, which was a luxury, and you didn't go on cruises or interstate holidays or stay in luxury resorts during the school holidays. Children were left to their own devices and made their own fun.

During school holidays, most children were out the door by 8 am, with warnings to be home by dark 'or else'. There were no mobile phones, of course, and in many cases no home telephones either. Basically children did what they wanted and visited places for the entire day. Walking or riding bikes to the beaches of Seacliff, Brighton and Glenelg were as normal as jumping off the jetty piers.

Adventuring into the Adelaide Hills behind the Golden Mile of the South Road service stations was an adventure, and there was never a thought that something bad could happen to you. What seemed perfectly natural and acceptable then must now seem dangerous and irresponsible. Back in the 1960s, there were no such concepts as Stranger Danger or Neighbourhood Watch. Certainly your parents warned you to beware of 'dirty old men', but they were more objects of ridicule than bogymen to be feared. The thought that athletic, sun-tanned 'surfies' or women could harm you never entered your mind.

Christmas in Adelaide was a magical time for children. Long lines of children waited patiently outside Santa's Cave at John Martin's department store in the heart of the city while parents secretly shopped for Meccano sets, Barbie dolls, toy cars and train sets. On long summer evenings, families would follow the different coloured lights strung along the beachfront at Glenelg, which was host to sideshows, a Salvation Army band in the roundhouse and a merry-go-round. The smell of pine trees and salt water filled the night air.

Many people have fond memories of Glenelg; it was bigger and busier than the other beaches, with lawns that stretched along the beachfront and sprinklers that children could run under when the sand became too hot. But now, the beach is remembered for other reasons.

On Australia Day 1966, thousands of Adelaide residents and visiting interstate tourists went to Glenelg beach on a hot summer's day. Three innocent children, who supposedly spoke to and played with a stranger at Colley Reserve, did not come home. What happened next, no-one knows.

Adelaide, the sleepy town, had taken a little part of the Australian dream and turned it into a nightmare.

For baby boomers growing up in the late 1960s, and for those who came after, the subsequent police investigation into the abduction and probable murder of the Beaumont children has been both repelling and haunting. On the fortieth anniversary of the children's disappearance, many questions still remain: What happened to Jane, Arnna and Grant Beaumont at Glenelg on the day they disappeared? Who was the man last seen with the children that day? Why has there never been a public inquest into the children's disappearance? What links are there to the abduction of two young girls from Adelaide Oval in 1973 and the infamous Family Murders in the early 1980s? Are the Beaumont children still alive, as many still believe, or buried in some unmarked spot?

A book has never before been published solely on the Beaumont Case — on the actual events of the day the children disappeared, the subsequent police investigation, the media coverage, the hoaxes, or the charlatans and religious fanatics who preyed on Jim and Nancy Beaumont. If the Beaumont children were alive today, Jane would be 49, Arnna would be 47, and Grant would be 44. The story of the Beaumont children deserves to be told.

The mere mention of the words 'the Beaumont children' brings so many memories of that time flooding back. For those who have come after, and know only the half-truths and the urban myths, there is a yearning to know more — to understand the unimaginable and try to answer questions that may never be answered.

For over four decades now, we have all been searching for the Beaumont children.

Alan J. Whiticker and Stuart Mullins*, January 2006

*Stuart Mullins was born in South Australia and acted as researcher for this book.

1
The City

The Australian city of Adelaide, geographically separated from the eastern state capitals of Brisbane, Sydney and Melbourne, has long been described as the City of Churches. To the casual observer there are more restaurants and pubs in Adelaide today than churches, although church spires still complement the cityscape. The City of Churches tag is an obvious reflection of Adelaide's colonial past, but therein lies the paradox.

Adelaide is not quite what it seems.

In the last forty years, 'quaint' Adelaide — a city planned and conceived by a convict but founded without convict labour — has also been the setting for some of the country's most bizarre and shocking crimes. No more puzzling crime has been committed in Australian criminal history than the abduction and probable murder of the three Beaumont children on Australia Day, 26 January 1966. The disappearance from Glenelg beach of nine-year-old Jane Beaumont, seven-year-old Arnna and their brother, Grant, aged just four, has haunted generations of Adelaideans and permanently stained the nation's collective memory.

Adelaide is situated on a narrow coastal plain called the Fleurieu Peninsula, and lies between the hills of the Mount Lofty Ranges and the Gulf St Vincent in South Australia. The city was named after Queen Adelaide, the consort of King William IV, who was the reigning King of Great Britain when the area was colonised in 1836. Divided by the Torrens River, Adelaide CBD is criss-crossed by wide streets, with King William Street and North Terrace forming the main inter-section points. In 1960 the historian Geoffrey Dutton described North Terrace as 'one of the most beautiful streets in the world'[1] but despaired that the street was being corrupted by commercialism. Today, it is closer to Dutton's original description and provides a stunning view of such city land-marks as the Adelaide Convention Centre, the Casino, Parliament House, Government House, the National War Memorial, the State and Mortlock Libraries, the South Australian Museum of Natural History and the campuses of the University of Adelaide and the University of South Australia.

The city has a Mediterranean climate, which generally means that it experiences a mild, wet winter and a hot, dry summer. The mean January maximum at the height of the Australian summer is 28.8°C, although the city's Kent Town weather station once recorded an extraordinary top of 44.3°C in 1977. The climate was well suited to the foundation of a world-class wine industry in the Barossa Valley, 70 kilometres north of Adelaide. German immigrants, many of them escaping religious persecution in Europe during the late 1800s (another reason for the early predominance of churches in Adelaide), brought grapevine cuttings with them to establish their vineyards. Increased migrant intake after World War II saw an influx of Italian, Greek, Dutch and Polish people, as well as Asian migrants in the late 1970s, which added to the cosmopolitan range of Adelaide's restaurants and eateries.

It has been said that Adelaide has the amenity of a major city but the feel of a country town.[2] The city's parklands and gardens form a huge expanse of open greenery that provides a buffer between the CBD and the suburbs. Within the parklands are the Adelaide Botanic Gardens and the Adelaide Zoo as well as many of the city's major sporting venues such as Adelaide Oval, Memorial Drive Tennis Centre and Victoria Park Racecourse. One of Adelaide's main attractions is Glenelg beach to the southwest, which is accessible by tram and has become a unique seaside resort just kilometres from the city centre.

It is important to remember that none of this developed haphazardly or by chance — it happened for historical reasons. And Adelaide, the City of Churches, has a unique colonial history.

In 1967 Adelaide historian Max Lamshed wrote: 'When the Reverend C. B. Howard, South Australia's first colonial chaplain, arrived in Adelaide at the end of 1836, he was a preacher with a flock but no church.'[3] The first 'church' in Adelaide was actually a shelter made from a ship's sail obtained by the Colonial Treasurer, Osmond Gilles, who had it dragged from Holdfast Bay in a handcart. A wooden church, brought out from England in sections, was built to accommodate 350 worshippers but was patently inadequate to service the colony's spiritual needs.

On 26 January 1838 — the fiftieth anniversary of the arrival of the First Fleet in Botany Bay (a day now marked nationally as Australia Day) — a foundation stone was laid for Adelaide's first official church. Named Holy Trinity in honour of Reverend Howard's alma mater, the church was built on a town acre donated by Pascoe St Leger Grenfell at the corner of Morphett Street and North Terrace. 'Old Trinity' Church, the oldest in the diocese of Adelaide, was altered and enlarged over the years but was superseded by St Peter's Cathedral in the latter half of the nineteenth century.

When English architect William Butterfield demanded that St Peter's Cathedral be built of brick instead of colonial stone he effectively tendered his own resignation (brick being too expensive and the Bishop wanting local stone). Besides, Butterfield's argument was moot because there were no suitable bricks in the fledgling colony. Bishop Augustus Short duly replaced him with E. J. Woods, who opted for Tea Tree Gully stone for the facings, Murray Bridge freestone for the dressings, and New Zealand Mount Summers stone for the caps and columns of the principal openings. The Bishop was keen on the project from the start, having been enthroned at the propriety chapel of the Holy Trinity Church — a rather humble place for a bishop — and he sought donations for his grand cathedral from far and wide. Queen Adelaide and British Prime Minister William Gladstone were contributors. A triangular block of land was bought for £1042, and the foundation stone of the choir, transepts and one bay of the nave was consecrated, at a cost of £13 360, on St Peter's Day 1869. Although its twin spires were not completed until the turn of the century, the Cathedral fulfilled Bishop Short's goal of becoming 'a noble vista to King William Street'.[4]

When Chalmers Church was built at the corner of Pulteney Street and North Terrace in 1851 (the name 'Scots Church' would not be used for another eighty years), the number of churches supposedly exceeded public hotels in Adelaide. (Traditionally, it was believed that for every church that was built, an inn or public house was also established to serve the needs of the less pious.[5]) Reverend John Gardner, who was the driving force behind the new church, had been sent to Australia by the Free Church of Scotland after the colonial Scots had asked for a pastor. The building of the church was commenced within twelve months of his arrival and completed at a cost of £2572 (although the 120-foot spire was not completed until 1858). Reverend Gardner ministered there for twenty years, and the early congregation contained many of the prominent families in Adelaide.

The title 'City of Churches' was well and truly adopted by the time the foundation stone was laid for St Francis Xavier Cathedral in 1856. The following year there were some 300 churches or chapels in Adelaide so that 'just a little less than half the population of the province could be seated in church at any one time'.[6] However, not everyone has been comfortable with the city's nickname.

In June 1999 Adelaide's Lord Mayor, Dr Jane Lomax-Smith, called for the City of Churches tag to be dropped because it put off tourists who 'must think that the city is a dull place'.[7] Dr Lomax-Smith viewed Adelaide as the cultural capital of Australia and felt it should be promoted as such.

'I don't know what the City of Churches means to an outsider but to me it means we're a quiet, staid and conservative city,' she told *The Daily Telegraph*. 'Clearly we need a marketing image that's not staid and conservative.' She pointed out that, approaching the new millennium, there were seventy-one taverns in Adelaide compared to just thirty-three churches.

While the move to change Adelaide's traditional nickname drew the considerable ire of various church communities, the modern city views itself as a multicultural community, with more than 100 cultural groups maintaining their own identity in a population that now numbers over a million. Adelaide could just as easily be referred to as the City of Festivals. More than 500 festivals are planned throughout the state during each year, including the Festival of the Arts (a biannual festival acknowledged as one of the three main cultural festivals in the world behind Edinburgh and Avignon), its sister festival the Adelaide Fringe, the Festival of Ideas, the Adelaide Film Festival, and the Barossa Music Festival.

Adelaide City Council was founded in 1840 to administer a city that has grown to be the fifth largest Australian capital behind Sydney, Melbourne, Brisbane and Perth. However, the city's rapid growth has not come without its social problems. In April 2001 Adelaide City Council voted to install a blanket ban on public alcohol consumption on every street and square in the CBD. ABC reporter Anne Barker commented: 'Walk down the main street in Adelaide, day or night, and chances are you'll be accosted, often by a drunk or drug addict — many homeless and usually asking for money or cigarettes. Drunkenness, begging and general harassment in any city are hardly new. But now Adelaide's civic leaders have had enough.'[8] Premier John Olsen demanded that if the city council did not act, then the state government would overrule it and enforce the dry zone itself. Adelaide could just as easily be called the City of Pubs.

Scratch below Adelaide's façade of respectability, as several prominent authors have attempted to do, and Adelaide reveals a dark underbelly. When the Indian-born English writer Salmon Rushdie visited the Adelaide Arts Festival in 1984, he caught a sense of this small town/big secrets paradox. On his return to London, Rushdie wrote: 'Adelaide is a perfect setting for a Stephen King novel or horror film. You know why those films and books are always set in sleepy conservative towns. Because sleepy conservative towns are where those things happen.'[9]

While sophisticated Adelaide citizens might take umbrage at Rushdie's generalisation of the city as being 'a sleepy, conservative town', there is no denying Adelaide's history of macabre and predatory serial crimes that one too readily associates with Europe and the Americas.

Consider the following cases.

THE SNOWTOWN MURDERS, 1999

In May 1999 the decomposing remains of eight people were found in six barrels inside the disused State Bank building in the Adelaide Hills township of Snowtown. Police discovered that 33-year-old John Bunting and his accomplices, Robert Wagner and John Vlassakis, had preyed on the victims, who were known to them via a network of family and casual relationships, in order to claim their unemployment benefits. The bodies of another four victims were found buried in Bunting's former backyard, bringing the number of victims to twelve — the worst case of serial murder in Australian history. Several of the victims were homosexuals and there were elements of ritualistic sexual sadism in the manner in which some bodies were dismembered.

The Snowtown murderers openly bragged and joked about the murders but used fear to silence others within their inner circle of 'friends'. Jodie Elliott, besotted with Bunting, but said to be of low intelligence, assumed some of the victims' identities in order to steal their Centrelink benefits. Bunting murdered Elliott's sister and her nephew, and was jailed for life for his involvement in eight of the killings. Bunting's wife, Veronica Tripp, also knew of one of the murders but was told not to say anything about it. (Tripp, who suffered from an intellectual disability, knew enough to be scared for her life.) Barry Lee, a convicted paedophile, took part in the disposal of one of the bodies before he too became a victim.

John Vlassakis was found guilty of four murders, including that of his stepbrother, David Johnson, and was jailed for twenty-six years. Robert Wagner, who had the physical strength to kill and dismember the victims, was found guilty of seven murders, while a fourth man, Mark Haydon, was convicted in 2005 of assisting Bunting and Wagner in the disposal of five bodies, including that of his wife Elizabeth.

The Family Murders, 1979–1983

During the late 1970s and early 1980s, a series of shocking crimes occurred that would shed light on the seedy side of the city: the surgically mutilated or dismembered bodies of five young men were found in various parts of Adelaide. In June 1983, fifteen-year-old Richard Kelvin was abducted from a bus stop near his North Adelaide home. On 23 July the boy's body was found in the Adelaide foothills. A post-mortem revealed that although he had been missing for seven weeks he had been kept alive for at least five weeks and his body contained traces of four different drugs.

The Adelaide media dubbed the killings the Family Murders when detectives revealed the existence, stretching back to the 1960s, of a small subculture of paedophilia and sexual sadism among the city's homosexual network. The network, it was alleged, protected its members in the same way that a family does. One of the names in that network was Bevan Spencer von Einem, who had once rescued a man from drowning in the Torrens during a rash of gay bashings in the city during the early 1970s. A tall, grey-haired 37-year-old, von Einem was a known paedophile but denied any knowledge of the five unsolved murders. When police searched von Einem's house, however, they discovered three of the drugs that had also been found in Kelvin's body, and they matched von Einem's hair to strands found inside the boy's clothing.

Von Einem was sentenced to life imprisonment for the murder of Richard Kelvin but, when he stood trial for the murders of the other victims, sensational allegations were made against him by associates at his committal hearing. One of the prosecution witnesses, 'Mr B' (whose identity was withheld for his own protection) told a shocked courtroom that von Einem had allegedly abducted the Beaumont children from Glenelg beach in 1966 and had performed some 'brilliant surgery on them'.[10] Mr B claimed that their bodies were buried in Moana or Myponga, south of Adelaide. Although no names were mentioned, von Einem also allegedly told Mr B that he had taken two young girls from Adelaide Oval — a reference to Joanne Ratcliffe and Kirste Gordon.

THE TRURO MURDERS, 1976–1977

On Anzac Day 1978, a man searching for wild mushrooms near Truro, eighty kilometres north-west of Adelaide on the outskirts of the Barossa Valley, found the body of a young woman, identified as that of missing eighteen-year-old Veronica Knight. It was not until a year later that the remains of Sylvia Pittman, aged sixteen, were found nearby. Investigating police realised that these crimes were undoubtedly linked to the 1977 disappearances of Tania Kenny, fifteen, on 2 January; Juliet Mykyta, sixteen, on 21 January; Vicki Howell, twenty-six, on 7 February; Connie Iordanides, sixteen, on 9 February; and Deborah Lamb, twenty, on 12 February.

Police received information that a man named James William Miller had incriminated himself and another man, Christopher Robin Worrell, in the murders of the women. Worrell, a 27-year-old convicted rapist and Miller's homosexual partner, had been released from Adelaide's Yatala prison in October 1976, only weeks before Veronica Knight went missing. After Worrell's death in a car accident on 19 February 1977 (a week after Lamb's disappearance), Miller confided to Worrell's girlfriend that the pair had shared a dark secret.

On 26 April 1979, searchers in a Truro paddock found two skeletons, later identified as those of Howell and Iordanides. Miller confessed to his involvement and took police back to Truro, where he identified the resting place of the remains of Juliet Mykyta. He directed police to Port Gawler beach, where Lamb's remains were found, and to Wingfield, an isolated area on the outskirts of Adelaide, where police found Kenny's remains. Although other women had disappeared during this period (and several bodies were found) the deaths of seven young women were attributed to Miller and Worrell. On 12 March 1980, after a six-week trial, Miller was found guilty of the murders of six of the seven Truro victims, but was acquitted of Knight's murder. He was sentenced to life imprisonment.

THE ADELAIDE OVAL CASE, 1973

On 25 August 1973, two young girls were abducted from the Adelaide Oval during a South Australian Football League match. Eleven-year-old Joanne Ratcliffe was at the match with her parents and was sitting next to four-year-old Kirste Gordon, who was watching the match with her grandmother. Although the older girl did not know the toddler, the younger girl's grandmother asked Joanne to take Kirste with her when she went to the toilet. The pair returned after several minutes but, about thirty minutes later, when Kirste again wanted to go to the toilet, Joanne volunteered once more to take her. This time they did not come back.

After fifteen minutes, Mr and Mrs Ratcliffe went looking for the girls and were quickly joined by the other adults in the group when no trace could be found. Ken Wohling, the assistant curator at the Oval, saw the girls leaving the ground in the company of a man. In the hours immediately after the girls went missing, four different sightings of the man and the two young girls were recorded in Adelaide. The description of the man, who was wearing a wide-brimmed hat, and the circumstances of the abduction were uncannily similar to the Beaumont Case seven years earlier: two young girls, who could easily have been mistaken for sisters, were taken from a public place and vanished without a trace despite an extensive police investigation.

THE BARTHOLOMEW FAMILY MURDERS, 1971

In the early hours of 6 September 1971, Clifford Cecil Bartholomew returned to his family farmhouse at Hope Forest, south of Adelaide, and murdered his wife, Heather; their seven children; Winnis Keane, his wife's sister-in-law, who was staying with her at the time; and

Keane's two-year-old son. The estranged forty-year-old
husband and father shot the ten family members with a
.22-calibre rifle he had bought for his eldest son, Neville.
The catalyst for this act of madness was a mixture of
financial and marriage problems that the Bartholomews
had faced during that wet South Australian winter. Cliff
Bartholomew had been laid off from work and his wife
had formed a relationship with a young boarder they had
taken in to help them support their seven children. The
hapless father left the family home to sort things out,
and clumsy attempts at a reconciliation had failed.
When he learned that his wife was intending to move to
Adelaide with the children and live with the boarder,
Cliff Bartholomew snapped.

Bartholomew broke into the farmhouse and attacked
his wife with a rubber mallet as she lay in bed. When
Heather Bartholomew woke screaming and called for her
sister, Winnis responded but was chased outside by
Bartholomew, who brandished the rifle and shot her. He
then returned to the bedroom and shot his wife dead.
Woken by the noise, nineteen-year-old Neville
Bartholomew was killed trying to disarm his father.
Bartholomew then went from room to room killing his
other children — Christine, aged seventeen; Sharon,
fifteen; Helen, thirteen; Gregory, eleven; Roger, seven; and
Sandra-Jane, four; He then remembered that his sister's
two-year-old son, Daniel, was also asleep in the house. The
little boy was the last to die. Bartholomew then covered
the bodies with blankets and rang his stepmother and told

her what he had done. When police arrived they expected a stand-off but found him drunk in the kitchen.

At his trial Cliff Bartholomew pleaded guilty to ten counts of murder, which was then the worst single case of mass murder in Australian criminal history. 'My mind was in a state of madness,' Bartholomew stated. He had returned home that night to murder his wife but couldn't stop himself when the killing started.[11] Justice Roma Mitchell had no alternative but to sentence him to death — later commuted to life imprisonment. Incredibly, Bartholomew was paroled on 10 December 1979, having failed to serve even one year for each of the murders he had committed. His release from prison caused a public outcry in South Australia.

THE BEAUMONT CHILDREN, 1966

On Wednesday 26 January 1966, the three children of G. A. (Jim) and Nancy Beaumont from the Adelaide suburb of Somerton Park asked their mother if they could go to nearby Glenelg beach for a swim. Jim Beaumont, who was a linen goods salesman, was in Snowtown to see customers that day but the temperature was expected to top 100 degrees on the old Fahrenheit scale and the children were persistent. Nancy Beaumont finally relented and allowed Jane, Arnna and Grant to make the short bus trip to Glenelg. She gave her children eight shillings and sixpence (85 cents) to buy some pasties for lunch and told them to be home on the midday bus.

The children left their Harding Street home at 10 am and caught a bus from the corner of Diagonal Road and Peterson Street, just 100 metres away. When the children did not arrive home on the midday bus, Nancy Beaumont was not immediately concerned — she presumed they would be on the two o'clock bus. When the next bus came and went, she felt she should go and look for them — perhaps they had missed the bus and were walking home. But the children could be walking several different ways back home, so she decided to stay and wait for the next bus.

Jim Beaumont arrived home from work at 3.30 that afternoon and, when told that the children had not returned, he immediately went to Glenelg beach and frantically searched for them. The children were reported missing later that evening and a full-scale investigation began. The lives of those involved in the case were changed forever — the shattered parents; the police who earnestly investigated the case; and the thousands of people who volunteered to look for the missing children. In the forty years that have passed, the case has remained an open, ongoing investigation and, in many ways, has become one of the defining crimes in the history of this country.

In August 2002 Britain's Channel 4 was forced to send a letter of apology to the Australian High Commission in London after it erroneously described Adelaide as 'the murder capital of the world'[12] in a documentary about the dangers of travelling in Australia. While the yearly murder rate in

Adelaide (1.9 per 100 000 people), or any other Australian city for that matter, was well below that of other cities (Washington being the actual murder capital of the world with a yearly rate of 50.8 murders per 10 000 people), that negative perception of the South Australian capital does exist. Even in Australia, there is real feeling that the people of Adelaide prefer to avert their gaze from the Snowtown murderers who tortured, dismembered and disposed of twelve of their fellow citizens in vats of acid in the 1990s; from the five young men who were mutilated in the 1980s in what became known as the Family Murders; from the seven teenage girls who were taken from the streets, strangled and buried outside Adelaide in the late 1970s; from the two little girls who were kidnapped at a crowded Adelaide Oval in 1973; from a father who murdered ten family members in one night of madness in 1971.

Are the people of Adelaide really indifferent also to the fate of the three Beaumont children, abducted from a public beach in the 1960s?

Former Adelaide-based author Susan Mitchell attempted to probe the psyche of the city in her book *All Things Bright and Beautiful: Murder in the City of Light.*[13] Mitchell wanted to discover why Adelaide boasts the best food and wine, promotes radical views on politics and the arts, and produces any number of imminent Australians (filmmaker Scott Hicks, actor Anthony LaPaglia, musician Jimmy Barnes, astronaut Andy Thomas, the cricketing Chappell brothers, tennis star Lleyton Hewitt and Nobel-Prize-winning scientists Howard Florey, William Bragg and W. L. Bragg, among others) and yet is the focus of so much social poverty, moral depravity and murder. 'People close off,' she told *The Sun Herald* in 2004. 'Adelaide sees itself as a multilayered village. It is a very different city to the other cities in that no-one arrived with chains around their ankles. Adelaide has always seen itself as a paradise. It still does.'[14]

How then did 'a snake' slither into the paradise?

One has to delve back into the very foundation of the city in 1836 to understand why many Adelaide residents might think this way. Unlike Sydney, Brisbane, Melbourne or Hobart, Adelaide was not established as a convict settlement. Instead, it was a planned colony from the beginning — a bold social experiment; the first of its kind — founded on Edward Gibbon Wakefield's principles of organised immigration and land sales. In 1829 Wakefield was serving a three-year jail sentence in Newgate, London (for the abduction of a young girl for amoral purposes) when he hit upon the idea of covering the cost of establishing a new colony with advance land sales.

Wakefield's scheme was based on sound ideas at the time, which were brought together in one plan known as 'systematic colonization'.[15] The foundation of Adelaide was proposed on the following guidelines: advanced land sales would be at a price that was neither too low nor too high; the settlers were to be drawn from all social classes, businesses, skilled professions and agriculture; the population was to be made up of 'capitalists' and 'labourers' in order to keep demand for workers (and wages) down, and should comprise an equal mix of men and women to discourage prostitution (it didn't); and, most importantly, the colony would be self-governing once the local Aboriginal community had been subdued and the area surveyed.

Britain was wary of French and Dutch interest in *Terra Australis* (referred to as New South Wales in the east and New Holland in the west) and so had rushed the 'free' settlement of Western Australia in 1829. The colony in Perth had been badly planned from the start, and the British Parliament wanted to ensure that the same mistakes were not made in South Australia. In 1830 the National Colonization Society was founded and the 'South Australian Land Company' was formed to oversee the development of a new colony. The *South Australian Foundation Act* was passed by the British Parliament in 1834 and a Board of Commissioners for Land Sales and Emigration quickly established.

Lieutenant Colonel William Light (1786–1839), the son of Captain Francis Light (founder of Penang in Malaysia) was chosen as the first Surveyor-General of the proposed city. Light was given the final responsibility of surveying and selecting the site of the new colony, based upon existing maps of the time and his own exploration of the area before the arrival of the first settlers in December 1836. A veteran of the Peninsular War (1808–1814) and a former officer in the Egyptian Navy, Light brought a military-style resolve to the task and ignored political interference in his choice of the best site for the colony.

South Australia had been 'discovered' as a suitable area for settlement after the explorer Charles Sturt travelled to the mouth of the Murray–Darling river system at Lake Alexandrina in 1830. The problem was that the ocean entrance into the sand-filled Lake Alexandrina, named Encounter Bay, was not accessible by ship. Sturt made it clear that the poor country around Nepean Bay and Port Lincoln, to the immediate north-west of Lake Alexandrina, was unsuitable for settlement, but news of his discovery reached England long before his official account could be published in 1833, by which time the decision had been made to colonise the area. Light found this out for himself in late 1836 when he came to choose the site of the proposed city. He ventured sixty miles north of Cape Jervis (opposite Kangaroo Island) on the eastern side of the Gulf St Vincent to find a safe harbour. The present day site of Port Adelaide was originally named Jones Harbour on old maps. The waterway that emptied into the harbour was labelled Sixteen Mile Creek, but was found to be a somewhat more significant waterway past the inlet and was renamed the Torrens River.

When the first settlers arrived in South Australia on 8 November 1836, Light had still not decided upon an actual settlement site, having only arrived in October himself. Light spent day after day surveying the terrain, visualising where the buildings, amenities, roads and parklands would be built. He was sure that the best site for the city was one and a half miles north of the harbour on a rising plain close to the water supply provided by the Torrens, but there was conflict over who had the final authority to choose the site (Light's papers confirmed that he, in fact, did). With emotions running high, the ceremony proclaiming the establishment of the new colony was held on 28 December 1836, on the hot plain near the beach, which the colony's new Governor, Captain John Hindmarsh, named Glenelg after his major sponsor Lord Glenelg. South Australians celebrate a public holiday, Proclamation Day, on this day each year.

The following day, Light revealed the site of the new city but was immediately pressured by Hindmarsh to move it downstream, closer to the harbour. A day later Light decided that his original decision was best and told Hindmarsh that the longer distance from the harbour was more than compensated for by its superior position. On the last day of 1836, the present-day site of Adelaide was officially adopted. John Morphett, the colony's land agent, wrote of the 'forlorn hope, as it might be termed, of a large, wealthy and intelligent community of Englishmen, who had fixed upon this country as the scene of an experiment in colonization'.[16]

Light died of tuberculosis just three years later, heavily in debt. Adelaide's civic leaders built a monument to him made out of local sandstone but unlike his city, the thirteen-metre gothic statue crumbled away within a few years (to be replaced by a bronze statue by Birnie Rhind in 1906). The fact that Light's city required little or no modification as it grew led to the locals' referring to the South Australian capital as the City of Light, highlighting the brilliance of its planning. Geoffrey Dutton noted: 'Unfortunately the various Governments of South Australia have not had the sense to realize that the benefits of Light's planning could be extended. While zealously prating about their "garden state" they have allowed suburbs to sprawl for mile after mile without a break, and the green belt that surrounds the central city has remained an obvious hint that was never taken.'[17]

Dutton saw something in the changing face of Adelaide in the late 1950s that speaks volumes today. Adelaideans have always had a very proper view of who they are — 'respectable' being the word that author Susan Mitchell uses[18] — and because the original settlers did not rely on convict labour to build their city there is no sense of inherited guilt. Adelaide citizens have always differentiated themselves from their eastern cousins because of this. It continues to infuse the city with high moral expectations that are often difficult to meet.

And if Adelaide does have the feel of a large country town, it may be because its inhabitants see themselves as one big family. There is the uncanny sense that the 'six degrees of separation' under which the rest of the world operates do not apply to Adelaide; it is almost as if everybody knows everybody else. And when something horrific happens in Adelaide, as has been the case every decade during the past forty years, the city subconsciously unites to keep its secrets hidden from the rest of the country. 'To spill the family secrets is tantamount to treason, especially in a city-state that considered itself a utopia,' Mitchell hypothesises.[19]

But Adelaide is more like Milton's *Paradise Lost* than Thomas Moore's *Utopia*. The South Australian capital has become 'a city of shadows and lost dreams' says Mitchell. 'In the shadows of those who still had employment, in streets where all the houses looked the same, spread the human debris, hidden in the ghettos of the lost, the forgotten, the disturbed and the deviant,' she explains. 'Underclasses can grow up under governments' noses. Even in paradise, you can't pretend they are not there.'[20] In suburban Adelaide in particular, the gap between the haves and have-nots has become a chasm. The Snowtown murderers, for example, came from the depressed western-suburb centres of Elizabeth and Salisbury, and they killed their associates not for millions or even thousands of dollars but because they hated homosexuals and wanted to steal their victims' dole cheques.

There are obviously other forces conspiring against Adelaide — more primaeval and post-modern than supernatural — but more powerful than even the Dutch clairvoyant Gerard Croiset (called in to 'solve' the Beaumont Case) could have foreseen. Author and academic Peter Pierce explored these themes when he wrote that Australia is a country where 'the innocent young are most especially at jeopardy'.[21] Pierce pursues these themes in two parts, first looking at the late nineteenth and early twentieth centuries, when children were highly susceptible to the perils of the bush. Pierce tracks this theme through highly sentimentalised newspaper and bush-ballad accounts of the rescue of youngsters (or the discovery of their bodies) who had strayed or were deliberately abandoned in the wilderness. Interestingly, Australia's best known case of 'disappearance without explanation', that of baby Azaria Chamberlain from Uluru in 1980, resonated with the entire nation because it tapped into this fundamental Australian anxiety.

Pierce then compares this theme with its modern counter-part — children 'lost' in suburbia. The anxiety expressed about the risk of 'losing' children is a national one, Pierce argues, and he quotes a generous body of evidence to support this, including the institutionalised abuse of English children (the 'orphans of the empire') evacuated to Australia during World

War II; the 1960 kidnapping of Graeme Thorne in Sydney; the disappearance of the Beaumont children in 1966; and the death of Moe toddler Jaidyn Leskie in 1997. Pierce's views evoke a particular poignancy in regard to the development of Adelaide. It is almost as if the sprawling, non-descript suburbs that encroached on the virgin bush in front of the Mount Lofty Ranges have, in turn, devoured Adelaide's children.

But, as the former Lord Mayor of Adelaide discovered, there is no easy way to change people's perception of the South Australian capital. But let's try. Adelaide should not be called the City of Churches, the City of Light or even the City of Restaurants.

Adelaide remains the city of lost children.

2

The Times

*The 1960s are remembered as a decade of immense social change:
the decade witnessed an explosion in youth pop culture, the
development of liberal sexual attitudes, the conflicting escalation
of the war in Vietnam and the peace movement. As the nation
celebrated New Year's Day, 1966, Australia was still something of
a conservative stronghold but there were signs that it was
awakening to the world beyond its shores.*

*People in Adelaide had every right to look forward to the New
Year: hot summer weather had seen temperatures soar into the
90s on the Fahrenheit scale, and tourists were expected to flock to
the city's beaches during the holiday season; at the end of the
month Adelaide would host the Fourth Cricket Test of the Ashes
Series between Australia and England; and a £16-million
program of public works promised to transform the city into what
many people already regarded it to be — the 'Athens of the
South'.*

*But in January 1966, Adelaide, and the entire nation, would
be shocked to its very core.*

In 1966, according to census figures published at the time, Australia's population was 11 550 462.[1] While the accuracy of that number ought to be assured, having been produced by the first Australian census calculated by computer, it did omit one important group of people. The 1966 census was the last one not to record indigenous Australians among the population. These 'non-citizens' did not have the right to be counted in census figures until the following year when a referendum was passed and 90.8 per cent of Australians voted in favour of altering the Constitution to not only have indigenous Australians counted in future censuses but also to allow the federal government to make special laws for their welfare.

At the same time, South Australia's population was 1 091 000, with the great majority (about 750 000) living in the city of Adelaide and outlying suburbs. A staggering twenty-two per cent of the population was made up of immigrants — mainly from the countries that make up Great Britain and Northern Ireland — but also significant numbers from Italy, Germany, Greece, the Netherlands, Poland and Yugoslavia. Since the end of World War II, many Britons had taken advantage of the federal government's assisted passage migration program. In 1956 the government modified its controversial immigration rules and commenced its Operation Reunion scheme, which was designed to reunite migrants from Eastern Europe with relatives who had settled here. In 1957 the 'Bring out a Briton' campaign encouraged the public to sponsor British families and assist in their settlement, and the following year the *Revised Migration Act* finally abolished racially biased language tests that had been compulsory for all prospective migrants.

But just whom did the federal government allow into the country? Although many Australians took a xenophobic view of immigrants from non-English-speaking countries, the question remains: did the government do background checks on all the immigrants it allowed to come to these shores after World War II? The short answer is no. History now shows that war criminals from Eastern Europe, members of Calabrian Mafia families and even people charged with kidnapping, murder and paedophilia came into the country when the great tide of immigration swept these shores after World War II. How easy would it have been for criminals to hide their past from Australian Immigration officials? An interesting statistic from that time is that South Australia's population had grown by twenty-five per cent in the previous ten years but its prison population had risen by seventy per cent.[2]

One of the English 'migrants' to take advantage of the relaxed immigration laws was 'Great Train Robber' Ronald Biggs. On 8 August 1963, a fifteen-man gang, led by London criminal Bruce Reynolds and including Ronnie Biggs, robbed the Royal Mail's Glasgow to London travelling post office train of £2.6 million. Most of the gang were captured but in July 1965, 35-year-old Biggs escaped from Wandsworth prison. After undergoing plastic surgery in Europe and assuming a new identity as 'Terry Cook', Biggs met up with his wife and children in suburban Adelaide. The Great Train Robber's identity was almost discovered when he and an associate were questioned by police at an Adelaide pawn shop.[3] Incredibly, Biggs talked his way out of an arrest and moved to Melbourne, where he was later discovered working as a builder, prompting him to flee the country to Brazil.

The South Australian state government did everything it could to make Britons feel at home in their new country. In the 1950s, as part of a bold government project to attract unskilled and semi-skilled migrants from Britain, the state government created satellite towns outside the Adelaide CBD. They even named one town in the north of Adelaide 'Elizabeth' after the Queen. Built with 'many of the mother country's trappings, down to faux-English pubs and streets named after the Queen, her relatives and her castles,' the radical social experiment disintegrated in the 1980s when economic depression sent many residents into the dole queues. Journalist Kerry-Anne Walsh commented: 'By the 1990s Elizabeth had become a sprawling isolated ghetto which acted as a magnet for the disenfranchised of South Australia and beyond.'[4]

In the 1960s, Adelaide was something of a British enclave.

Over the Christmas holiday break of 1965, The Beatles held the number one position on the national top forty with their hit *Day Tripper*. Barely eighteen months before, an estimated crowd of 250 000 people — effectively a quarter of the state's population at that time — crammed King William Street as the four English moptops were given a civic reception at Adelaide Town Hall. Australia had not witnessed anything like it, and the immense crowd that turned out in Adelaide on 12 June 1964 to see the four Liverpool lads was attributed to the high number of British immigrants living in the state.

Adelaide was well and truly engulfed by Beatlemania. During that summer, many of the drive-ins and cinemas showed The Beatles' second film, *Help*. Early in the New Year, 22-year-old George Harrison, the youngest Beatle, broke the hearts of millions when he married model Patti Boyd in London on 21 January.

During January 1966, national expectations were heightened by the exchange of pounds and pence for dollars and cents on C-Day — 14 February. After three years of planning by government, industries, banks and businesses, the new currency was ready to roll out on Valentine's Day. Originally there were just five new notes and six coins: the $1, $2, $5, $10 and $20 notes (the $50 and $100 notes would not come until much later) and the 50c, 20c, 10c, 5c, 2c and 1c pieces. Early in the New Year, $240 million in notes and $20 million in coins were minted at the National Mint in Canberra and distributed throughout Australia.

The federal government launched an extensive media campaign to educate the population about the currency changeover. One tune, sung to the traditional folk song *Click Goes the Shears*, warned people:

> In come the dollars and in come the cents
> to replace the pounds, the shillings and the pence.
> Be prepared folks when the coins begin to mix
> on the 14th of February 1966.

Because there was no 'halfpenny' as there had been with the previous currency system, it was expected that the rounding up of totals would confuse many people. 'Housewives are to be largely affected by the changeover,' wrote one newspaper report at the time, 'having the household spending power and being the ones to deal with the day-to-day problems of conversion.'[5]

On 26 January 1966, Adelaide's famed choreographer and international ballet star Robert Helpmann was named Australian of the Year for 1965. Helpmann, born in Mount Gambier in 1909, made his professional debut in Adelaide in 1923 before studying with Anna Pavlova's touring company and going to Britain in 1931. The first dancer of the newly founded Sadler's Wells Ballet, the elfin-like Helpmann had also transferred his talents to dramatic roles in several major films, most recently *55 Days at Peking* in which he played a Chinese advisor to the Dowager Empress at the time of the Boxer Rebellion. Joint artistic director of the Australian Ballet in 1965, Helpmann premiered the ballet *Yugen* in his home city of Adelaide and was 'thrilled more than I can say by the wonderful reception'.[6] At the time of his award as Australian of the Year, Helpmann was preparing his ballet *Electra* for its premiere at the Adelaide Arts Festival.

That same day the English Cricket Team arrived in Adelaide for the Fourth Test of the Ashes Series. Fans were waiting at Adelaide Airport to obtain autographs from the English team — Geoff Boycott, Colin Cowdry, David Larter and Ken Higgs were pictured in the morning papers — while news of Australian openers Bill Lawry and Bob Cowper's unbeaten centuries playing for a Combined XI against the touring English team in Hobart had set the scene for the vital test match at Adelaide Oval. With each of the first two tests finishing in a draw, and England winning the New Year's Test in Sydney by an innings and ninety-three runs, the Richie Benaud–led Australians needed a win in Adelaide if they were to tie the series and retain the Ashes.

But the big news story that the Australian media followed during the first month of the New Year was the imminent retirement of long-serving Australian Prime Minister Robert Menzies. The leader of the Liberal Party since its formation in 1944, Menzies had first been Prime Minister from 1939 to 1941, when he was unceremoniously dumped by the Australian electorate at the height of World War II. Menzies then moulded the Liberal Party out of the remnants of the United Australia Party and fourteen other anti-Labor parties and regained government in 1949. On 20 January 1966, Menzies resigned after seventeen consecutive years in office. At the age of seventy-one 'one becomes tired,' Menzies told the nation in an 8 pm television broadcast that lasted fifty minutes, 'not quite 100 percent ... It is something that doesn't happen very frequently ... to go out of office before today under someone else's steam, this time it's under my own.'[7]

Menzies was variously known as Pig-Iron Bob (for selling steel to the Japanese after the war), and Ming, or Ming the Merciless, by university students angered by the Prime Minister's commitment of troops to the Vietnam War. (This name was based firstly on Menzies' discovery that his Scottish surname was pronounced *Mingis*, and secondly on a character in the Flash Gordon comic strips and films.) Menzies had achieved many things in his record eight successive election wins — establishing the medical welfare scheme, sponsoring state aid for private schools, offering financial assistance for tertiary education and starting programs for National Service between 1951 and 1965. But his leadership will always be associated with two issues: an immigration scheme based on the White Australia Policy and a cloying, almost sycophantic relationship with Great Britain and the British Royal Family.

On Wednesday 26 January — Australia Day — Harold Holt was sworn in as the country's new Prime Minister along with his cabinet ministers, who included future prime ministers John McEwen, John Gorton, William McMahon and Malcolm Fraser. As the group of ministers stood alongside Holt that hot Wednesday afternoon, the party was attacked by a swarm of flies. Menzies resigned from the federal seat of Kooyong on 10 February and was replaced by a young Liberal 'colt' named Andrew Peacock, who would come achingly close to being elected Prime Minister in 1987.

Another milestone was passed that day when Australia's first female cabinet member was included in the Holt ministry. Senator Dame Annabelle Rankin, born in Brisbane in 1908 and a Liberal Senator since 1946, had been the Government Whip for the past fifteen years. Senator Rankin, the newly promoted Minister for Housing, was one of twenty-five ministers of the Crown who assembled on the lawns of Parliament House to have her photo taken. 'Beauty and the Beast,' one minister quipped to photographers. Did she foresee any special problems for a woman taking charge of a government portfolio and sitting on the front bench?

'I think that sort of thing has long since gone,' Dame Annabelle said. 'Women work at almost everything today. I feel that it is a very great responsibility and I was very pleased to accept the post.'[8] Only days before, India, the largest democracy in the world, had witnessed a woman ascend to the position of Prime Minister. Indira Gandhi, the daughter of foundation Prime Minister Jawaharlal Nehru, was elected by her party to succeed leader Lal Shastri when he died suddenly. When it came to political opportunity for women, Australia was still fifty years behind one of the most undeveloped countries in the world.

In Adelaide, women were making their own inroads into a conservative, male-dominated society. The previous September, Adelaide barrister Roma Mitchell became the first woman in Australia to be appointed to a state Supreme Court. Announcing her appointment, the South Australian Attorney General, Don Dunstan, said that he believed Miss Mitchell was only the second woman to be appointed a judge in the whole of the British Commonwealth. However, court protocol demanded that Miss Mitchell still be referred to as 'His Honour Mr Justice Mitchell'.[9] It was Justice Mitchell who handed down the death penalty to Cliff Bartholomew after he murdered ten members of his family at Hope Forest in 1971.

But it was the legal and political career of Don Dunstan that was to have the most significant impact on the lives of ordinary South Australians over the next decade. Born in Fiji of South Australian parents in 1926, Donald Allan Dunstan studied law and classics at Adelaide University before entering politics as the Labor member for Norwood in 1953. In 1965, when Labor was swept to power under leader Frank Walsh, Dunstan was appointed Attorney-General, Minister for Social Welfare and Minister for Aboriginal Affairs. In June 1967, when Walsh resigned as Premier, the thirty-year-old former lawyer became the youngest Premier in the state's history. Although his government was defeated the following year, Dunstan's Labor Party was returned to government in 1970 and he served as the state's Premier for the next decade.

Dunstan was a curious mix. A social, cultural and political reformer and a non-conformist, he was also a passionate supporter of the arts and an active anti-war campaigner during the Vietnam War. Some of his key progressive policies included land rights for Aborigines, greater consumer protection, equal rights for women, and relaxed liquor legislation that would allow women to hold liquor licences and pubs to stay open after 6 pm. Arguably his greatest achievement was to decriminalise homosexuality among consenting adults, but it was a decade-long battle that only came to fruition after his government's election victory in 1975.

The young Premier cut a contradictory figure among the Adelaide establishment; he preferred to wear open-necked shirts, shorts and long socks at a time when a collar and tie were *de rigueur*. But he was also a rarity in politics. Don Dunstan changed lives at a time when not everyone in South Australia was ready to change. Even today, many older Adelaide residents blame him for the problems that continue to confront their state.

In 1966, Adelaide was changing, even if many people were not aware of it. This was particularly true of the seaside suburb of Glenelg, south-east of Adelaide.

Glenelg, the birthplace of South Australia, was already host to an unsolved mystery that had become part of Adelaide's urban folklore. On 30 November 1948, a man aged about forty-five was seen near the edge of the seawall at Somerton, north of Glenelg. At first locals thought the man was merely sleeping but when he was still in the same position the following morning — lying on his back, his feet facing the ocean and a half-smoked cigarette in his right hand — police were called. The man was indeed dead but no form of identification was found on him. Named the 'Somerton Man' in the media, the man's death was put at about 2 am the previous night.

A search of the man's pockets did reveal an unused rail ticket to Henley Beach, a bus ticket stub to Glenelg and cigarettes and matches. The man had no money on him and, interestingly, all the identification labels on his clothing had been painstakingly removed. A post-mortem two days later established that the man had a large amount of congealed blood in his stomach — a sign that he might have ingested poison — and that his heart had failed. No known toxin or puncture marks could be found on the man's body. Police began an extensive investigation into the man's identity, but photographs and fingerprints sent around Australia and overseas did not help in revealing who he was.

In January 1949, an unclaimed suitcase lodged at the cloakroom in Adelaide Railway Station on 30 November the previous year was forwarded to police. The suitcase was new but the brand label had been removed. The clothing inside it was similar to that worn by the Somerton Man and also had the identifying labels removed. Three of the items had the name 'T. Keane' on them but an Australia-wide search of the name revealed nothing. Also in the case was a brush used for stencilling names on cargo, a knife and scissors — items that may have been used by an officer on a merchant ship.

In April, after another examination of the clothing left in the cloakroom, a rolled-up piece of paper was found in the fob-pocket of the trousers. On the piece of paper were the words *Taman shud*, which were the final words of a poem written by the Persian poet Omar Khayyam 900 years before. *Taman shud* means 'the end' or 'the finish' and, in the context of Khayyam's poetry, it may have meant 'no regrets'. Later a Glenelg doctor came forward with a copy of the book *The Rubaiyat of Omar Khayyam*, which he had found thrown on the front seat of his car outside his beachside home the previous November. A section of paper had been torn off the final page and tests later confirmed that it was the same paper as the piece found in the pocket of the Somerton Man. Examination of the cover of the book found faint pencil outlines of four lines of capital letters but detectives could not determine if it was a code or even if it could be deciphered.

Adelaide Museum taxidermist Paul Lawson was asked to make a plaster cast of the still unburied Somerton Man. Lawson made a cast of the man's head and shoulders but also found that the dead man had been tall and athletic, having wide shoulders, a narrow waist and well-formed calf muscles. Although strong and robust, the man had well-cared-for hands and manicured nails, and his little toes were wedged close together like those of a dancer.

The body of the unidentified man was quietly buried in June 1949 in the West Terrace Cemetery. The South Australian

Grandstand Bookmakers Association paid for the funeral and the service was conducted by the Salvation Army. An inquest into the death of the man was held shortly after the burial but was quickly adjourned because of lack of evidence. The discovery of the Somerton Man raised many more questions than it could answer. Who was he and how did he die? Was he Australian or an immigrant? (His clothes were made in America.) Did he commit suicide or was he murdered? Why did he go to such pains to keep his identity secret? Was he a refugee, a war criminal or a spy? (The Woomera testing range was being established at the time.) He was in such great physical shape when he died ... was he a dancer, an athlete or a soldier?

Did the Somerton Man take his own life after a failed love affair or did he die of a broken heart? The mystery remains.

In more ways than one, Glenelg can be seen as Adelaide's oldest suburb. The landing place of the foundation fathers of the state in 1836, Glenelg developed into a popular seaside resort at the turn of last century with its own unique jetty. Many of the streets in the seaside township were named by Colonel Light. Some were named after English seaside resorts: for example, Brighton Road, and Ramsgate, Margate, Hastings, Broadstairs, Scarborough, Penzance and Torquay streets. Colonel Light, as he had done in Adelaide, followed his habit of giving the same street two or more different names. Partridge Street, Gordon Street and Tapley's Hill Road — all actually the same street — originally had nine different names.

Adelaide's urban sprawl engulfed Glenelg in suburbia by the 1950s. The building boom that had started after World War II pushed Adelaide's suburbs into the foothills in the east and south and to the beach in the west. Glenelg became 'an island of old houses and mansions in a sea of small stereotyped urban houses'.[10] Nevertheless, the fact that the Anzac Highway allowed quick and easy access to the city centre made Glenelg a desirable residential area.

Because most of Glenelg's prime real estate was taken, the conversion of mansions into flats and the development of new multi-tiered buildings met the housing needs of younger people. So Glenelg was left to the flat tenants who worked in the city and to the aged who wanted to be close to the beach for health reasons. It was a unique mix. The therapeutic benefits of living near the sea had not been lost on the people of Adelaide. At Glenelg many of the old mansions were converted into private hospitals.

Glenelg beach was badly in need of a facelift in the mid-1960s. In February 1966, one Melbourne reporter observed:

> The development of other beaches and the spread of the city along the miles of foreshore round St Vincent's Gulf has lessened Glenelg's popularity. The wealthy have found better beaches, leaving the Glenelg sands to the children, the retired and the elderly, the social outcasts and the seagulls. The area is pockmarked with boarding houses, flats and private hotels [among] fine homes of Mount Gambier stone with neat bright fences.

The Glenelg beachfront, seven miles from the city, resembles a down-at-heel St Kilda — a long promenade, a couple of pubs, a wide beach filthy with litter and flocks of hungry seagulls. There are ugly clumps of rock and the remains of a washed away jetty. There's a small sideshow alley where music blares from the merry-go-round ... where you can buy fairy floss, your aim at the shooting gallery or ride a dodgem car.[11]

The people of Glenelg, and boat owners across the state, had been given a major economic boost when the mouth of the Patawalonga Creek was transformed into a large boat haven in the late 1950s at a cost of £255 000. Originally given the ostentatious name 'River Thames' by Colonel Light, the tidal estuary that meandered into Holdfast Bay was later renamed Patawalonga. The Pat, as it is popularly known, regularly flooded with the overflow of stormwater from the Sturt River after heavy rains in the south-eastern Adelaide Hills. It was finally decided in 1956 that the mouth of the Patawalonga would be turned into a boat haven with the building of gates and a lock at Glenelg. The haven was opened by the Governor of South Australia, Sir Robert George, on 13 February 1960.

The transformation of the Pat was seen as a better use of state government and local council money than the rebuilding of the jetty. In April 1948, the ninety-year-old Glenelg jetty, described as 'one of South Australia's best-known institutions and landmarks'[12] was destroyed by a huge storm. 'Overnight the state and Glenelg had lost a friend, a gathering place and traditional symbol of the seaside resort the world over,' wrote the historian W. H. Jeanes.

Glenelg had battled hard to establish its harbour facilities. Back in 1859, a jetty, 1250 feet long and eighteen feet wide, had finally been completed. A kiosk and an aquarium were later added. Both additions survived the 1948 storm but were useless without pedestrian access along the jetty and so were demolished. The loss of the jetty affected local businesses, tourism and boat enthusiasts. It was as if Glenelg locals, who had long identified with the jetty, had lost part of their own identity when the jetty was washed away. More than twenty years would pass before the Glenelg jetty was rebuilt.

Immediately to the west of Moseley Square, on a grass area named Colley Reserve (after a former mayor of Glenelg), the Glenelg Amusement Park was established on land reclaimed by the erection of a seawall in 1920. Glenelg's first merry-go-round, a steam-operated 'riding gallery', was installed in 1895. In 1902 an English-built merry-go-round, previously in operation at Manly in Sydney, was brought to Glenelg. Originally steam-powered, it was converted to electricity in 1949 but only after its boiler was stolen.

In 1929 the Luna Park amusement complex was established at Glenelg along the lines of a similar park in operation at Melbourne's St Kilda Pier. One of the main attractions of the sideshow area, the Big Dipper rollercoaster, was later dismantled and taken to Sydney's Luna Park. However, following another huge storm in 1953 that completely demolished the sea wall and much of the internal reclamation, the amusement park declined into a hotchpotch[13] of tin sheds that comprised nothing more

than a cluttered sideshow alley. As 1966 approached, Glenelg
Council had already recognised the need for redevelopment of
the amusement area west of Colley Reserve and had requested
architectural consultants to submit plans.

Glenelg constantly fought both natural and human forces
to retain its sandy beaches. In the early 1960s, storms turned
the popular beach into a bare-rock foreshore; the immediate
effect was to reduce beach patronage and undermine the
popularity of the Glenelg Surf Lifesaving Club. A rock groyne
built on the south side of the Patawalonga outlet acted as a
buffer so that nature could replenish the sand on the beach,
which it duly did after huge seas in 1965. The crowds
returned to Glenelg, and renovations to the Glenelg Surf
Lifesaving clubhouse began the following year.

Local police always had a significant presence at Glenelg
beach. According to council records of the period, their brief
was to 'perambulate the beach between 6 to 8 in the morning
daily, on Saturday afternoons from 2 to 5, and during the
greater part of Sunday'.[14] A police station had been built in
Moseley Square in 1865 but the constable was withdrawn
after three years and the station was placed under council
control. Locals protested the lack of police protection, and
another constable was hastily sent from Adelaide. The old
police station had to be demolished in 1933 and was replaced
by offices in the Glenelg Court House. Glenelg Police Station
was divisional headquarters for the Number 1 Division in the
Adelaide CIB. In 1966 a detective sergeant was in charge of
nine plain clothes officers, with two uniformed sergeants
supervising seven uniformed personnel.

As a harbour town, Glenelg had its fair share of law and order problems. A memorial mounted in Moseley Square states that on 29 March 1908, 'Foot constable Albert Edward King was shot and killed in the execution of his duty trying to reason with an armed offender at Miller's Corner at the intersection of Gordon and Partridge Streets in Jetty Road, Glenelg.'[15]

Although Glenelg was going through a tough period in the mid-1960s, it had one major advantage over its neighbouring suburbs in that its business and commercial centre was already highly developed. The lines of shops stretching from the beach up along Jetty Road comprised the fourth largest shopping centre in the Adelaide metropolitan area. The fact that it also had the last tramline in Adelaide made Glenelg even more unique as a shopping destination. The historian Tom Brown wrote: 'Although Glenelg could never regain its name and character as a seaside resort, it did achieve a new burst of popularity as a pleasant residential suburb in the late 1950s and early 1960s.'[16]

One of the historical features of Glenelg's housing development was the introduction of the War Service Homes Act in 1918. The scheme initially provided finance through the federal government for houses built by the State Bank of South Australia. However, after World War II, the War Service Homes Branch of the Department of Housing set out terms and conditions for successful applicants and specified what were acceptable designs and specifications for the houses that could be built. There were thirty-nine basic floor plans for small, ninety-square-metre homes, usually with two bedrooms and distinguished by red brick or cement-rendered walls and gabled front roofs. These were built *en masse* in the Adelaide suburbs of Blair Athol, Plympton, Novar Gardens and Glenelg North, as well as some larger country towns.

One of the many war veterans who took advantage of the War Service home scheme was G. A. Beaumont. Christened Grant but known to most of his friends as Jimmy, Beaumont had served in the 2/74th Battalion in Borneo while still a teenager and had been wounded in battle in the final year of the war in 1945. In December 1955, Jim Beaumont married an Adelaide girl named Nancy Ellis (who referred to her husband by his more formal name, Grant), and they started a family together — relatively late in life for that time. Surrounded by their family and friends, the Beaumonts raised their three young children in a pretty, white 'State Bank bungalow' on the corner of Harding and Peterson streets in a Glenelg North subdivision named Somerton Park, roughly halfway between Glenelg and Brighton beaches.

The Beaumont's eldest daughter, Jane Nartare Beaumont, was born on 10 September 1956, when Nancy was in her late twenties and Jim was already thirty-one. The unusual middle name was picked by 'Nance', as Nancy was popularly known, and was derived from a Latin word meaning 'to swim'. The Beaumonts' second child, Arnna Kathleen, was born on Remembrance Day, 11 November 1958 — a fitting tribute for a war veteran — with Nancy changing the traditional spelling of Anna so that people would pronounce the name with a formal Adelaide accent. Lastly, Nancy presented her husband with a son on 12 July 1962. They named the child Grant after his father and gave the boy his mother's maiden name, Ellis, as his middle name, both common traditions for the time.

Jim Beaumont had a number of occupations, including owner–driver with the Suburban Taxi Service. However, with his wife busy with 'domestic duties' and three children under the age of six, he took on a position as a travelling salesman for the Lincot Linen Company. Although there was still a lot of travelling involved, and regular overnight stays in the country, it was a lot more stable than driving a taxi, with better hours and the prospect of earning more money. Nuggetty and balding, Jim Beaumont looked older than his forty years but was a doting, loving father.

Jane and Arnna Beaumont attended Paringa Park Primary School, which was about two kilometres from the family home. In an innocent age, the two girls used to walk to school and back, often by themselves. They also played with schoolmates, such as the Smith children in Wilton Avenue in Paringa Park and, like countless other groups of kids, explored the vacant blocks and creeks that peppered the area in the mid-1960s. Their small backyard at Somerton Park had fruit trees, a swing and even a go-kart. They were normal, Australian kids.

'They used to make their own beds and dress themselves,' their mother later said. 'They were capable kiddies, even though they were little.'[17]

Jane was a bright girl. At a time in education when marks mattered, she had missed topping her grade-four class at Paringa Park Primary School by a single point. Shy and

reserved, she stuttered when she got excited. Jane was also a
pretty girl with sun-bleached, ear-length hair with a wisp of a
fringe, freckles and prominent teeth. Arnna, the middle child,
was going through a plump stage. She had brown eyes, dark
hair and a fringe like her big sister. Both girls had olive
complexions like their mother. Even the youngest, Grant,
with his big toothy grin and little boy fringe cut neatly across
his forehead, turned brown during the summer months.

However, the children suffered from the same fears as
others of their age: they were afraid of the dark.[18] Grant, at
the age of four, still wore a nappy to bed.

The Beaumont girls received bicycles for what was to be
their last Christmas together, in 1965. These were much
better than the old three-wheelers the older children used to
ride around the streets of Somerton Park. Jane and Arnna
became very confident on their new two-wheelers, while
Grant mastered his sister's three-wheeler. The children even
rode as far as the Broadway — a row of shops at the top end
of Glenelg, some two kilometres away — and had walked
their bikes down to the beach before. That summer, the
children were becoming increasingly independent and the
eldest, Jane, had proved to her parents that she could look
after her younger sister and brother.

During his summer break, Jim Beaumont often took his
three children to Glenelg beach. Jane was a competent
swimmer but her younger sister and brother were not, so the
three of them tended to swim in the shallows near the
collapsed jetty. They would then run up to the grassed area
on Colley Reserve and wash off the salt water by running

through the council sprinklers. Although their father had to go back to work on Tuesday 25 January, Jane, Arnna and little Grant were keen to continue their sojourns to the beach. On his first day back at work, Mr Beaumont tried a little experiment. He offered to drop the children off at Glenelg on his way to Snowtown, allowing them to catch the bus home from Moseley Street at midday. But secretly, away from the children, the concerned dad watched for another half hour to make sure his children were settled before he left for work.

'I left about 8.30 or 9 o'clock for my usual routine trip up north to Snowtown,' Jim Beaumont recalled. 'But on my way I dropped the children at the beach just up from Glenelg Town Hall. [The children] had spent just about every day on the beach with me ... On that Tuesday morning I told them "Don't go in deep water. Don't talk to any strangers."

'After I dropped them, I watched them for at least half an hour where they couldn't see me. They were enjoying themselves with some other children. I was quite confident they were OK at the beach.'[19]

The children returned to their Somerton Park home on the two o'clock bus.

Two nights before the children disappeared from Glenelg beach, nine-year-old Jane babysat her two younger siblings while her parents went out for a couple of hours. Jim Beaumont had taken the children to the beach that day — the last day of his holiday break — and he had to go to Snowtown on business the following day. Mr and Mrs Beaumont had drinks with friends while Jane put her brother and sister to bed. When the parents returned home, they found this note written by their eldest daughter:

24-1-66

Dear Mum and Dad,

I am just about to go to bed and the time is 9.00. I have put Grant's nappy on so there is no need to worry about him wetting the sheets. Grant wanted to sleep in his own bed, and so one of you will have to sleep with Arnna. Although our rooms are not in very good condition I hope you will find them as comfortable as we do.

Goodnight to you both.

Jane XXX

P.S. I hope you had a nice time wherever you went.

P.S.S. I hope you don't mind me taking your radio into my room, Daddy.[20]

The letter reveals a lot about the obviously tight-knit Beaumont family. The parents had to play 'musical beds' with their young children, just like thousands of other families. Jane was a polite, mature young girl for nine and handled responsibility well. Lastly, Mr and Mrs Beaumont were used to leaving their children on their own, so allowing the children to go to the beach unaccompanied was not out of character for them or for the times.

Jim Beaumont was proud of his eldest daughter, calling her the family's 'little mother'.[21] Nancy Beaumont later said that she put this letter away safely after she read it and intended to show it to her daughter when she grew up and tell her what a beautiful child she was.

Mrs Beaumont would never get that opportunity.

3

The Disappearance

On Wednesday 26 January 1966 — Australia Day — the three young children of Jim and Nancy Beaumont of the Adelaide suburb of Somerton Park caught a bus to Glenelg beach. When they had not returned by 3.30 pm, their father went to the beach and searched for them. With no trace of them found, the panic-stricken parents contacted the police at 5.30 pm.

The ensuing search and extensive police investigation resulted in one of the most baffling mysteries in Australian criminal history.

For the generation born in Australia after World War II, Australia Day 1966 is indelibly etched in their memories. For many, it was the day our national innocence came to an end — Australia would never be the same. But most importantly it was the day three Adelaide siblings on a visit to the beach had their childhood stolen from them.

In 1966, the actual day on which Australia Day fell was not a public holiday for the millions of Australian workers; the holiday was tacked onto the Monday of the nearest weekend so that families could enjoy a three-day weekend. Wednesday 26 January may have been Australia Day, but as far as the three Beaumont children were concerned it was just another chance to go to the beach during the school holidays. With their father away for the remainder of the week on business, the Beaumont children woke early and pressed their mother to allow them to go down to Glenelg.

'I can't remember who was up first that day,' Nancy Beaumont said of that Wednesday morning.[1] 'Jane was the early riser. When I say she'd be first up, she wouldn't necessarily be first out of bed. She'd be first to wake, but she'd read, you see. But the other two were the ones! As soon as they woke up they would be up and into my room. Jane would read first and then come in.'

Jane was reading a paperback copy of Louisa May Allcott's *Little Women* at the time.

Nancy Beaumont tried to curb her children's enthusiasm for the beach. She was not one for 'beach outings' and she had her housework to do. If they would just be patient, she told them, they might be able to go later. But their eagerness wore her down. 'It was just hot enough then to realise it was going to be a scorcher,' Nancy later said.

'The children wanted to ride their bikes to the Broadway and then walk to the beach,' Nancy recalled but she wasn't keen on that idea. No, they could catch the bus from Diagonal Road. Explaining herself, she later said, 'The bus stops right in the heart of Glenelg, you see ... they could swim close handy so they could go to the shop, get a drink, and then [go] back [home] on the bus.' She told her children that they had to be back on the midday bus.

The children quickly got ready for the beach. Jane dressed in her pink one-piece bathers, pale green shorts and tartan canvas sandshoes with white soles. Jane dressed herself that morning, and her mother could not remember if she was wearing a yellow ribbon and tortoiseshell hair band in her hair. Arnna wore her one-piece red and white striped bathers, tan shorts and tan sandals. She also sported a bright orange hairpin in her hair. Grant, the youngest, wore only green and white bathers under green cotton shorts and red leather sandals. 'It was really hot the day before,' Nancy recalled. 'That is why little Grant, for instance, didn't have a singlet or shirt. I thought they would be home in a few hours. I know what little ones are like. They wouldn't be bothered with underclothes.'

This was long before the days of sun-safe clothing, 15+ sun-screen and the hole in the ozone layer.

'I know perhaps other people think it's rather odd to send kiddies to the beach not fully dressed,' Nancy explained when she was later questioned about her decision. 'If you came [to the beach] from the other side of town, naturally you would be dressed. But down here [at Glenelg] they would be in bathers. You wouldn't even worry about shorts.'

Jane Beaumont carried three 'drying' towels inside an airline-style shoulder bag. Nancy gave her eight shillings and sixpence — about 85 cents in pre-decimal currency — for bus

fares and lunch. As Jane placed the money into her white
purse, her mother told her to bring a pastie home for her,
knowing that the children would more than likely buy a drink
or an ice-cream with any leftover money. Lastly, Jane packed
her trusty paperback to read on the bus. Then, shortly before
10 am, Nancy Beaumont stood at her front gate at the corner
of Harding and Peterson Streets and waved goodbye to her
children as they walked barely 100 metres to the bus stop.

It was the last time Nancy Beaumont saw her children.

From their investigations, the detectives were able to piece
together the final known movements of the three children that
morning. Jane, Arnna and Grant caught the red and white
Seacombe Gardens–Glenelg bus to the beach at 10.10 am. The
driver, Mr I. D. Munro of South Brighton, remembered the
children getting onto the bus at the Diagonal Road–Harding
Street bus stop, although he did not recall them getting off.
However, the children did not return from Glenelg on any
other bus that Mr Munro drove that day. It is assumed the
children got off the bus at the Jetty Road–Moseley Street bus
stop, outside the Wenzel's cake shop, and walked down to the
beach, because the police were able to confirm their movements
with at least seven eyewitnesses, including a nine-year-old
school friend of Jane's who saw the children at Glenelg at about
11.15 am.

Some witnesses confirmed that the children followed their
usual routine and swam in the shallows near the run-down
Glenelg jetty before running up to the Colley Reserve
sprinklers directly behind the Holdfast Bay Sailing Club on
Moseley Square. A 74-year-old Glenelg woman told police that

she saw the children 'frolicking' with a tall, thin man at Colley Reserve at about 11 am. The man was described as a 'sun-tanned surfie' or 'beachcomber', about six foot one (180 centimetres) in height, and thirty to forty years old. The man's hair was originally described in the press as blond and 'in need of cutting',[2] but this was soon contradicted. A Broken Hill man who had come to Adelaide to watch the Fourth Cricket Test with his family, and had seen 'the man' with three children at Glenelg beach that day, came forward only after the suspect's description was modified to 'fairish to light-brown' hair.

The man seen by witnesses had been lying face down on his towel on the grass area watching the children as they ran up from the beach and washed themselves off under the Colley Reserve sprinklers. He was wearing brief, dark blue bathers but had his clothes on one of the white seats near the sailing club. The children had laid out their towels near two trees and were running in and out of the sprinklers. The spot was described as a 'quiet corner of the foreshore, hidden by the sailing club and the sideshows'[3] to the north-east.

The elderly woman told detectives that the man started talking to the children and very soon they were playing with him. The younger of the two girls and the little boy were jumping over him as he lay on the grass and the older girl was flicking him with her towel, the woman said. 'They were all laughing.'[4] When she left the area shortly before noon the children were still playing with the man.

An elderly couple told police that they had a conversation with the man when they were at Glenelg beach with their teenage granddaughter on Australia Day. After midday the

man and the children were standing on the grass area behind
where they were sitting when he approached them and asked,
'Did any of you people see anyone with our clothes? We've
had some money taken from our clothes.' Another witness, a
middle-aged woman sitting near the elderly couple thought
the man said, 'Have you seen anyone messing with our
clothes? Our money has been pinched.'⁵

The man's use of plural pronouns — 'our' and 'we' — was
of concern to the police. It gave the impression that the man
was not only friendly to the children but was *with* the
children. And yet something wasn't quite right. As the
middle-aged witness watched the man help the children put
their shorts on over their bathers she thought it was especially
strange that he did this for the eldest child. Surely she was old
enough to dress herself? Nancy Beaumont would also express
her amazement at this discovery ... Jane would never let
anyone else dress her, even if it was just putting her shorts on
over bathers.

And another point: if the children had indeed lost their
money — their lunch money and their bus fare home — it
gave the stranger a reason to give them a lift in his car and
make him appear sympathetic to their needs. As police were
later to discover, the issue of money proved crucial to their
investigation.

Having obviously won the confidence of Jane Beaumont, the
man must have felt secure enough to leave the children and go
to the changing sheds to dress. The three children crossed the
path that cut through Colley Reserve and stood near a seat
apparently waiting for the man. They were still standing there

when the elderly couple left the beach at 12.15 pm with their granddaughter. The woman was able to describe the children's clothing, right down to the airline-type bag the oldest girl was carrying, and her description was confirmed by the middle-aged woman sitting near them.

It was most definitely the Beaumont children. They had missed the midday bus home.

The last corroborated sighting of the three children was in Wenzel's cake shop on Moseley Street, outside of which was the bus stop where they should have caught the bus home. A shop assistant remembers the children coming in around midday and buying their lunch with a one-pound note. They bought pies and pasties but then asked for another lunch in a separate bag. This information was not widely circulated in the press, nor was it officially confirmed by police until twelve months later, because it was known that the children had left home with only eight shillings and sixpence. The clear implication was that someone else, most likely the man they were seen with, had given them the money to further win their confidence.

Mr Tom Patterson, the local postman from the Adelaide suburb of Glengowrie, told the police that he saw the children 'holding hands and laughing' in Jetty Road *after* midday.[6] The three children were walking east, towards the beach, and 'appeared to be about to cross the road towards Moseley Street'. The postman recalled, 'We all stopped and they said, "It's the postie."' However, the elderly 'postie' could not recall whether he saw the children at the beginning of his rounds, at 1.45 pm, or at the end, at 2.55 pm. Further investigations by police, who checked Mr Patterson's shift for the day, determined that this sighting was at 2.55 pm — three hours after the children had bought their lunch.

If this is true, where had the children been all that time and why had no-one else seen them?

The failure to find anyone else who could corroborate Tom Patterson's claim made it difficult for investigating detectives to accurately determine the children's final movements in Glenelg. There were other sightings of 'children' after midday, but one by one these were eliminated. It was originally reported that the children were last seen in the company of 'the man' at about 1.45 pm, but this could not be corroborated by the shop assistant who served the children at midday or by the postman. The official police line has always been that the children 'disappeared into thin air' after leaving Wenzel's cake shop at midday.[7] They either tried to walk home and were offered a lift by a person or persons unknown or were driven away from the beach — most likely by the man they were seen playing with at Colley Reserve.

As the South Australian heatwave consumed the afternoon, there was no immediate sense of panic in the Beaumont household. 'I came back inside and did a few jobs,' Nancy later recalled. 'Then about half-past ten, or somewhere about then, I rode my bike over to see a girlfriend of mine. She lives just on the other side of Diagonal Road. I left her place at about five to twelve to meet the bus. They weren't on the bus, but I wasn't particularly worried. The bus might have left a minute early, or the kiddies might have been a minute later and there wasn't another one until two o'clock. So I went home.'

Later that afternoon, some of Nancy's friends dropped in to the home unexpectedly. The friends shared a beer with Nancy on that hot afternoon.

'It was just after two I started to worry,' Nancy later said. 'My friends offered to go with me and have a look, but I said, "Well, there's not much point, because if they decided to walk, which they have done before, we won't know whether they're coming along Moseley Street, Partridge Street or Brighton Road. And if they're on their way we may miss them anyway." So I said, "It's best we wait for the three o'clock bus."'

Shortly after 3 pm Jim Beaumont arrived home unexpectedly from Snowtown. 'Normally I get home on Thursdays,' Jim told police, 'but I came home earlier that week because I didn't do well. It was my first week back after the Christmas break and, besides that, it was so hot and the children were still on holidays.' When he walked in the door Nancy was worried that the children had not returned home. Maybe there had been an accident? Jim calmed his wife and told her not to worry. 'You would have heard if anything was wrong by now,' he told her.

Nancy Beaumont immediately thought that an accident couldn't have happened to the three of them. Surely if one of them had got hurt — a sting, a cut or a graze — the other two would have spoken up and the St John Ambulance service would have brought them home. It's only a couple of minutes away by car, Nancy thought. 'That's what kept me thinking from two o'clock that I needn't be terribly worried ... about an accident.'

'Of course I didn't think that anything else may have happened,' she said. 'I always thought there was safety in numbers.'

The temperature was quickly climbing past the old century mark (39°C) when Jim Beaumont drove down to Glenelg beach. Although it wasn't a public holiday, it was still school holidays in South Australia and the heat had drawn thousands of people to Glenelg. Jim Beaumont later remarked, 'There were so many people that I wouldn't have seen the kiddies if they were there.'

Jim Beaumont rushed home again to see if he had missed them on the way to the beach but the children still hadn't arrived. 'That decided us. Nan came with me and we went and searched again. Then we reported it to the police at Glenelg. I went to the police station because it was the only thing to do ... if you can't find your children you'd logically go to the police station. They had never been missing from home before. I knew there was something wrong if they weren't at home.' Two hours had passed since Jim Beaumont had arrived home from Snowtown. It was now 5.30 pm.

The Glenelg Police Station was situated in Moseley Square not a hundred metres from where the children had been playing at Colley Reserve. If they had been abducted — and Jim and Nancy were already starting to think this as waves of anxiety washed over them — incredibly, their children had been stolen from within sight of the local police station. 'I didn't think they could have been drowned because there were so many people down there ... the thought was going through my mind that they had been taken away.'

Jim Beaumont recalled being 'very upset at this stage' when he spoke to the constable on the front desk at Glenelg CIB. 'He took a full description of what they were wearing, and details of their ages and heights ... [the constable] rang up head office [in Adelaide] I think. I waited there.'

Shortly after 6 pm, at about the time Jim and Nancy arrived back home, the temperature again hit the century mark under the old Fahrenheit scale. Jim immediately went out by himself to look for the children while Nancy waited, hoping that the children would walk through the door. 'Next thing the police came here and asked me to tell them just what did happen,' Nancy said.

'I didn't know who they were but they were uniformed police. They searched the house because they felt perhaps the kiddies might be hiding. You know, these things have happened [before] and the police are experienced at looking for people.

'Then there was some questioning here about the bus and when they left home and what they were wearing and their physical descriptions.

'Everyone started to worry then.'

Jim Beaumont searched for his children throughout the night while his wife was comforted by neighbours and friends. 'To be honest, from there on I'm pretty vague,' Nancy Beaumont later admitted. 'I think it just started to sink in then. Although I was walking around and talking, when I look back now it was just as if I looked through people.'

News of the three missing children from Glenelg beach broke into radio and television programming at about ten o'clock that night. In Somerton Park, where Nancy Beaumont kept a restless vigil for her children, friends and neighbours arrived at the house and offered to help in the search. 'They didn't come in because they didn't want to worry me, but they just did it quietly on their own.' Some of the people knew them personally; others had merely heard it on the news and wanted to help.

Nancy started to doubt herself as uncontrollable thoughts crossed her mind. Had her three young children fallen in a big hole, or down a cliff, in the dark?

'I was thinking all night. During the day I was thinking, "Perhaps ... well ... although you tell a child something, they are not adults are they?" Even at five o'clock I thought they were [just] overstaying their day at the beach. And I thought they would even catch the five o'clock bus.

'But at night I was very worried because my children were never out at night. They were frightened of the dark. And when it came nightfall, to be honest I thought, "There is only one reason the kiddies are not home: somebody is holding them back, stopping them from getting here."'

The prospect of a kidnapping was totally foreign to her. 'After all, they were three children together. If there was only one ... perhaps that would have entered my mind. But who would think in a million years anyone would kidnap three?'

During that long night, Jim Beaumont rode in police patrol cars looking for his children among the thousands of Adelaide inhabitants still trying to escape the heat. 'I left from the Glenelg Police Station,' he remembers. 'Then I came home in a patrol car to see if the kiddies had come back. And then I went out with the different patrol cars all night ... I was either in them or walking along the beach at Seacliff, Brighton, Somerton, Glenelg, West Beach ... right along.'

Late in the night, the Police Emergency Operations Group was called into the search. Five boats from the Sea Rescue Squadron were sent out to sea from the Patawalonga boat haven, sweeping searchlights across the water and onto Glenelg beach, hoping to pick up a glimpse of the missing children. Arrangements were made during the night to bring a four-wheel-drive vehicle into the search as soon as dawn broke. During the night, members of the emergency operations group searched the suburbs surrounding Glenelg. Police from city and suburban patrols joined the search — looking in backyards, checking sheds and exploring stormwater drains just in case the children had fallen asleep. Police cars scoured the streets in the suburbs near the beach, with amplifiers blaring out the call: 'Have you seen three small children?'[8]

But it was such a hot night and thousands of people were still on the beach at midnight, which didn't help matters. In an era before extensive street lighting, it was also very dark. Jim Beaumont just couldn't imagine his young children wandering the streets by themselves. As he searched for them he started to rationalise his own fears. 'I ruled out drowning altogether,' he later said. 'The beaches were packed and the sea was calm. One kiddie, perhaps, could be drowned, but three together — I just can't imagine that. There would have been some evidence. They had their green beach bag with them. They had their clothes. I found nothing like that [at the beach] at all.' No, they were not drowned. A more tragic fate had befallen them.

Jim Beaumont did not sleep that night. The police took him home in the early hours of the morning before sunrise, which was at about 4.30 am in the middle of the South Australian summer, but he got into his own car and continued searching by himself. 'I don't know how long I searched. All I was intent on doing was to keep on searching. I wouldn't have known if it was the next day or the day after.' Jim Beaumont vowed that he would not go to bed until he found his children.

As morning dawned, and with it the reality that the children were now officially lost, Nancy Beaumont was in such an anxious state that doctors had to be called to her side. Dr Cowling, a local GP who had treated the Beaumont children for their simple childhood coughs and colds, sedated Mrs Beaumont. Another family doctor, Dr Steele, prescribed sleep for an exhausted Jim Beaumont. For the next fortnight, the doctors voluntarily visited the house and continued to sedate Nancy Beaumont as police failed to find any trace of her children.

The search headquarters were situated not far from the scene of the children's disappearance, at Glenelg Police Station, and run by Superintendent Jack Vogelesang. Sergeant B. Fuller coordinated the Police Emergency Operations Group and the Sea Rescue Squadron, and Detective Sergeants Ron Blight and Peter Vogel were the investigating detectives at Glenelg CIB. Blight, a nuggetty, chain-smoking ball of energy who was nicknamed 'Wings' by his colleagues because he waved his hands wildly when he talked, looked very much the 1960s detective with his white shirt, black tie and porkpie hat. Blight and Vogel were under the direction of Detective Sergeant Alex Palmer, the chief of Adelaide Homicide Squad. The

Superintendent of the South Australia Police, Inspector Noel 'Knocker' Lenton, oversaw the entire police investigation.

At 5 am the Glenelg police launch *William Fisk* set out and searched the shoreline from Glenelg to Aldinga in the north and back to Henley Beach. Police checked hollows and caves in seaside cliffs for any evidence of a cave-in, while colleagues on foot searched several stormwater drains that opened into the sea. The *William Fisk* was joined by another police launch from Port Adelaide. Members of the police 'aqualung squad' used snorkels to search the Patawalonga boat haven, immediately south of where the children were last seen playing, but murky water hampered their efforts. That afternoon, fifty-six police cadets were called in to comb the sandhills behind the Glenelg Treatment Works all the way up to the West Beach Caravan Park. Every clump of thick scrub in the area had to be searched individually because it provided a potential hiding place for clothing items or, at worst, a body.

In the initial stages of the investigation, detectives explored three scenarios that could explain the disappearance of the three children:

- *The children drowned.* This was quickly discounted by their father and by the police after the sea search on the first night. Glenelg beach was also tightly patrolled by lifesavers, and none of the children's belongings were found at the beach.
- *The children had run away from their home and were hiding.* This was also dismissed because of the ages of the children and the fact that nothing in their previous behaviour brought their home life into question.

- *The children had been abducted and had met with foul play.* This possibility came into strong focus as the likely fate of the three children on the very first day of the investigation.

A telephone was installed at the Beaumont home so that police could contact the family more easily and keep them in touch with the investigation. After being interviewed by Detective Sergeant Palmer — a standard operational procedure — Jim Beaumont was regularly briefed by police during that first day. While Mrs Beaumont lay sleeping, it was left to an increasingly ragged and emotional Jim Beaumont to speak to the media and make public appeals for the return of his children.

'Somebody must be holding them against their will. They would otherwise have come home by now,' Jim Beaumont told the press in the front yard of the family home the day after the children were reported missing.[9]

When it was realised that Mr Beaumont had previously been an owner–driver with the Suburban Taxi Service, forty of his former colleagues volunteered to use their vehicles to search for the children. The manager of the taxi service, Bill Lay, told the press: 'As soon as the boys heard that it was Jimmy's children who were missing, they came to me and asked that I ring the police and seek permission to join in the search. Jimmy is a very likeable chap, and was very popular with the drivers when he was with us.' The taxi company later started up a public fund for the family, donating $130 to Jim Beaumont to support him and his wife while he was unable to work.

That night detectives showed photos of the missing children to other youngsters at the Glenelg sideshow while calls kept coming in to the operations room of the Glenelg CIB. With descriptions of the missing children circulating across the state via the media, 'sightings' of the children at the beach, in the suburbs and even in the city were reported to operation headquarters. Some of the police spent thirty-five hours straight investigating reports from the public; residents in West Richmond told police that on Wednesday afternoon 'children' had been going to houses looking for odd jobs; a woman reported seeing three children in the company of two men on a bus at Semaphore Park on Wednesday afternoon; others merely wanted to ring and offer their services. Although police described the public response as 'astounding' they asked that no more people volunteer.[10]

At 10 pm that night, friends and relatives comforting the family at the Somerton Park home used the newly installed telephone to talk to the police and seek some hopeful news for Jim and Nancy Beaumont. There was none.

However, press reports describing the missing children on the first day prompted a 74-year-old Glenelg woman to come forward and speak to police of what she had witnessed at Colley Reserve on that Wednesday morning. She was now sure that it was the three Beaumont children she saw 'frolicking' with a tall, suntanned man. Investigating detectives saw this as the first real break in the case. Detective Sergeant Alex Palmer, the chief of the Adelaide CIB, commented: 'At the moment we see a picture of the man striking up a conversation with the children. Arnna, the younger girl, would approach anyone and held no fear. She would have frolicked with the man with her young brother Grant and when Jane, the quiet, sensible one, had her confidence bolstered, she may have joined in.

'At this stage or some time later, he could have offered to take them home ... and from then on we are in the dark. It is quite feasible the children accepted the invitation because they had spent all their money on ice-creams and drinks. The children had walked home on previous occasions when they had run out of money.'[11]

Now the large team of detectives working on the case were relying heavily on information from the public. Detective Sergeant Palmer implored all people owning 'packing cases, cold rooms, industrial and shop refrigerators and similar items to check them ... There are many vacant homes — both old, ramshackle buildings in the old area of Glenelg, and new houses in the nearby suburbs — and the children could have been lured into them and anything could have happened.'

That day a group of church women visited the house to tell the parents of the prayers being said for their missing children. Jim and Nancy hardly had the strength to talk to them. Friends and relatives caring for the couple appealed to people not to come to the house. That night a friend came and took Mr Beaumont out to a local hotel to have a drink just to get him out of the house. The many telegrams sent to the family were held back instead of delivered, as continual knocks on the door of the Somerton Park home could have caused added distress. The Beaumonts had many offers of assistance — money, transport, petrol, 'anything' — and took pains to officially thank all the volunteers who were searching and the police who were coordinating the investigation.

On Friday 28 January, police divers moved their search to the Patawalonga Creek after a woman came forward and told police that she had seen three children sitting on the steps of a landing on the river's edge at about 7 pm on the Wednesday night. Although the woman could not remember whether it was two girls and a little boy — and the children told the woman that they did not live in the area — the police could not take the chance that this sighting wasn't the Beaumont children. For most of the day, police divers searched the river, up to a depth of four metres in places, but found nothing.

As the long weekend approached, police watched airline flights out of Adelaide. 'Passengers on at least two flights were scrutinised closely today,' wrote a not-too-convincing report in *The Sunday Mail*.[12] Following the release of the artist's sketch of the man seen playing with the children on the Wednesday they disappeared, the public inundated the police with potential sightings. By 31 January, the police had taken approximately 1000 calls. Police had checked the files of known sex offenders in the area in order to find clues to the identity of the man seen with the children.

All of South Australia was on alert. A man in Unley suggested that, in case the children were still hiding, local volunteers organise groups of searchers to look in their local areas because they had a better knowledge of their own backyards. A group of youths chased a grey sedan in Rundle Street in the city to the suburb of Glynde merely because the driver had three children in the car. It was another false alarm. The hills behind North Glenelg were searched for the fourth time in five days. Jane Beaumont had recently joined the Third Somerton Brownie Pack. Girl Guides from Somerton roamed streets on their bicycles looking for the three children.

All the while, Jim Beaumont kept in constant contact with Glenelg police for news of his children.

On 31 January, Jim Beaumont asked the *Sun News-Pictorial* to publish his favourite photograph of the three children, taken on a country trip the previous October, hoping that it would also be published in Victoria. 'It's a good photograph,' Jim Beaumont said. 'And maybe someone will see it and recognise the kids. You can see Jane's teeth are a little more prominent in the front and the fringe of hair on Grant's forehead. And that's Arnna to a T with the big grin . . . well, we were all happy then.'

Jim Beaumont's voice broke off and after five sleepless nights of worry, the conversation changed tone: 'What sort of mongrel would keep children away from their home for that long? Grant is only four and he'd get frightened at night. He still wears a nappy at night. Who could keep a little boy like that away from his mother?

'Jane is a very sensible kid . . . She'd look after the little ones as long as she could. But it's been six days now. They must be so frightened. I'm not a religious man but the only thing I can do now is pray. A lot of people are praying for us.

'I'm OK but my wife couldn't even eat or sleep until last night,' Mr Beaumont softened again. 'She cries all the time and the doctor has had to give her sedatives. If I could give my life right now for my kids to be returned safe and sound I would . . . and no questions asked.'

Jim was hoping that the 'mongrel' who took his kids might have taken them to Victoria because he couldn't keep them hidden in South Australia. If this photo of his children was published interstate, maybe a miracle would happen. He was clutching at anything now; he had lots of friends in Victoria — 'mates he trained with in the 74th Battalion' — they might find his kids.

Journalist Tom Prior observed: 'Mr Beaumont was speaking less wildly than most men in similar circumstances.'[13]

On 2 February, sixty officers conducted a house-to-house canvass of over 400 homes in the Glenelg–Brighton area in the hope of finding additional information about the man reported to have been with the children. A man with a 'striking resemblance' to the police artist's sketch, and who lived in the Glenelg district at the time, was questioned three times by police: once at Adelaide Airport; once when he was walking along North Terrace; and lastly when he voluntarily went to Adelaide CIB to clear up the matter once and for all.[14] The man seen by witnesses at Colley Reserve remained the police's main suspect. If he had merely been playing with the children, surely he too would have come forward and cleared up the matter. Jim and Nancy Beaumont were equally sure that neither they nor the children knew anyone fitting that man's description.

At a meeting of the Glenelg Council in February, it was suggested by a local ratepayer that the Patawalonga boat haven should be drained so a more thorough search for the children's bodies could be conducted in the black, oozy haven bed. It was an unprecedented move: the haven had not been emptied since its completion in 1959. The haven covered a surface area of seventy acres but had an average depth of about two metres, and it was conceivable that the children could have accidentally drowned (although no sign of their belongings had come to light) or that their bodies had been weighted and dumped there. After conferring with Detective Sergeant Ron Blight, the council alerted local boat owners to remove their craft or to prop them up to avoid capsizing when the gates of the lock were opened at 8.30 am on 3 February. The haven would then be refilled at the next high tide.

While the boat haven emptied, police on the *William Fisk* watched for any evidence of the children as the flow of water and debris poured into the sea. About thirty police, members of the Emergency Operations Group and another thirty-five police cadets conducted a shoulder-to-shoulder search of the boat haven bed from mid-morning to late afternoon. The men waded across the boat haven bed in a straight line, moving knee-deep through the pools of water left behind after the haven was drained and often sinking up to their thighs in the mud. Hundreds of spectators watched the muddy search from the catwalks of the lock and the banks of the haven. Police used poles to probe the mud while divers explored the deeper pools of water. By the afternoon, the line of searchers had travelled from the lock gates to the King Street bridge. Later in the afternoon, the team of exhausted men continued the search upstream of the Patawalonga Creek but the exercise unearthed no new leads in the investigation.

On the day the boat haven was drained — the ninth day of the investigation — Nancy Beaumont ventured outside into the sunshine and spoke to the press for the first time. Sitting at a small table in the shade of her fruit trees in the backyard of the Somerton Park bungalow, Mrs Beaumont was comforted by her husband Jim. 'I don't think they're alive, but I haven't lost hope, and all I want is that they come back,' she began. When her husband tried to console her, Mrs Beaumont shook her head. 'I've got to look at it at both sides, but it's the time that is getting to me … it has been too long. I can't be stupid and say that they're going to come in with a skipping rope. I've got to feel that the little things are huddled up somewhere and nobody has found them.

'Excuse me for crying in front of you fellows,' she paused. 'I've got to keep busy. I do little jobs … mop floors, clean ashtrays and smoke cigarettes. I've done my little bit of praying all to myself.' Mrs Beaumont spoke of the children in the present tense. 'They're very affectionate — they're lovely to one another. If the other two were very keen to go with somebody, Jane would go with them to look after them, and wouldn't leave them alone.'

Nancy had not read any newspaper accounts of the search for her children. 'My husband has been telling me about it,' she said. 'I believe they've just finished the 'Pat' [Patawalonga boat haven] and there's nothing there. I'm inclined to think it was all over on the Wednesday afternoon [that the children disappeared]. Whoever it was [who took them] had nothing to lose.'[15]

But, as happens in such cases where mysteries are not solved quickly, many Adelaide citizens had already made their minds up about Jim and Nancy Beaumont. Despite being supported by the police, relatives and a loyal circle of friends, the parents of the Beaumont children would soon be subjected to reckless gossip, malicious innuendo and callous indifference.

4

The Media

The disappearance of the three Beaumont children was the biggest news story in Adelaide since the Rupert Maxwell Stuart murder trial. In 1958 an Aboriginal man named Max Stuart was charged with the rape and murder of nine-year-old Mary Hattam, but the trial was hijacked by the print media, who discarded the facts and turned the case into a public debate about the death penalty. The media, largely from the Rupert Murdoch–owned News, tried the case in public and attacked the prosecution case, the Liberal government of the day and the Premier, Thomas Playford.

A series of appeals was made, right up to the Privy Council in the United Kingdom, all of which were rejected. A royal commission found allegations that Stuart had been wrongly convicted were not justified. However, Stuart's death sentence was commuted to life, and he was released a decade later.

The Beaumont Case was heartbreaking, but the cold hard fact was that a scoop on the investigation was worth another 10 000 copies to a newspaper's circulation. Despite this reality, many in the media became emotionally involved in the case.

The people of Adelaide slept uneasily on the night of Wednesday 26 January. At midnight, the temperature was still a stifling 32°C, and the cool change that many hoped for did not eventuate. The temperature dropped to a minimum of 25°C at 7 am before steadily rising again. Because the Beaumont children were not reported missing by their parents until the evening on Australia Day, news of the evolving tragedy did not filter out until the following day, when it made the morning newspapers. *The Advertiser* led off its nine-sentence coverage with: 'Police parties last night were searching Glenelg and nearby beaches for two girls and their four-year-old brother who left home for the beach yesterday morning and failed to return.' [1]

The Advertiser misquoted the names of the two girls as 'Joan' and 'Anna'. But that afternoon, the evening paper *The News* broke the immense scope of the story. Under a huge, eleven-letter headline, Adelaide residents were informed of the unfolding drama:

THREE VANISH:
Vast hunt at beach

Three Somerton Park children — a nine-year-old girl, her sister 7, and brother 4 — have disappeared. All night searches by a large squad of police and civilians in boats, vehicles and on foot have failed to trace the children who went to Glenelg beach 24 hours ago. [2]

The report not only named the children but also gave the address of the family at Harding Street, Somerton Park, which quickly became a magnet for journalists, searchers and even the religious. The report also noted that 'Some sandals were found on the beach at Glenelg this morning. They are being taken to the parents' home for identification.'[3]

Mr and Mrs Beaumont confirmed that the sandals did not belong to their children, and the theory that the children had drowned was quickly discounted.

With the police investigation gathering momentum, ADS7 (Channel Seven in Adelaide) took the unprecedented step of broadcasting the 6.30 news on Thursday night from a mobile broadcasting van set up outside the Glenelg Police Station. Television had the power to enter many households in South Australia and to show, with pictures and interviews, the immediacy and desperation of the situation. Anchored by newsman Brian Taylor, a graduate of Channel 9's *In Melbourne Tonight* with Graham Kennedy, the Seven news remained at the search headquarters over the weekend and broadcast special appeals from Jim Beaumont and the Police Commissioner, J. G. McKinna.

Black and white flickering images of people searching dunes and drains for the missing children were sent around Australia that long weekend. It was through this medium that Jim Beaumont made his first heartfelt address to the Australian public on Sunday 30 January: 'Today is a world of prayer throughout Australia for Australia Day. I hope whoever is holding my children will return them.' The strain of the past four days made the big man break down emotionally. 'My wife is not too good,' he struggled. 'She is still under sedation.'[4]

For the genial Brian Taylor, the disappearance of three young children from a crowded beach hit hard. Taylor became a confidant of Jim and Nancy Beaumont in the early days of the investigation and provided private and public moral support for the grief-stricken pair. After work finished, Taylor would spend long hours searching the Glenelg area for traces of the missing children. The unknown fate of the Beaumont children became an obsession, his private mission, but he was not the first or the last individual to be personally affected in this way by the case. Taylor would continue to look for Jane, Arnna and Grant Beaumont long after he walked away from his television career.

It had been expected that news on Friday 28 January would be dominated by predictions of cooler weather and final preparations for the crucial Fourth Test of the Ashes Series between Australia and England. Instead, *The Advertiser*'s banner headline jumped off the front page:

NO CLUE IN MASSIVE HUNT:
Father fears three abducted

The three Somerton Park children, who disappeared at Glenelg on Wednesday, were still missing early today despite a massive search ... Their father, Mr. G. A. Beaumont, 40, said yesterday: 'Somebody must be holding them against their will. They would otherwise have come home by now.'[5]

The *Advertiser* article showed a map of the Glenelg area and pinpointed the time they went to the beach: 10 am. This report prompted the 74-year-old Glenelg woman, whose name was withheld by police for her own protection, to come forward and tell police that she saw the three young children 'frolicking'[6] with a tall, blond man at Colley Reserve. She was even able to give the *Advertiser* sketch artist Peter von Czarnecki enough of a description to draw the first likeness of the suspect. This sketch of a man with a thin face, swept-back hair and piercing clear eyes, has become the defining image of the abductor whom no-one knows.

The only problem was that the sketch relied more on von Czarnecki's artistic invention than the old woman's recollection. As early as 31 January, just five days after the children went missing, the Adelaide artist warned the public that his rough sketch was not an accurate likeness of the man seen with the children. 'From the description the woman had given the police [von Czarnecki] prepared a sketch of the outline of the face of the man wanted for questioning,' reported *The Advertiser*. 'Throughout the weekend the artist was on call to the police and late yesterday was whisked to Glenelg for a second interview with the woman. While she described in detail as much of the face as she could remember, he prepared the sketch.' Although von Czarnecki altered the sketch after another meeting, the final likeness of the man wanted by police was largely the artist's. '[The woman] agreed that the artist's outline and structure of the face *resembled* the man she remembered. However, she could not recall the shape and colour of the eyes and shape of his mouth and nose ...'[7]

That night ADS7 printed copies of the sketch to be distributed around Glenelg, and broadcast the image on its television news coverage. The depiction of the unknown man's face, which has survived forty years, is most likely an inaccurate one.

The Sunday Mail newspaper, a joint venture of Rupert Murdoch's News Limited and the *Advertiser* newspaper group, with a circulation of 228 000 (the highest in South Australia at the time), played on every parent's fear with its 29 January coverage:

SEX CRIME NOW FEARED:
Police in search for blond man

Police fear that a sex pervert with an unruly mop of blond bleached hair has slain the three missing Beaumont children and may strike again. The pervert may have a woman accomplice.

A man answering his description accompanied by an attractive dark-haired woman in her late thirties was seen leaving Glenelg beach on Wednesday.

Police are investigating the possibility that the man is the same one wanted for last year's Sydney Wanda Beach Murders. Detectives say some of the aspects of the case are similar to the Sydney murders.

Detectives have urged parents to watch children closely, especially at beaches.

After four days of pleading, prayer, radio, and television broadcasts and police inquiry, no positive trace of the children or their clothing has been found. Their disappearance is one of the most baffling mysteries in South Australian police history.[8]

Though sensationalistic, the *Sunday Mail* story does reveal several prominent themes in the early days of the case. First, the reference to the 'woman accomplice': did the man responsible have help in luring the children into a car? Second, was there a connection with the unsolved murders of two fifteen-year-old schoolgirls at Wanda beach, south of Sydney, in January 1965? Lastly, even after four days, investigating police labelled the crime 'a baffling mystery'. The Beaumont Case remains so forty years later.

Although the theory of a female accomplice could not be corroborated by any of the eyewitnesses, there were distinct similarities with Sydney's Wanda Beach Murders. Both involved schoolchildren missing from a crowded beach during January school holidays, the only difference being that the bodies of teenagers Christine Sharrock and Marianne Schmidt were found raped, mutilated and buried in a sand dune the day after they went missing. The Sydney *Sun* newspaper thought there was such a strong link that they sent a 'special investigator' to Adelaide. On 10 February, the Adelaide press reported: 'One of Australia's most famous detectives, ex-Inspector Ray Kelly, who closed a colourful police career with the capture of Pentridge escapees Ryan and Walker in Sydney, is in Adelaide to try and find the three missing Beaumont children ... Mr Kelly made an unofficial visit to police headquarters yesterday to visit the Chief of the CIB (Superintendent Noel Lenton) who is a close friend, and other SA detectives who know him well.

'He dined at an Adelaide restaurant last night with senior SA detectives who know him well. Police here stress, however, that Mr Kelly is here as a private citizen.'[9]

Kelly stayed only one more day in Adelaide, conducting his own door-knock along Brighton Road, investigating a claim by a woman that she saw 'the man' and the Beaumont children at about 2.45 pm, and interviewing local postman Tom Patterson, who now claimed that he saw the children closer to three o'clock on 26 January and not earlier as he had first thought. Kelly's claims were given only polite consideration by local police and, after wishing the South Australia Police 'all the success they richly deserve', he returned to Sydney the following day.

One of the interesting aspects of the case was the posting of the original reward for information by the South Australian government. Two days after the disappearance of the children, the state government offered a paltry £500 reward. Over the ensuing months, the value of the reward grew like some bizarre public fundraiser. Interestingly, when the Wanda Beach Murders outraged Sydneysiders in the early months of 1965, Robert Askin's Liberal state government offered a record £10 000 reward.

'If Nan and Grant [Beaumont] had a million pounds they would give it to have their children back,' countered a close friend of the family.[10]

Announcing the modest sum, the South Australian Premier Frank Walsh said, 'We hope that as many people as possible will help wholeheartedly and join in the vital search during the long holiday weekend and that this will result in the safe return of the children to their parents.

'The government appreciates that the police are doing all they can, but a general search by the public may help to throw light on the question of whether the children are being held somewhere against their will.

'The government is much concerned to try to relieve the anxiety that is being felt not only by the children's parents but by all of us.'[11]

Almost immediately, Mr Walsh was contacted by a private citizen who was willing to offer another £250 but wanted to remain anonymous. Dr Keith McEwin of Seafield Avenue, Kingswood, offered £100 but did not ask to remain anonymous and, for his troubles, had his picture published beside those of the missing children like a police mugshot. Dr McEwin, an invalid pensioner who could not help with any physical search, hoped that his offer of a reward would prompt others to do the same. 'I feel the poor parents are entitled to know what has happened to their children, and my offer may assist in that direction,' he said.[12]

However, any reward will flush out the desperate, the unscrupulous and the opportunistic. In early February, two men were prosecuted for making false reports about the children to the investigation. One had been drinking, and the other had taken a keen interest in the case and wanted to test his own theory that the children had been taken to Nuriootpa in the Adelaide Hills. On 9 February a man 'with a foreign accent' — an echo of the Graeme Thorne kidnapping in Sydney in 1960 — contacted *The News* but obviously confused the word 'reward' with 'ransom'. The man phoned the receptionist at the newspaper and said, 'I have got Jane, Arnna and Grant Beaumont. I want reward money for them. It will have to be a good reward.'[13] The man hung up when the receptionist tried to connect him to the newspaper's editorial department.

After decimal currency came into circulation on 14 February, the reward was converted to $1700. A Mr J. H. Ellers and Le Cornu's Furniture Centre each contributed a further $200 and a Melbourne newspaper made a $2000 donation, taking the reward over the $4000 mark. In July a family friend of the Beaumont family, Barry Blackwell, offered $2000. The Brighton car dealer was unimpressed with the state government's original reward. 'I don't think enough incentive has been offered to urge anyone knowing the details of the children's mysterious disappearance to come forward,' he said from his office at Midway Motors on Brighton Road.[14]

But, poignantly, the bulk of the reward came from Jim Beaumont himself. Mr Beaumont confirmed to a Melbourne newspaper that if information was brought to light that resulted in the return of his children then he would sell his Somerton Park home. 'It is a War Service house and I think my share would be about $4000.'[15] The $10 100 reward for information leading to a conviction for the person or persons responsible for the abduction and probable murder of the three Beaumont children was created out of a bureaucratic sense of duty, the hopes of private citizens and the broken dreams of Jim and Nancy Beaumont.

By early February 1966, with the investigation stalled, news coverage was, to use a newspaper term from the time, starting to go 'off the boil'. The headlines got smaller and less dramatic: 'No respite for police in search', 'Search still at impasse' and 'Search goes on for children'. This did not sell newspapers.[16] Even the exploration of a new theory, that the Beaumont children knew their abductor, could not unlock any doors. Who? Had the man befriended the children over the summer or was he clever enough to gain their confidence on the day they disappeared?

Journalists working at *The News* recall 'grabbing at straws' in order to create an angle to keep the story in the newspapers. 'After a few days we were interviewing each other,' one journalist said. Without the slightest hint of irony, he then added: 'The children had disappeared ... the story was dead.'[17]

Something sensational — and nothing short of a confession — needed to happen. Instead, the Beaumont Case took a left turn into the 'twilight zone'.

At about this time, a printer named Jan Van Schie, who worked at *The Advertiser*, wrote to Dutch clairvoyant Gerard Croiset to ask if he could help solve the mystery. 'Dad was like the rest of Adelaide: he wanted to help in some way,' his son Jan told me. 'Croiset was well known in Holland for cracking murder investigations, but not so much here. Dad wasn't an advocate for Croiset's "powers" — they had never even met — but if there was any possible way he could return those children to their parents, Dad would have done it.' Van Schie showed Croiset's reply to the editor of *The Advertiser*, who published the clairvoyant's 'visions' in early August.[18]

From his home in Utrecht, Holland, Gerard Croiset stated that he believed the children were buried 'about half a mile from where they were last seen'.[19] The clairvoyant asked that the photographs and news footage of the Glenelg beachfront where the children disappeared be sent to him so that he could pinpoint in his 'visions' where the children were buried.

Brighton businessman Barry Blackwell, who had already contributed $2000 to the reward, tried to charter a helicopter to film the Glenelg area. 'We hope to shoot the film on Wednesday,' Blackwell told the press on 2 August, 'but we are still waiting for permission from the Department of Civil Aviation. I really don't believe in this sort of thing [clairvoyants],' Blackwell confided, 'but I am told that Mr Croiset has had uncanny success in finding missing children.'[20]

The introduction of Gerard Croiset into the investigation created a media storm. Not wanting to be scooped, John Kroeger, the editor of *The News* in Adelaide, instructed his London correspondent Jules Zanetti to fly immediately to Holland with photos of the Glenelg area and to interview the Dutch clairvoyant. Croiset did not let him down. 'I see an overhanging rock plateau under which there are stones of a nice colour and behind is a cave or hollow,' he said.[21] The mere reporting of this in *The News* on 3 August saw people flock to Glenelg beach, 'probing, prodding and digging' as they looked for any evidence of the missing children. The police were diplomatic about this renewed activity. Any action that led to the discovery of new evidence, they said, was worthwhile.

That night ADS7 newscaster Brian Taylor spoke to Gerard Croiset via radio-telephone live on television. With the help of an interpreter, Taylor had a long conversation with Croiset after tracking him down at his holiday home in Zandvoort, Holland. Croiset told Taylor that he had been working on the disappearance of the children 'for some time now'. Taylor asked whether clothing belonging to the children would help pinpoint his vision of where the children were. No, Croiset said, 'a good picture' would be enough. The Dutch clairvoyant had written a long letter about the case and had asked for a detailed map of the area but begged off being asked any more questions because, he told Taylor, 'The faint [telephone] line was making him tired and interfering with his ability as a clairvoyant.'[22]

Croiset's thoughts on the case reignited public interest in the fate of the missing Beaumont children. Dozens of people reported the existence of various caves and hollows along the Brighton beachfront, which they thought resembled the area described by the Dutch clairvoyant. ADS7 news cameraman Terry Clifford filmed the stretch of coastline from Port Stanvac to West Beach from a Cessna aircraft chartered by the television channel. Newsman Brian Taylor accompanied Terry Clifford in the plane and also felt that part of the area filmed matched the description provided by Croiset. The film, plus more recent photographs of the three children and some background information on the case were sent to Croiset in early August.

On 7 August, the noted *Herald and Weekly Times'* London correspondent Leigh Bottrell went to Holland armed with photos of the children, maps of the Glenelg area and film from ADS7. After viewing the material, Croiset said that he believed the bodies of the three 'lie buried in sand two kilometres from where they were seen near a merry-go-round at Glenelg beach'. More importantly, the Dutch clairvoyant concluded that the man seen frolicking with the children on Colley Reserve had nothing to do with their disappearance. Bottrell, who was with Croiset when he watched the film of Glenelg, noted that the clairvoyant mistook the pavilion at Colley Reserve for a merry-go-round.

'From the area around the merry-go-round and memorial and looking ... from the sea,' Bottrell wrote of Croiset's 'vision', 'the children walk [fully] dressed 800 to 1000 metres to the right, away from the beach. They then turn right and walk about 600 metres back towards the beach. In this area there is a warning sign, about a foot square, around it. Close to this pole is a hollow or a hole surrounded by dead grass. The children look at this then go another 200 metres through some sort of fence or barrier. In this area there is another hole, again surrounded by dead grass.'

'They crawl through a little hole,' Croiset told Bottrell. 'Suddenly the whole lot tumbles down — instantly. I cannot see if it is water or sand. They crawl towards the end of the hole and suddenly I don't see them anymore.' Croiset then said that the Beaumont Case — the first time that he had tried to see the disappearance of three children at one time — was the most difficult he had attempted. But if searchers went to the area and failed to find any trace of the children, Croiset said, then he would study still photos and maps of the area because film filled his head with too many 'tumbling images'.[23]

'He was an interesting sort of fellow,' Leigh Bottrell told me in a recent interview. 'He was very highly regarded in Europe and he seemed to "check out". His film projector wasn't wired for sound and so we went to a television studio in Hilversum with an American woman who had latched onto him and was going to make a documentary about him. She was more excited about the whole thing than I was, but nothing ever came of the documentary. Croiset had a ruddy face and was very intense. I remember him speaking fairly good English though. He became very flushed and agitated when he saw the photos of the children and touched them. I visited him later at his holiday home, a very simple place as I remember, and he had become very interested in the case. After originally not wanting to come to Adelaide, he was now rather keen to make the trip.'[24]

On 9 August, as a result of Croiset's vision of the Beaumont children's 'last walk', volunteers armed with a fire hose tried to flush out rubbish from a stormwater drain at the south end of Glenelg beach. Barry Blackwell, who led the search, was joined by Brian Taylor as they retraced Croiset's directions and came to two stormwater drains. The first was clear but the second was blocked with rocks and sand 200 metres from the beach. The Glenelg Fire Brigade then lent a hose to wash about ten metres of sand from the drain, which had been caused by recent storms and high tides. A woman in the beach kiosk pointed out that the drains had been clear when the police searched them on the day after the children disappeared.

Nancy Beaumont, though, was pleased that the search was still going on. She had always felt that the children could have met with an accident and, if they were dead, 'their death had been quick and that they had not been kidnapped.'[25] Even though she had no idea whether Croiset was right or wrong, she was willing to clutch at even the slimmest of hopes.

Seven months after the children's disappearance, and with the search advancing the case no further, Barry Blackwell now considered bringing Gerard Croiset to Australia. When he was told the airfare to Australia was about $1200, he said that he was willing to cover half of the cost if someone else was willing to 'come to the party'.[26] That person was Con Polites, company director and successful Adelaide real estate agent.

Polites was the city's wealthiest landlord and later one of a handful of Greek immigrants to enter the *Business Review Weekly* Rich 200 list. He stamped his buildings with his family name inside large blue and white boxes that would light up all over Adelaide at night. Distinctive with his large moustache, and known for his habit of arriving in a white chauffeured limousine to inspect his many properties, the Greek millionaire was something of a city landmark himself. He would sponsor Croiset's visit to Australia in 1966 and become the clairvoyant's chief advocate for the next thirty years.

Despite the fear that the Dutch clairvoyant's arrival would turn the investigation into a three-ring circus, Blackwell and Polites came to an agreement with Dutch airline KLM and arranged Croiset's airfare to Australia. When Jim Beaumont cabled Croiset and requested that his arrival in Adelaide be kept secret, Barry Blackwell expressed his concern about the impact Croiset's involvement in the case would have on the children's parents: 'I know from family friends of the Beaumonts that the parents are concerned about the publicity given this affair lately,' Blackwell told the press in September 1966. 'All they want is that Mr Croiset visit Adelaide quietly, to make his on-the-spot investigation.'[27] When several media organisations tried to get in on the act and 'sponsor' Croiset's visit, thereby giving them exclusive rights to the clairvoyant's trip, Blackwell could see that it was going to be impossible to keep the media out of the clairvoyant's visit. In the end, Con Polites paid Croiset's $1200 airfare, although it is believed another Adelaide businessman contributed $500.

For Croiset's part, he refused to sell the rights to his story while in Adelaide, and came to Australia in good faith. 'I will stay two days,' the Dutchman told reporter Reg MacDonald. Although he still held the view that the children were dead, he thought it best to come to Australia and 'start again'. 'I have received so many photographs and [so much] information from people in Adelaide that I am a bit confused,' he said. 'There is a big chance I will be able to find them. That is the only reason I am going to Australia. But of course, I cannot be 100% certain that I will succeed ... all I want to do is go there and help.'[28]

However, a series of small diversions sidetracked the Beaumont investigation before Croiset arrived in Australia in November. In August a Brighton undertaker reported that a 112-year-old crypt on the beachfront near the Minda Home for the Handicapped had been demolished in 1954. Eight bodies were removed from the crypt before it was filled in with rubble and buried by sand. Could the Beaumont children have walked up the esplanade from Glenelg and crawled into one of the openings to the crypt — or even another crypt, for that matter? An intensive search of the area was conducted but no trace of the children or any crypt was found. But the Minda reference raised a darker doubt in the minds of many people living in Adelaide.

Could one of the so-called 'retarded' patients have kidnapped the Beaumont children as they walked home that hot afternoon and buried their bodies on the sandy foreshore in front of the Minda Home? It was a fear largely borne out of ignorance. In the 1960s, children in the area often called each other 'ya Minda!' if they did or said something stupid. The notion of one of the disabled residents of Minda being the abductor of the Beaumont children was an idea that was quickly latched onto by the media.

A man who also entertained the theory that the Beaumont children met their deaths on the hospital grounds was Dr Douglas Buxton Hendrickson, who worked at Minda. Hendrickson was described as 'the last of the natty men — small, compact and intense ... bow-tied ... [he wore] spats ... Donegal and Harris tweeds ... and the royal blue and white diagonal tie stripes of St Peter's College, Adelaide.'[29] In September 1966, Hendrickson cabled Gerard Croiset in Holland and informed him that he, his fourteen-year-old son and another member of staff had spent much of the previous month scouring the foreshore in front of the Minda oval for evidence relating to the three Beaumont children. They had found three items: a battered straw hat, the remains of a dead bird and a piece of black material. Could these relate to the missing Beaumonts?

Croiset validated Hendrickson's search, even acknowledging the doctor's own 'paranormal powers', and told him he should continue digging within half a metre of where the straw hat was found. But, in the interim, maintenance staff had dumped tonnes of soil in the area to stop the edge of the oval being eroded by sand and wind. Although the superintendent of the home was going to instruct Hendrickson to stop digging, these new developments meant that something more coordinated now had to be done. Front-end loaders were used to remove tonnes of soil and sand, but nothing of material interest could be found at Minda. An ADS7 cameraman filmed the excavation and photographed the area so that images could be sent to Croiset in Holland.

It wasn't the first or last time the Dutch clairvoyant would change his mind. Maybe when he arrived in Adelaide, Croiset could mark with an 'X' the spot he saw in his 'vision' and lead investigators to the children's remains?

Croiset replied that his cable had been misunderstood. He had meant '*14 to 16*-and-a-half metres' from where the straw hat was discovered.[30] Searchers should look for a *kinderwagen* (a child's pram) as a marker. Soon after this was reported, a child's pram was found in a thicket by a 21-year-old patient. It was quickly established that the young patient had planted the *kinderwagen* because he wanted to help the search.

Meanwhile, Dr Hendrickson conducted his own search and led a group of volunteers wielding shovels and spades in an attempt to shift tons of rubble and sand in a vain search for the remains of the children. For several hours, the group of five diggers followed what appeared to be 'a tunnel' — even diverting the driver of the front-end loader from his task of excavating the edge of the oval. Hendrickson's group found the bones of some sheep, articles of rotting clothing and a purse — but nothing relating to the children. The digging was a public embarrassment. The Minda superintendent, Mr Lennon, forced the doctor to sign a memorandum that he would discontinue any more 'after hours' digging on the hospital grounds and limit his involvement to the areas sanctioned by investigating police.

Dr Hendrickson, who now believed firmly in his own psychic ability, refused to sign the letter and withdrew from the formal search altogether.

On 28 September, a country policeman based in Kaniva, 257 miles west of Melbourne near the South Australian border, overheard a disturbing conversation when he got a 'crossed' line while trying to ring his superiors in Russell Street, Melbourne. Senior Constable Ron Grose overheard another voice on the line say, 'We're bringing the Beaumont kids back from Hobart.' Victorian police immediately viewed the incident as a hoax; someone had been previously investigated in Hobart but the Victorian PMG said that it was impossible to get a 'crossed line' from Hobart to Melbourne when ringing from Kaniva to Melbourne. More than likely the person knew they had crossed telephone lines with a police call and threw the reference about the Beaumonts into the conversation for 'shock value'.

'We are not taking the matter seriously,' said Detective Inspector F. Holland, the Victorian Chief of the Homicide Squad, 'except that we think that it is a pretty despicable act to exploit such a tragedy for amusement.'[31] However, Jim and Nancy Beaumont did not so easily dismiss this as a hoax; they clung to the incident with renewed hope.

Talking to the media after a self-imposed absence, the Beaumonts spoke to ADS7's Brian Taylor. Stating that the 'Kaniva connection' had been her first ray of hope since the disappearance of the children, Nancy Beaumont appealed to her children's abductor as only a mother could: 'Please, whoever you are, please listen with your heart,' she said. 'I feel that in different ways you have been kind to our children but I beg you, show a greater kindness by letting them come home. Perhaps you could let them go to a household or shop and tell the people their names and address so they can be safely returned to us. We do love and miss them so.'

Jim Beaumont added that he and his wife had never given up hope that the children were still alive. 'We have always been praying and hoping the children will come back soon.'[32] The newly appointed chief of the Adelaide Homicide Squad, 41-year-old Detective Sergeant Stan Swaine, also seemed to disregard the views of his Melbourne colleagues.

'We don't know for sure, but our investigations would point very strongly toward it being a bona fide call,' Swaine said. 'We are pinning great hopes on this lead.' Swaine was said to have launched an 'intensive investigation' into the phone call.[33]

On 10 October, supported by Adelaide detectives who believed that the phone call was not a hoax, Mr Beaumont drove with the ever-reliable Brian Taylor to Kaniva to talk to Senior Constable Grose. 'I am convinced that this telephone

conversation is no hoax and my children are alive,' Jim
Beaumont said. 'Senior Constable Grose is a very sincere man
and although he thought my children were dead before the
telephone conversation, he is now convinced they are alive . . .
I am sure that whoever has them must have looked after them
well, since it is now eight months and fourteen days since we
last saw the children.' Jim Beaumont was said to be a 'thrilled'
man when he returned home to Adelaide.[34]

Finally, on 12 October, the matter was laid to rest. Two
South Australian women came forward and told police that
they did have a conversation in which the Beaumont children
were mentioned but that Senior Constable Grose had simply
misinterpreted it. The two women had first discussed two
children whom they both knew personally. These children
had been on a holiday to Hobart and had recently returned to
the mainland. When the Senior Constable first heard the
crossed line, the women were finishing talking about the
Beaumont children and then seamlessly started talking about
the Hobart trip. It was a simple error, but Ron Grose believed
what he heard with all his heart. Superintendent Noel Lenton
was forced to announce in the press that the 'Kaniva
connection' had been cleared up. After building up their
hopes, Detective Sergeant Swaine had to go and break the
news to Jim and Nancy Beaumont.

Gerard Croiset arrived in Adelaide from Holland, via
Singapore and Sydney, at 9 pm on 8 November 1966. While
on the plane to Adelaide, Croiset had a new vision: 'The sea,

then land covered with dead grass ... in the background, a broken fence with a sign prohibiting entry, a house with an unusually shaped porch, a child's pram and a dead tree.'[35] Croiset was travelling with interpreter Gary Smeding, a Dutch-born cabinet-maker from Glenelg, whom Con Polites had arranged to escort Croiset to Adelaide. The interpreter told press reporters he thought he knew the area that the clairvoyant was describing. There was no media waiting at Sydney Airport when the pair left for Adelaide but it was a different story when they arrived.

The Advertiser wrote, 'As Mr Croiset stepped from the plane at Adelaide Airport, he was met on the tarmac by a surging group of people calling questions to him in Dutch and English. More than 30 reporters and cameramen were in the crowd. Told by reporters that he had been met by more members of the press than the Beatles when they visited Adelaide, Croiset said (through his interpreter), "Yes I know of the Beatles. That is very nice of you to say so but I am here to try and solve a tragedy ... this reception is too much for me. I have not come here for [a] sensation but to try and find the children."'[36]

The News ran a full-page close-up of the Dutchman's face under the banner headline, 'The searching eyes of Gerard Croiset'.[37]

After being swept into an interview room, Croiset added, 'I want to solve the unhappiness of the parents and release this city from a fearful feeling ... I will start my work tomorrow but I hope you will leave me alone.'[38] Outside, people tried to talk to the clairvoyant, shake his hand or give written notes and letters to him. All this time, the South Australia Police watched impassively, willing to move in only if trouble started.

That night ADS7 broke into its usual programming with a newsflash of Croiset's arrival. The film finished with vision of a large black car, with Croiset inside, speeding from the airport while a black sedan followed and prevented press cars from following. Croiset was then driven to a secret location, ready to start his work the following day.

A new sideshow had rolled into Glenelg. A Dutchman with 'magnetic hazel eyes, chiseled artistic profile and thick mop of halo-like, auburn hair'[39] was the main attraction.

Adelaide, and the rest of Australia, would not forget Gerard Croiset in a hurry.

5

The Clairvoyant

In November 1966, Dutch clairvoyant Gerard Croiset came to Australia to try to solve the case of the missing Beaumont children. Today it is hard to fathom how a failed grocer with minimal English could play any part in a possible murder investigation. But last century, spiritualists, clairvoyants and paranormal healers played an integral role in the daily lives of many Europeans and often helped police in their criminal investigations.

For decades scientists had studied whether the 'powers' of alleged clairvoyants had any scientific basis in fact. Professor Willem Tenhaeff, Director of the Parapsychology Institute of the University of Utrecht in Germany, was the appointee to the world's first professorship in psychic research. In the 1920s Tenhaeff had coined the term paragnost *(from the Greek para meaning 'beyond' and gnosis meaning 'knowledge') to describe a form of extra sensory perception (ESP), or sixth sense for want of a better term. For the next thirty years, Tenhaeff studied forty-seven paragnosts — twenty-six men and twenty-one women — but the best known of Tenhaeff's paragnosts was Gerard Croiset.*

Tenhaeff met the then 36-year-old Gerard Croiset at a university lecture in Enschede, Germany, in December 1945 and invited him to visit his parapsychology laboratory at the University of Utrecht to undergo further scientific study. Tenhaeff spent the remainder of his life studying and promoting Croiset's powers and, as a result, the flamboyant Dutchman became one of Europe's best known psychometrists — the term now used to describe someone who seemingly has the ability to reveal facts about people or events merely by holding an associated object.

During his lifetime, Gerard Croiset was variously known as 'The Wizard of Utrecht', 'The Dutchman with the X-Ray Eyes', 'The Miracle Man of Holland', 'The Man Who Mystifies Europe' and simply 'Croiset the Clairvoyant', which was also the title of his 1964 biography. For four decades Croiset battled another Dutch clairvoyant named Peter Hurkos (who supposedly played a role in solving twenty-seven murders in seventeen countries, including the infamous Boston Strangler Case in the early 1960s) for international recognition of his 'powers'. However, Croiset's psychic career, which continues in the form of his son, Gerard Croiset Junior, was shrouded in controversy.

When Croiset's fame started to grow in the late 1940s, a time when spiritualists and clairvoyants were supposedly consulted more in Europe than psychiatrists in the United States, the Dutchman's 'powers' seemingly broke through the barriers of space and time. 'The past, present and future are difficult to separate for me,' Croiset said.[1] It was reported that Croiset did not accept financial reward for his work and paid his own expenses when involved in a murder or missing persons case. Originally he preferred to spontaneously 'read' an object or predict an event from his native Holland, and to be a considerable distance from an actual crime scene, because he felt that going to other countries 'chokes all the impressions'. As history now tells us, he later changed this stance in the 1960s and 1970s.

'My work has to help society,' he said in his 1964 biography. 'I have a gift from God I don't understand. I can't use it to make money from it myself. If I do, I may lose it. I can't force it. I have to feel it is useful before I can help anybody.'[2]

The reasons why Gerard Croiset was able to establish an international reputation as a 'psychic detective' are threefold: he was involved in several highly publicised cases and enjoyed varying degrees of 'success' over the years; his powers were vouched for and promoted by a respected professor of parapsychology who had years of research to support his findings; and, most importantly, Croiset was a born actor and a shameless self-promoter. It is now clear, twenty-five years after his death, that Croiset's 'success' relied heavily on vague, verbose, rambling statements and his ability to draw often contradictory conclusions from them.

Gerard Croiset was born in Holland in 1909. His parents were involved in the theatre, his Jewish father, Hyman, working as an actor and his mother as a wardrobe mistress. They had a common law marriage but Hyman was mostly absent from the family home. When he was eight years old, Gerard was placed in a foster home. A sickly child who suffered from rickets, he escaped his troubled upbringing by imagining and talking about people he had never met and places that he had never visited. Croiset moved from foster home to foster home and obtained only an elementary education before quitting school at the age of thirteen.

When he was a young child, Croiset almost drowned and he attributed his 'success' with locating missing children (especially those who had drowned) to this traumatic event. At the age of eleven, he was reunited with his mother, who had since married, but after leaving school he worked and lived on a farm. Later he progressed from junior clerk in the office of the local harbour master to shop assistant and sales representative for a grocer. He married Gerda ter Mersche and they had their first child, whom Croiset named Hyman after his errant father. Croiset then opened his own shop, but the budding clairvoyant was a failure as a businessman; declared bankrupt, he suffered a complete nervous breakdown.

In 1937 Gerard Croiset's mother died of cancer. Croiset, who always believed he had 'spiritualist' powers, suddenly became more in tune with his 'gifts'. His early efforts were not all that inspiring: a half-eaten peach left on his mother's bedside table when she died came to symbolise, to him, cancer in other people (although it is unclear whether this was anything more than a case of association, in the way the smell of a sterile hospital may evoke the memory of a sick or dying loved one). In 1938 he foretold that the Nazis would invade the Netherlands (not that this was too difficult, considering Europe was a powder keg after Hitler came to power in 1933). He advised a neighbour to delay a move to the Dutch East Indies for another two years if she wanted to avoid the war (the Japanese invaded the colony in 1942), and he later said that he aided, with his 'psychic' impressions, not only members of the Dutch underground but also Jewish families hiding from the Nazis.

Croiset shifted his focus to more 'interpersonal' visions when he informed his friend, a pilot named Albert Plesman, that his missing son had been killed in an aeroplane crash during the war. In another vision, Croiset 'saw' the death of Plesman's youngest son, Hans, in a civil aviation accident after the war but could not bear to foretell this second tragedy to his friend. Instead, he decided to write a letter to himself and kept it confidential. Croiset's premonition was only revealed after Plesman's youngest son did indeed perish in a plane crash. It is unclear how many other premonitions Croiset wrote to himself and how many remained confidential.

After meeting Professor Tenhaeff in 1945, the unschooled grocery clerk moved to Utrecht with his wife Gerda and his three young children to be close to the professor's clinic. Tenhaeff, a scientist trained to record the results of clinical testing, originally found that Croiset had 'great vanity, aggressiveness, strong craving for power, and a lack of social propriety, which occasionally brought him into conflict'. A non-smoker who drank milk (possibly because of stomach ulcers), Croiset liked to wear loose-fitting, comfortable clothing. He refused to wear a belt or suspenders and often left his trousers undone because of constant stomach pain, and took his shoes off to relax during a psychic episode. He would frequently act out his visions and talk incessantly before pausing mid-sentence when he received another vision. It was said that Croiset competed with his younger brother Max, an actor, for attention and recognition both within his own family and in the media.

Croiset was reportedly subjected to 'comprehensive' studies by German, Swiss and American psychological tests at Holland's Para-psychological Institute, but the evidence doesn't support this. When Dr J. B. Rhine of America's Duke University Parapsychology Laboratory visited Holland in May 1951, he offered to test Croiset using his celebrated twenty-five Zener (ESP) card system made up of five symbols — a cross, circle, square, star and wavy lines — but Croiset declined. 'I do not like just to guess cards,' the Dutch clairvoyant declared. 'I have to be emotionally involved in a case, like that of a missing child ...'[3]

The Dutchman was obviously a complex man. He had the reputation of being humble among the scientific community ('I am just a simple, ordinary man,' he would say. 'Everybody has the same gift as I have — only in me it is more developed.') But when he was with ordinary laypersons, he assumed the role of a superman. 'I am the great Croiset,' he would declare. When a room full of people was ready to meet him he would say, 'Let them wait! There is only one Croiset.'[4] His personal bluster was matched only by his lust for attention. Croiset kept a scrapbook of his press clippings and he hung, on the walls of his home, signed testimonials from people he had 'helped'.

Croiset's 'powers' first brought him to national prominence when he conducted his chair test at a meeting of the Dutch Society of Psychical Research in 1947. A chair number was allegedly selected at random for a forthcoming meeting of parapsychologists, and Croiset described 'with amazing accuracy' the appearance, personality and major characteristics of the person who would sit in that chair. What appeared to be a remarkable look into the future was actually not all that remarkable. The great majority of scientists were men, and Croiset would generalise, stating that 'the man sitting in this chair was away for a few weeks in another country [the conference was made up of members of an international scientific community] ... I see him walking in a large city and a gentleman is walking up behind him and bumps into him.'[5] The trick was repeated in 1951, at a private residence in England after he was interviewed by the BBC, and allegedly on another '400 occasions'.

Croiset first made himself known to Dutch police in 1949 when he offered to assist them in the case of a murdered girl. When handed a sealed box, Croiset correctly revealed its contents as being a blood-stained shoe belonging to the dead girl, 'unknown' details of the crime scene and even the name of the murderer, 'Stevens'. The police were allegedly impressed with Croiset's ability and confirmed that they were holding a suspect by the name of Stevenson. Croiset went on to help the police in many other cases of missing persons, but because Dutch police were less prejudiced than their American counterparts about the use of clairvoyants — especially one as colourful as Croiset — the high-profile Dutchman became known as Holland's chief 'psychic detective'.

The truth is, Croiset had access to confidential police information that was not available to the general public, and that obviously helped him in his 'predictions'. The following case is another example of how easy it would have been for police to 'feed' him information.

In June 1958, Croiset was asked to hold a pair of red slippers. The clairvoyant allegedly revealed that the shoes belonged to a young woman who had been murdered in 'a big city in America' near a body of water by a 'bushy-haired man'. The slippers actually belonged to Marilyn Sheppard, who had been killed four years earlier in her home in Bay Village, a suburb of Cleveland, situated on the shores of Lake Erie. Her husband, Dr Sam Sheppard, was jailed for the crime but denied he was the murderer. The real murderer was a 'bushy-haired man' the doctor maintained (Sheppard was balding) but after spending ten years in jail, the US Supreme Court overturned the verdict and Sheppard was released. The Sheppard Case was one of the highest profile police investigations during the 1950s, and when Croiset was asked to 'intervene', Dr Sheppard was fighting for his release. It would have been easy for the police to give Croiset clues to the case he was being asked to solve, and the 'clairvoyant' could then have used the known facts of the case to fill the gaps.

Croiset used a very simple ploy to narrow the boundaries of his predictions when dealing with missing people. He would say that a person was either 'under the ground' or 'in the water' and that their body would be found within six days. Croiset knew that it took several days for a submerged body to bloat and then float to the surface, so if someone had gone missing near water there was a good chance that the body would eventually be found. If he said a body was buried, it was unlikely ever to be recovered, so he could not be proven wrong. Despite these obvious ploys, Croiset's international reputation was secured when he allegedly solved the following case.

On 18 October 1959, the daughter of a Kansas professor disappeared from a hospital where she had been admitted because she was suffering nervous exhaustion. Local and state police could not locate her, and the woman's family contacted Professor Tenhaeff in Holland, who put them in touch with Croiset. Walter Sandelius, a professor of political science at the University of Kansas, spoke by phone to 'The Dutch Wizard', who asked if the hospital where the girl was staying had a lawn or whether there was a viaduct nearby (echoing his favoured 'water' theme). Croiset also mentioned a truck and a red car but asked the professor to send him a photograph of his daughter and some local maps of the area. He was confident that the professor's daughter would turn up 'within six days'.

When the daughter inexplicably returned to her parents' home six days later, Croiset took the credit for her discovery. She had in fact crossed a lawn (most hospitals are surrounded by landscaped gardens) and a viaduct (Lawrence, Kansas, has several — a fact that could easily have been looked up on a map), and had hitched a ride in a truck. It was just too good to be true.

As Croiset's fame grew, he received requests to search for lost children, a missing Picasso painting valued at £10 000, and even the stolen questions from a medical exam. Based on a series of conversations that Dutch journalist Willem Oltmans had with Croiset in the early 1960s, the journalist became convinced that Baron George De Mohrenschildt (an associate of Lee Harvey Oswald's) had masterminded the assassination of John F. Kennedy. And yet, allegedly, the

Dutch clairvoyant did not earn a living as an 'international man of the mysterious'. How did Croiset feed his own family, let alone spend so much time helping the police, without an income? The answer is not so mysterious. Predominantly, Croiset promoted himself as a 'paranormal' healer.

Croiset discovered *this* gift during World War II. The struggling businessman had been ambivalent about his Jewish ancestry until forced to wear a Star of David during the Nazi occupation of the Netherlands. 'I never felt so proud,' he later stated.[6] Not only did he predict that other Jewish families were in 'grave peril' of being deported, but when he himself worked in a labour camp in Emmerich from October 1944 to March 1945, he often 'laid hands' on fellow internees and treated everything from eczema to cancer. When he moved to Utrecht to be studied by Professor Tenhaeff, Croiset opened his home to the sick and needy, and people travelled from all over Europe to be treated by him.

'Utrecht's busiest healer sees 100 to 120 patients a day,' wrote Croiset's biographer Jack Harrison Pollard. 'Treatment is often as brief as a minute. Because he accepts no money for his clairvoyant work, Croiset earns his living from his healing. Though it is illegal for healers to charge fees in Holland they can accept contributions — usually five guilders [A$1.40] for the first visit ... some patients leave cheese, eggs, ham and wine' while Croiset's wife would often resort to 'passing the hat around for donations'. 'Some of his greatest successes have been polio victims,' the biographer continued unashamedly. 'One afternoon a week, Wednesday, when school is out, is set aside for children.'[7]

Croiset was what is known as a 'magnetic' healer, but he wasn't afraid to evoke the power of God, use the name of 'Jesus Christ', lay his hands on ailing people, or use electro-magnetic radiation (an age-old pain remedy) to achieve results. 'I can't help everybody,' he admitted. 'All I can often do is try to reduce pain.' Croiset would also integrate 'telepathic powers' into his cure. 'If I get an impression, I can help. I tell the patient to come back once a week, for six weeks. If there is an improvement I go on. Otherwise I send them back to the doctor.'[8]

The implication was clear: if there was any improvement in a patient's condition, Croiset would take the credit (and a fee) for it; if there was no such improvement, it was the doctor's problem and the clairvoyant washed his hands of the matter. At the very least, Croiset used the power of suggestion to give hope to his patients, and there is some medical evidence to suggest that psychology — simple 'mind over matter' — can play a positive role in the treatment of some illnesses. But these were vulnerable people ... as were the Beaumonts in Australia.

When he was contacted about the three Beaumont children six weeks after their disappearance, Gerard Croiset promptly stated that 'There was no foul play, nor were they kidnapped. The children are dead. I am almost certain they suffocated; smothered alive. There was some sort of collapse.'[9]

Croiset's assertion that the children were dead was met with this stinging rebuke from Jim and Nancy Beaumont: 'If Mr Croiset had said he could find the kiddies alive I would have gone to Holland to meet him and bring him out here. But I just can't stand the thought of him sitting in his chair in

Holland and saying our children are dead. Nancy and I are very upset about this statement and if we meet him, we'll tell him so. As parents we believe our children are still alive and we don't like people saying that they are not.'[10]

The problem of communicating with Croiset on the other side of the world was solved by Brighton car dealer Barry Blackwell and local businessman Con Polites, who paid for the Dutchman to fly to Adelaide on 8 November 1966. Nancy Beaumont commented: 'This man is coming 12 000 miles to help us and I suppose we should be grateful for that. [But] we are built to such a pitch of hope and anticipation, and then — always — we are let down and the children are still missing. Mr Croiset has been coming for so long and we are waiting and waiting. We'd like it to be cleared up — or his prophecies cancelled out.

'If we see Croiset it will be when he visits us here at home. We may be able to help him. We will if we can. But we are not going out to the airport to meet him and help make a carnival out of our tragedy.'[11]

But Croiset's prophecies could not be 'cancelled out'. If the children's bodies were not found, this didn't necessarily mean that he was wrong; it was just that he hadn't been proved right. This is how Croiset always worked.

Croiset declared that he would stay in Australia for only two days. But on his arrival in Adelaide, he quickly became engulfed in the growing media circus. Croiset was pictured in the media as some sort of Svengali walking along Glenelg beach and talking into a tape recorder while being followed by a trail of spectators and newsmen.

Adelaide police, who had no previous experience or success with clairvoyants, viewed Croiset as 'just another searcher'. While the rest of the world was getting carried away with Croiset's powers, Glenelg Detective Sergeant Ron Blight put the situation in Adelaide into perspective: 'Naturally we hope that he finds the children and we're prepared to appeal to the public to give him a fair go, but we aren't particularly hopeful. From what I have seen on the correspondence with Croiset and what has been published about his theories, I feel he has no idea of the size and nature of the country. He has no idea of the distances involved and all the sandhills to be searched if we are to follow his directions. If Croiset finds the Beaumont children it will be sheer luck.'[12]

On Gerard Croiset's first day in Australia, on 9 November 1966, he started at 10 am at the spot on Colley Reserve where the Beaumont children were last seen. The clairvoyant, who was accompanied by an interpreter, walked three kilometres southward along the Glenelg beachfront while Con Polites, Barry Blackwell, Dr Douglas Hendrickson and a large press contingent followed a respectful thirty metres behind him. At every opportunity, Croiset stopped and took a number of photographs. Towards midday he was driven through the streets of Glenelg, stopping here and there to talk to locals. Croiset continued to look for signs that had meaning only for him: a yellow truck, a block of land with a dismantled sign, a wrecking yard with merry-go-round equipment. When he went into Moseley Street where the children went missing, the Dutch clairvoyant, forever the showman, got out of the car and leaned up against the wall of one of the shops as if willing the walls to speak to him.

Croiset and his entourage then returned to the streets, driving past the children's Harding Street home without stopping, until they came to the Minda Home in nearby King George Avenue. Croiset confirmed to an eager press that he had 'recognised' the Minda Home from his visions and he was now 'very close' to finding the children. 'It is where I saw the children under the sand in a vision,' he said. During a lunch break at the Hotel Australia, Croiset had marked an 'X' on a hand-drawn map but once on the Minda grounds he declined to identify where the mark actually was. Speaking to the press through his sponsor, Con Polites, Croiset stated that he had 'a very strong feeling' that the children's remains were buried there. It was now five o'clock in the afternoon and the search ended for the day.[13]

The following day was a frustrating one filled with tension. Croiset was looking for the block of land that he had seen in his 'visions' but now complained that he could not pinpoint where the children's bodies were because there were too many people following him. Then, when the press contingent formed a long motorcade of ten cars that tailed him through the streets of Brighton, Croiset abruptly ended his search. The Dutch clairvoyant was 'exhausted' and announced that he would leave Australia the following day.[14]

However, in a surprising development that night, Con Polites was contacted by a woman living in the nearby suburb of Paringa Park, not far from where Jane and Arnna Beaumont attended primary school. After talking to the woman, Mrs G. Goldsworthy, for about half an hour at her Wilton Avenue home, Gerard Croiset quickly formed a new theory. Mrs Goldworthy told the Dutchman the implausible story that in the early hours of 27 January, the day after the children went missing, she heard children's voices in the street. She was sure someone had called out the name 'Grant'. There was more. The woman knew the Beaumonts had played with the children of her neighbour on a vacant block next to a warehouse at the end of the street. The warehouse had previously been used as a brick pit, and it was possible that one of the 'chutes' leading to the long-demolished brick kiln still existed. Could the children have crawled into one of the chutes, been buried in a cave-in and their bodies entombed in concrete when the warehouse floor was completed the previous September?

As unlikely a scenario as it seemed, Croiset nevertheless believed it was possible.

At a hastily organised press conference at the Hotel Australia on Friday 11 November, Croiset told everyone that he had formed the opinion that the children were not buried at Minda. Instead, on his final day in Australia, Croiset now promoted a third claim: that the bodies of the children were buried two to three metres underground in 'a bunker' or 'well'.[15] Croiset then took newsmen and sceptical police on one final trek to a newly built warehouse in Wilton Avenue, Paringa Park.

The 'revelation' of the possible resting place of the remains of the three Beaumont children caused a sensation.

The warehouse was situated roughly halfway between the children's home in Somerton Park and the primary school they attended in Paringa Park. So many people flocked to the warehouse that many of the police who went there to investigate Croiset's claims were reduced to directing traffic. The Deputy Commissioner of Police, G. M. Leone, had a forty-minute meeting with the South Australian Premier, Frank Walsh, so that a practical response could be made to the allegations. The part-owner of the warehouse, Mr Saint, said that all the disused brick chutes and the kiln itself had been checked thoroughly before they had been filled in with rubble and concreted over when the warehouse was completed the previous September.

The warehouse in Wilton Ave had been extensively renovated during August 1966, and the ten-centimetre-thick concrete floor was poured the following month. When Croiset took the media throng to the warehouse on 11 November, the premises were being used as a grocery warehouse. When the group went inside, the 1200-square-metre floor was obscured by rows and rows of cardboard boxes. It was now all or nothing for the Dutch clairvoyant: he was going to stake his reputation on this one decision. Croiset, who had been to the warehouse earlier that morning, took detectives Jack Zeunert and Bob O'Brien to the north-west corner of the floor. Walking directly to a point about three metres from the north wall of the warehouse, Croiset pointed to the floor and stated definitively: 'This is where they are buried.'[16]

Croiset later qualified his claims, saying that the children were within a radius of forty metres from where he had pinpointed — effectively the whole warehouse. The clairvoyant, who was due to fly to Sydney that afternoon and then leave the country, gave a highly romanticised version of what happened to the three children: 'When I came to the storeroom [warehouse] I got a very strong positive reaction,' Croiset began. 'They [the children] were looking for shelter near friends because it was dark. They were afraid to go home in the dark ... I never thought the children were murdered ... they were looking for shelter. They were huddling behind a fence on some planks and the planks caved in. All this time I had been looking for rocks but I realised I was looking for concrete.

'Yesterday, I found them,' he finished. When asked what needed to happen next, Croiset replied, 'It is up to you. My work is done.'[17]

Interestingly, Croiset did not reveal any of these developments when he had visited Jim and Nancy Beaumont earlier that morning. After originally wanting to have nothing to do with Croiset's visit, Jim Beaumont had changed his mind and asked for the Dutch clairvoyant to visit the family home before leaving Adelaide. The meeting, which lasted about fifteen minutes, ended amicably with both parents 'very relieved' that Croiset did not find anything. Jim Beaumont told the Dutchman, 'I know you have feelings, just like anyone else and I have my beliefs that my children are alive ... Until any evidence is found that they are not alive, my wife and I will go on believing that the children are alive.'[18] Jim and Nancy even bought him a gift — a writing case covered in kangaroo skin.

The day held a special significance for Jim and Nancy Beaumont: 11 November was the birthday of their second child, Arnna. She would have been eight years old.

Croiset, who did not ask the Beaumonts to attend the press conference at the Hotel Australia later that day, was determined to have the last word on the children's whereabouts. It is now widely felt that Croiset 'panicked' and named the Paringa Park warehouse because he had no idea where the children were buried and he knew that a building could not be entirely demolished on a whim. Although there was no evidence to substantiate Croiset's claim that the children were buried there, the warehouse theory quickly took on a life of its own.

Before he expediently left the country later that day (Croiset claimed in Sydney that he was flying to Bogotá, Columbia, to solve 'a family tragedy'), the Dutchman backed a plan to partially excavate the concrete floor of the warehouse.[19] However, Mr Saint, the warehouse owner, doubted the clairvoyant's claims and originally resisted calls to excavate the floor. The South Australian state government even debated the merits of digging up the floor of the warehouse but abandoned the issue when police refused to make a formal recommendation. (A citizen's action committee later raised $7000 for the specific purpose of ripping up the concrete floor on the first anniversary of the children's disappearance, but nothing was found.)

Croiset had been given a generous amount of information, both before and after he came to Australia, which would have enabled him to make an educated guess about what happened to the missing children. Yet he was ultimately no wiser than anyone else. Croiset's only contribution to the case was to give the Beaumont family false hope. They were not the only people he would disappoint during his psychic career.

Croiset's reputation became increasingly tarnished during his later years by the number of well-publicised failures he experienced. In the mid-1970s, Croiset was invited to Puerto Rico to find the two missing daughters of a local businessman. The Dutch clairvoyant stated that the children were no longer on an 'earthly plane' and he could advance the case no further. Shortly afterwards he was asked to locate a woman missing in Scotland but once again failed to provide any clues. When Croiset tried his chair test in Denver, Colorado, in 1969 a journalist rightly pointed out that if he was truly clairvoyant he should be able to name all the people in the room and not just give a broad description of one or two scientists.

In May 1976, at the request of a Japanese current affairs program, Croiset agreed to go to Tokyo to find another missing child: seven-year-old Miwa Kikuchi, who had gone missing in the town of Chihara in Chiba prefecture. Any success in this case would certainly have improved his international standing. Upon his arrival in Japan, Croiset allegedly locked himself in a room and was given a photo of the young girl. 'Perhaps I have ideas,' Croiset said, 'but this girl already died.[20]

Croiset then drew a picture of where her body would be found: down a trunk road, in a lake or pond near a place of recreation for children and within metres of the shore. He made his standard statement that the girl's body would be found 'within the week'. Incredibly, a local news team located the body in a reservoir in Yamakura before the police could get to the scene and seal it off. That afternoon 'Croiset the

Clairvoyant' appeared on a Japanese television program where they showed film footage of his premonitions and of the little girl's body floating in the water before it was retrieved by police. Seemingly, he had solved the case. Or had he? Did the television crew sit on their discovery of the girl's body and leak the details to Croiset so that he could prepare his 'clairvoyance' in advance? Or did the ageing psychic simply get lucky at last?

Croiset travelled to Japan again in December 1976, but was not as fortunate a second time. He first said that the body of a young boy was buried in the banks of the Tsurumi River, but when no trace could be found at the place he identified, Croiset changed his mind and said that heavy rain had washed the body downstream. (Thirty years after he introduced himself to Professor Tenhaeff, Croiset still liked to use water and land in his predictions.) Whether the body was found or not (it wasn't), Croiset had not advanced the case at all.

Gerard Croiset, 'The Dutch Wizard', passed away on 20 July 1980, aged 72. His son, Gerard Croiset Junior, seemingly inherited his father's 'gifts', along with the family psychic-detective business. But as soon as Croiset Senior was dead, the media began to deconstruct his international reputation.

In September 1980, Professor Tenhaeff wrote what was thought to be an 'ironclad' account of Croiset's powers in the German publication *Esotera*.[21] In 1979 Croiset had been asked to uncover the identity of an arsonist in the Woudrichem area. Croiset's description ('sometimes wears a uniform ... lives in an apartment building ... and has something to do with toy airplanes') apparently led directly to the arrest of a man. The police chief, named Eekhof, was shocked by Croiset's description because it matched a member of his own police force.

An investigative journalist who reviewed a tape recording of Croiset's interview found that:

- Croiset was asked about the case in 1977, not 1979
- the suspect was not apprehended until 1980
- Croiset did not mention 'toy airplanes' but spoke of large commercial aeroplanes, airfields and aeroplane construction
- police originally arrested the wrong suspect, based on Croiset's description
- the police chief Eekhof was not 'shocked', because he could not possibly identify the suspect — even a member of his own force — from Croiset's vague description
- the suspect was a member of the police force, but did not live in an apartment and was suspected for reasons other than Croiset's visions.

When Dutch authorities were contacted by author C. E. M. Hansel for his 1989 book *ESP: A Scientific Evaluation*, they told him that Croiset's psychic endeavours in most cases 'had been of no use' to them.[22] Just as importantly, and despite the fact that it had been written about in several publications, the staff of the University of Kansas knew nothing of the 'missing daughter' case upon which Croiset had won his international reputation.

In a 2004 article on psychic detectives, author Harry Edwards wrote that Professor Tenhaeff was 'absent-minded' and 'sometimes led astray by his own enthusiasm'. More importantly, Tenhaeff was also 'not beyond fraudulent editing and making false claims and statements, and wherever it has been possible to check his reports against ... police files and the testimony of impartial witnesses, those reports have proved to be utterly unreliable.' Edwards also debunked Croiset's powers and concluded that, 'like all other psychics who have claimed to [be] able to help police in their investigations, when the evidence is objectively examined, the claims made on behalf of Croiset remain unsubstantiated.'[23]

Given what we know about Gerard Croiset, and even taking into account what we still don't know about parapsychology, it is difficult not to draw the following conclusions. At best, Croiset believed his 'visions' and was therefore a dangerous and deluded man. At the very worst, he was a fake and charlatan.

6

The Aftermath

After the disappearance of their children, Jim and Nancy Beaumont were visited by a steady stream of religious fanatics and paranormal pests who exploited their tragedy for their own purposes and tore away at what peace of mind the distraught parents may have had left. After the clairvoyant Gerard Croiset left Australia at the end of 1966, several new developments kept the Beaumont Case in the public eye for the next eighteen months. The first of these was the public-sponsored excavation of the Paringa Park warehouse identified by Croiset, before he left the country, as the burial site of the missing children.

In September 1967, claims that a former mental patient knew the whereabouts of the remains of the three children were investigated by the police. It was first believed that the man had been admitted to hospital shortly after the children disappeared in January 1966, but police quickly ruled him out as a suspect. This particular development involved someone whose life and career would inexorably become linked to the Beaumont Case: Detective Sergeant Stan 'Tonner' Swaine.

Lastly, and most heartbreakingly, in February 1968 there were the 'Dandenong Letters': four letters allegedly sent by Jane Beaumont, the eldest of the missing children, and by the man who took them from Glenelg beach. These letters instructed Jim and Nancy Beaumont on what they had to do if they wanted to see their children again. Were the letters a real attempt by the children's abductor to return them unharmed or were they a callous hoax?

Dutch clairvoyant Gerard Croiset was not the only 'seer' to visit the Beaumont family in their moment of tragedy. One report stated that with the disappearance of the three children from Glenelg beach, '[it] became open season for spiritualists, clairvoyants, pendulum swingers, vision-seekers, hypnotists, religious fanatics, scatterbrained theorists and plain cranks who came up with their own solutions to the mystery.' They pestered the couple, the police and even members of the press. The Beaumonts 'suffered these people — many of them fools — perhaps not gladly, but certainly not impatiently'.[1] The Beaumonts had no choice but to listen, because who could tell who was fake and who might be genuine?

When the mystery of the children's fate was not solved in the first month, people started to come forward with their own theories. Some had good intentions but others were blinded by their own 'powers'. Glenelg detectives knew that it was going to be a long, difficult investigation when a man walked into Glenelg CIB and spoke to Detective Sergeant Ron 'Wings' Blight. 'I am Jesus Christ,' the man pronounced, 'and I know where the Beaumont children are.' Blight, a no-nonsense detective who certainly did not suffer fools, asked the man where his beard was. 'It's invisible,' the man replied. Blight had the man taken into custody for his own protection.[2]

Jim and Nancy Beaumont became victims of their own decency and sense of propriety. They answered every knock on their door. 'When a person knocks on your door you just can't sum him up in a minute and decide, "You're sick" or "You mean well" or "You don't." You just listen,' Nancy said. Others left her wondering how she could even stand politely at the door and listen to them. 'I will admit there were times when some of these people were talking to me and I was looking at them and wondering, "I wonder if you've got anything to do with it?"'[3]

This was certainly the case when a man knocked on the door of the Beaumonts' home in Somerton Park and told them that the Marist Brothers of the Sacred Heart College in nearby Brighton had the children hidden in an underground room. 'He kept on in this vein,' Nancy recalled, 'and when he had said his piece he asked me, "By the way, what religion are you?"' When Nancy Beaumont said she was Catholic, the man said he was 'terribly sorry' and 'shot off'.[4]

Another man dropped by with religious pamphlets for the family and then started canvassing neighbours about the Beaumonts. Nancy asked the man to please refrain from doing this but neighbours called the police when the old man again appeared on their doorsteps. Adelaide police threatened to jail the man as a public nuisance, and he wrote a letter to the Commissioner of Police demanding that the police investigate the parents more closely. Nancy later reflected, '[The old man] turned out to be very mean but he wasn't to start with.'[5]

Then there were the letter writers. A Victorian woman wrote to the couple:

> You have every reason to think of me as an eccentric, but I will never have peace of mind if I don't write to you. If what I say to you is not to your liking or your belief, then forgive me. But please believe, love prompts me to try and help you both . . .
>
> Mr and Mrs Beaumont, I have seen a white house on the beach . . . quite close to the water . . . My spirit guide tells me your children walked along the beach all day, alone. It was late, they were tired, so they dug a hollow in the sand very close to the fence around the house or shed. While they slept, the waters rose up over them and the soft sand covered their bodies.

A New South Wales man wrote:

> From my experience of visions I have had over a period of 50 years, your children are still alive and being well cared for by an elderly lady who speaks very little English. No doubt her lack of knowledge of English precludes her from being able to realise that a nationwide search is being conducted to locate them . . .
>
> It is quite possible, too, that the children were handed over to the lady by the blond surfie, no doubt a man of foreign origin — possibly a countryman of hers . . . I trust the time is not far distant when you will be re-united with your three lovely children . . .[6]

A Sydney man named Tom Fear, who was a self-described 'futuristic dreamer', made his own way to Adelaide to help with the case. Fear, who had allegedly found the body of a seven-month-old child 'in a dream' and collected a New South Wales state government reward of £1000, told police that he had dreamed the Beaumont children were buried in the Adelaide Hills in the area near the Torrens Gorge. Police made the mistake of saying to Fear that if he felt the children's remains were up in the hills then he should go and find them. When he was stopped for digging up a stretch of bitumen road, Fear told local police that he had permission to do so. He was quietly encouraged to return to Sydney.

Several 'pendulum swingers' arrived at the Beaumonts' home. One placed a pendulum over a map of Glenelg and studied the way in which the pendulum swung in order to determine where the children's remains were buried. Jim and Nancy refused to see another pendulum swinger from interstate, who wanted to swing a pendulum over black and white photos of the children and see if the pendulum gave off a 'positive or negative reaction' to whether the children were alive.

A water diviner from New Zealand arrived in Adelaide, believing he could trace the bodies of the three children because he had the power to receive vibrations on his divining rod in areas where human bones were buried. After an unsuccessful demonstration of his ability, members of the press dissuaded him from calling on the family. Jim Beaumont despaired that people with these beliefs called them relentlessly with their theories. 'The latest to call on us,' he said in a February 1968 interview, 'was a hypnotist. While he was welcome to call, I

told him he was only upsetting us, and would he mind ...'
After the Croiset fiasco, Jim Beaumont had made up his mind.
No more. 'I've got no time for beliefs in crystal balls,
pendulums, the stars, spiritualism ... Let them go to the police
and tell *them*.'[7]

On 14 November 1966 — just one week after Croiset had
left the country following his claim that the bodies of the
three Beaumont children were under the concrete floor of a
warehouse in Paringa Park — the South Australian state
government met to decide whether to finance the excavation
of the site to end the matter once and for all. Cabinet
ministers were briefed by police, who had been able to
determine the history of the site, locate the original building
plans and interview those responsible for the renovation of
the warehouse the previous August. That night, ministers
slept on their decision before announcing it to a waiting press
and an eager public.

Adelaide businessman Con Polites tried to pre-empt the
decision when he was quoted in *The Advertiser* the following
morning. 'I am convinced the children are there. I will be very
disappointed if the work of the very dedicated Mr Croiset is
not supported by the government.'[8] But Polites' views were
not supported by police investigations, the parents of the
missing children or, finally, the state government.

On 15 November, state cabinet declined to authorise
excavation work at the Paringa Park warehouse. Announcing
the decision, South Australian Premier Frank Walsh stated that
a police investigation had shown 'conclusively' that there was
no possibility that the children had been buried there. Any

excavation would be 'a waste of time, money and effort'.[9] Police determined that the warehouse had been built in 1955 by the Paringa Press Brick Company. Part of the site's infrastructure included two steel-lined sand pits (3 × 3.5 metres square, and 2.5 metres deep) and an L-shaped concrete chute, with steps leading down to a depth of about three metres, for the conveyance of bricks. Another pit, some two metres away, housed the brick conveyance machine, which had a small excavation of about one metre by half a metre underneath it. The only other pits on the site were a large concrete-lined motor pit (1 × 4 metres square, and 2 metres deep) and a water soakage pit (1.2 × 1.2 metres square, and 1 metre deep). Five steam kilns situated at the rear of the premises had been built on a concrete floor at ground level. There were no tunnels leading to the kilns.

The brickworks had fallen into disrepair between 1961 and June 1965, when they were bought jointly by Western Joinery and Screenings Limited. The premises were used to store furniture until renovations began in August 1966. Mr Saint and Mr Starr, co-directors of Western Joinery, regularly visited the site during 1966, including the period in which the Beaumont children went missing, and did not notice anything untoward. In August the remains of the brickworks were demolished, and this included the excavation and filling in of all pits on the site. Lastly, the floor of the warehouse was laid to a depth of ten centimetres and the single-building warehouse constructed.

It was impossible for the children to have crawled into one of the chutes, or for their bodies to be hidden there, state cabinet was told, because of the removal of the steel-lined super-structure and the inspection of excavated pits before concreting. Mr R. L. Golding, the original builder of the brickworks, even took members of the press to the warehouse and showed them where the brick pits originally were and how they had been filled in. 'It would have been impossible for the bodies to have been in the pits from the time the Beaumont children disappeared until the rebuilding without their having been discovered,' Mr Golding said.[10] There had been no cave-in.

Jim Beaumont supported the cabinet's decision and reconfirmed his confidence in the South Australia Police. 'If they decided not to dig then that is fine by me. I have more faith in the police than I do in Mr Croiset and I go along with the police here.' However, others were not so sure. 'I would like to see a vote taken of the people on this,' said Con Polites. 'I feel sure they would be in favour of Mr Croiset's decision.'[11]

Despite the government's decision, a citizen's action committee that had been formed to investigate the excavation of the warehouse and to raise funds from public donations was flooded with offers of help. Mr Saint, the owner of the warehouse, originally agreed with the government's decision not to finance a dig but came under increasing pressure to allow a partial excavation during the summer of 1966–67 leading up to the first anniversary of the children's disappearance. When Con Polites came on board as 'patron' of the citizen's action committee, he implored Mr Saint to allow the excavation. Allegedly, 13 000 people contacted the committee in support of an excavation, while only thirty voted 'no'.

Finally, on Thursday 26 January 1967 — one year to the day after the three Beaumont children went missing from Glenelg beach — a group of about forty people (half of them journalists) met at the Paringa Park warehouse in Wilton Avenue. The excavation would begin on 1 March and last for a maximum of two weeks, but only after the $7000 cost had been raised. In his enthusiasm to prove Croiset right, a spokesman of the citizen's action committee, Mr G. R. Dawson, spoke as if the children were nothing more than three lost coins. Dawson told the press: 'Let's find out once and for all if the children are here as Gerard Croiset said. Should the search for the children prove fruitless, it should strengthen the conviction of Mr and Mrs Beaumont that their children are still alive ... They must be interested in the outcome — if nothing is found it will give their belief strength.'[12]

Members of the committee asked for donations from the crowd as Mr Dawson made his announcement.

In February 1967, when donations stalled at $3000, the committee again approached the state government to subsidise the excavation but the Premier again declined. No, the government was satisfied 'beyond doubt' that the remains of the children were not buried beneath the floor of the warehouse and it was not prepared to spend public money on a proposed excavation. However, a concert held by members of the Dutch community in Unley raised money and, by the time March approached, the committee was only $795 short of the minimum amount needed to start the dig ($4800).

A condition of the owner's support for the excavation was that the work had to be done by professionals, the costs had to be fully audited, and the police had to be in attendance. On 1 March 1967, a single brick internal wall measuring approximately four metres by three metres was demolished and a machine with a water-cooled diamond blade started cutting through a section of the ten-centimetre floor in the north-west corner identified by Gerard Croiset. The following day workmen used jackhammers to dig down to a depth of two metres and excavated one of the former sand pits. On 3 March the workmen discovered a number of small 'tunnels' and followed them down to a level of four metres.

During the next few days, the dig continued but could not spread outward beyond the cavity where the concrete floor had been cut. Some rubbish was found at the bottom of one of the holes: paper bags, greaseproof paper, a chocolate wrapper, bottle tops, a shirt cuff, a rotting towel and orange peel. In the minds of some of the citizen's action committee who watched the excavations, these somehow became pie and pastie bags, part of a beach towel and a little boy's shirt. (Grant Beaumont did not wear a shirt to the beach the day he disappeared.) Idina Probyn (later Dame Idina Probyn) found the rubbish after a workman smashed through a brick foundation below the concrete floor. Police took the precautionary step of showing the rubbish to Jim and Nancy Beaumont, who confirmed that none of it had any tangible connection with the missing children.

From his home in Holland, Gerard Croiset implored the citizen's action committee to keep digging, so posthole diggers were used to excavate to a depth of five metres. However, the project was quickly stopped when funds ran out after ten days of digging, with nothing to show for the committee's efforts except a large hole that quickly filled with water. The failure to find any sign of the missing children was enough to remove doubt from the minds of most people; citizen's action committee chairman Mr G. R. Dawson stated that the excavation showed 'the police were correct in their analysis'[13] of the merits of the dig.

Premier Frank Walsh put the entire project into some perspective when he said that he 'could not agree at any stage that the warehouse search was a step in the right direction'. He then extended his government's sympathy to Mr and Mrs Beaumont for their 'continued anxiety and sorrow'.[14] But Gerard Croiset was clever enough to realise that the failure to find anything of the children did not mean they weren't buried there. The lack of success at the Paringa Park warehouse would fuel decades of speculation, the growth of an urban myth, and yet another excavation attempt thirty years later.

The Beaumont Case, which often defied logic, would not remain off the front pages for long.

On 6 September 1967, Adelaide police received an anonymous letter stating that a man of similar appearance to the suspect seen with the Beaumont children the day they disappeared had later been a mental patient at Glenside Hospital. The informant had seen the man at Glenelg beach after the children had disappeared and recorded his licence number. Based on this information, Detective Sergeant Stanley Swaine, recently promoted to Chief of Homicide, started a new line of inquiry but it was quickly established that the man had been questioned twelve months before. He had lived in the Glenelg area (his parents running a local business there) and had indeed been to Glenelg beach. Swaine took it upon himself to retrace the route the children might have taken if they had tried to walk home after missing the Moseley Street bus, in order to determine whether they would have passed the business run by the man's parents. However, Adelaide CIB Superintendent Noel Lenton denied that police were seeking any particular person in relation to the continuing investigation.

It was not the last time 'Tonner' Swaine would take it upon himself to investigate leads in the Beaumont Case, nor was it the last time he was to come into conflict with his superior officers. A decade later, Swaine told author Alan Dower about this particular suspect: 'Let's not name him publicly. He died in the early seventies. We questioned him early in the case and tried to break through again some nineteen months later. This man had made himself a voluntary mental patient at Glenside Hospital only a few days after the children vanished. It was said that he had sex-deviate tendencies and so on. We went into it thoroughly but could not nail anything down. But despite any supporting evidence then or since, I still feel it possible that he knew something.

'It was said that at the time of the children vanishing, the man had been living alone in a street only one away from the Glenelg beach. The Glenside Hospital where he was admitted a few days later is roughly eight miles away, slightly north of east by going along Anzac Highway.'[15]

Could the man have taken the children up into the Mount Lofty Ranges, which were another five or six kilometres away, and disposed of their bodies down one of the thousands of mine shafts there? Swaine, who was obviously a man who could not let go of a hunch, regardless of the available evidence, certainly thought so.

On 29 February 1968, a curious report was posted in the Melbourne *Herald*: 'Adelaide Homicide detectives made a secret visit to Melbourne this week. It is believed that Mr and Mrs Beaumont came with the detectives. They booked into a south-east suburban motel. None of the other guests recognised them. Melbourne police were not aware of the visit. It is believed the detectives were following what they believed was a worthwhile lead ... the detectives checked the lead and returned to Adelaide yesterday.'[16]

Not surprisingly, given that the Beaumont Case was a continuing investigation, Superintendent Lenton refused to confirm or deny the report. 'There has been nothing to make us believe there was likely to be any developments in the Beaumont case,' Lenton told *The Advertiser*. 'Nothing has happened in recent weeks to cause us to review our attitude and no relevant or material information has come to light.'[17]

What prompted Adelaide detectives to make a clandestine trip to Victoria with Jim and Nancy Beaumont? Why was nothing revealed at the time? The true story behind this aspect of the case, which became known as the 'Dandenong Letters', was not pieced together until several years later.

In February 1968, the Melbourne *Herald* ran a series of articles entitled 'The Beaumont Disclosures' as part of a News

Limited serialisation to mark the second anniversary of the children's disappearance. In these articles, which ran over three days, Jim and Nancy reiterated their belief that their 'kiddies' were still alive.

Almost immediately, they received the following letter written in a childlike script in blue ink:

Dear Mum and Dad,
We are safe, so there is no need to worry about us! Oh, we really missed you in the last two years. At the beach on that day, we were walking to the bustop [sic] when a man in a car stopped us and asked us if we wanted a ride. I said that we did and that is how it all started. The man would not let us write before. He is letting us write tonight because he saw the story in the Herald tonight and felt sorry for you both. He watched us a lot for about six weeks and then he did not watch us so much. Arna [sic] and I often talk about you but Grant does not remember you at all after more than two years. We have been well fed all the time. I as well as Arna and Grant hope that you are both well. The man said to me just now that he will willingly let us go if you will come over to Victoria to get us as long as you do not call the police. He said that if you do the deal is off. You have to pick us up in front of the Dandenong post office at ten minutes to nine o'clock next Monday, the twenty sixth of February. You, Dad, have to wear a dark coat and white pants so that the man will know you. The

man told me to tell you that the police must not know at all. He said that if you do tell them, you may as well not come, so please do not tell them. The Dandenong post office is in Victoria in case you did not know. We are all looking forward to seeing you next Monday. Please do not tell the police. The man did not mean to harm us. We still love you both.

Love Jane, Arna and Grant. (This is Jane who is writing.)[18]

Despite the fact that one of their daughters' names was misspelt 'Arna' and that the writing did not match the handwriting style of their eldest daughter, for the second time since their children went missing Jim and Nancy Beaumont were again filled with hope. Like the 'Kaniva' phone call in September 1966, the arrival of this letter fed the Beaumonts' innermost belief that they would one day see their children again. 'Children are life,' Jim Beaumont once said. 'You can't get away from that, can you?'[19] Now, they had a letter to cling to.

Against the wishes of whoever wrote the letter, Detective Sergeant Stan Swaine became involved in the affair. Swaine later said that he forensically checked the handwriting of the letter against one of Jane Beaumont's exercise books stored at Glenelg CIB and that there were 'many characteristics' that were similar.[20] (Even to the casual observer there is little similarity between the letters, but sometimes one sees what one wants to believe.) Swaine did not tell Superintendent

Lenton of his plans, but talked the Beaumonts into allowing him to organise a secret trip to Dandenong with them in order to keep the appointment with 'the man' on Monday 26 February.

Trusting Swaine was the Beaumonts' next mistake; the first was believing that the letter was real.

Stan Swaine asked an associate named Bill Cotton to drive him and the Beaumonts to Melbourne in a borrowed 1966 brown Dodge Phoenix. They left Adelaide at 3 am and changed cars once they reached Melbourne. The Beaumonts were booked into the Commodore Motel six kilometres outside Dandenong under Nancy's maiden name of Ellis. However, Swaine made the stunning error of booking himself and Bill Cotton in at the Dandenong Hotel under their real names. The following morning, Swaine planned to dress in a khaki shirt and slacks and pose as a window cleaner in front of a light-coloured 'Hemco Industries' van, within sight of the post office. But without him even knowing it, matters quickly swung out of control.

Some time on Sunday afternoon, Douglas 'Stainless' Steele, a former Adelaide reporter who was chief of staff for the Melbourne *Herald*, was contacted by a local Dandenong police sergeant. 'Funny thing,' the sergeant told Steele. 'I got a call not long ago from a local publican. He knew that we have had a lot of safe busts around here recently and rang me to say a stranger had booked in at his pub and would I check him out. So I checked him out and found he was a detective sergeant named Swaine from Adelaide. I didn't know he was here, but he checks OK.'

'Swaine?' Steele thought. '"Tonner" Swaine? He's been on the Beaumont case!'[21]

The following morning, Steele sent two *Herald* reporters to Dandenong to see what was going on. But even he had been beaten to the scoop. John Kroeger, the chief of staff for the Adelaide *News*, had been informed on the Sunday night that Jim and Nancy Beaumont had left for Dandenong with Stanley Swaine to meet an unknown man who was going to return the Beaumont children after two years. Ken May (later Sir Ken May), the head of News Limited in Adelaide, actually received the tip-off from someone close to the Beaumonts, and he then told Kroeger to follow up what could have been the story of the decade.[22]

Kroeger quickly contacted police roundsman Ken Anderson, journalist Doug Easom and photographers Bert Stansbury and Mick Conrey, and the group of five newsmen rushed towards Melbourne in two cars. They arrived in Dandenong, thirty kilometres south-east of the Melbourne CBD, at five the following morning. After freshening up in a motel room, Kroeger took his men to the Dandenong Post Office and staked them at several vantage points shortly after 7 am in order to record what was about to unfold.

Photographers Stansbury and Conrey shot the scene with their 'Long Tom' cameras from about 150 metres away. Some time before 9 am, a light-coloured van pulled up near the post office, which was situated on a sharp corner in the middle of town. All five Adelaide newsmen immediately recognised the man who got out of the van in work clothes as Stan Swaine. At about nine o'clock, Jim Beaumont took up a position in front of the post office; as instructed, he was wearing a blue bowling blazer and white slacks.

Alice Parker was working at the post office on that searingly hot summer's day, and she remembered the day 'of some commotion' many years later. Mrs Parker recalled that there were two calls made that morning: 'The speaker was a man [and] sounded like an Australian. It was masculine and the message sounded genuine. "Hello, is that Dandenong Post Office? Look, I wonder if you could do me a favour? Can you see a man standing outside your office, wearing white cricket slacks and a blue blazer? Well, would you mind popping out and telling him I won't be long? I've had a bit of trouble but I'll be there as quick as I can.'

Mrs Parker did just that, and the man was very thankful. 'When I reached my counter I said: "You know, that man looks like Mr Beaumont, who had his kids stolen . . . Just after that, one of our messenger boys came from the telegram room [and] said: "I've had a telephone call to tell a man outside that someone will be there shortly." I was sure then that the gentleman was Mr Beaumont. He listened to the boy [and] waited there for a long time.'[23]

The second message said that Grant was sick and that they would be delayed until after lunch.

During the next six hours, Stan Swaine changed positions many times, moving the van to Patterson's store across the road, whistling the time away while keeping his eyes and ears open, ready to 'scoop [the children] up and whisk them back along the Melbourne road to the motel where Nancy was waiting'.[24] At one stage Jim Beaumont crossed the road to retrieve another message from one of the shops opposite the post office. But when no-one came by three o'clock, Jim Beaumont walked away despondently. Something had gone wrong with the plan.

The newsmen drifted away to a nearby pub, where they came face to face with Stan Swaine and Jim Beaumont. Bert Stansbury later told author Alan Dower: 'And "Tonner" looks at us and goes white — dead white — with shock and anger, and he cries out, "What are you bastards doing here?" . . . We went back to our motel, then up to the Dandenong Hotel to make our peace. "Tonner" seemed to be living it down a bit. And Jim said he bore no malice. And Nancy was there too. I didn't know she came over. Anyhow, she joined us in a drink or two and we even had a little dance before the five of us packed up and started for home. And that was my last connection with the Beaumont Case.'[25]

The press were now onto the story and Swaine, AWOL from his official duties as head of Adelaide CIB, hurriedly returned to face Superintendent Lenton. Dandenong, Melbourne and Adelaide police were able to suppress news of the Dandenong Letters with a curt 'no comment' but Jim and Nancy Beaumont remained in town for several more days. The following day, Jim Beaumont again stood in front of the post office waiting for the man who would never come, and on the third day he shifted to opposite the post office, in front of Patterson's store, just in case he had made a mistake.

The day after the Beaumonts' Dandenong rendezvous came to naught, other letters, written in the same round hand, were posted to Jim and Nancy Beaumont's family home in Somerton Park. One of them was written in red ink. The first read:

Dear Mum and Dad,
We had a really beautiful lunch today. We had some turky [sic], and a lot of vegetables. They tasted really nice. The man is feeding us really well. The man took us to see the Sound of Music yesterday. Little Grant fell asleep in it though. He could not understand it. The man was very disappointed that you brought all those policemen with you. He knew all the time that they were there, he says that is why he sent the message to go across the street so that it would disturb the positions of the policemen. The man said that I had better stop now, so I will. Grant and Arnna send you their love.

Love Jane, Arnna and Grant.
𝗑 𝗑

A second letter, also posted on 29 February, was from 'the man':

Dear Mr. and Mrs. Beaumont,
I am terribly sorry that I could not hand you your children back to you when you were in Dandenong, but I knew that you had detectives with you, and the main street was so busy.
 I am taking extra good care of the kiddies for you. I took little Grant to the doctor because of his gashed knee. He is feeling a lot better now. (Gashed to his ankle.)

Actually, in a way, it is your own fault that I did not return them. I saw the letter that Jane wrote before she sent it and it definately [sic] said that there were to be no police (and you know that that includes detectives as well).

I apologize also for all the phone calls at the post office, William's and Roger David's, but I had to contact you somehow. Like William's, the post office soon became quite 'BITCHY.' I got frantic when they would not give you any more messages. Then I got into contact with whom I believe was the Dandenong Post Office master.

I guess it is too late now, isn't it. I will put them on the train to Adelaide one of these days in the near future, so you had better have their rooms cleaned up!

The assumed Postmaster gave me a phone number to ring. I did so in a hurry. But the girl there lied miserably by saying that a Mr. G. A. Beaumont had not been registered there. If only I could have talked to you then, you might have had your children safely by now!

Isn't it a pitty [sic] you brought those Detectives!

I will write to you as often as possible. I will let Jane and perhaps Arnna write to you.

I am sorry for all the inconvenience I have caused you over the past two and a quarter years (nearly).

Yours faithfully, 'THE MAN'

A third letter, with the Dandenong postmark faded and the date indecipherable, arrived some time later.

> Dear Mum and Dad,
> I wish you could have got us when you were over here but the man said that you brought some policemen with you. I wish that you had not done that. If you had not, we might have been home by now with you both. The man said that he will let us come home on the train one day. I want you to know and never forget, no matter what happens, that we still love you both very much.
>
> Love,
> Jane, Arnna and Grant.
> *x x x x x x x x x x x x x x x x x x x x x* [26]

The letters tugged at the consciences of Jim and Nancy Beaumont ('isn't it a pity you brought those Detectives?') and were filled with references to current events (the popular film of the time *The Sound of Music*) and the health of the children ('I took little Grant to the doctor because of his gashed knee'). They gave the reader the impression that the three 'kiddies' were alive and well and living in some bizarre parallel universe just out of reach. Tragically, the Beaumonts also believed this.

Jim Beaumont gave photocopies of the letters to an Adelaide journalist, the aptly named Dick Wordley, who in turn gave them to Alan Dower, the famed police roundsman on the Melbourne *Sun*, who published them for the first time in their entirety in his 1979 memoir *Deadline*. Dower stated that although the postmarks on the letters were genuine, the

Dandenong Letters were most likely a hoax. When he tracked down Stan Swaine to discuss this view with the now former Adelaide detective, Swaine was not so ready to concede defeat: 'To this day [1979] it cannot be proven conclusively whether the Dandenong affair was a hoax or a genuine plan which some circumstances rocked off the rails. I have private reasons — private only to the general public — for suspecting often that it was a setup. And yet one cannot help wondering still — unless someone confesses and risks charges of conspiracy and public mischief — whether there was substance in it.'[27]

Instead, Swaine was sure that someone from his own police department had 'fizzed' to *The News* in Adelaide about the secret mission to Dandenong. But Swaine did not tell his superiors of his trip to Dandenong nor did he inform local police of his presence in Victoria. It is highly unlikely that he even had the handwriting of the letters checked, because he was determined to solve the Beaumont mystery by himself.

The embarrassment Stan Swaine suffered over the affair led to his eventual retirement from the police force and fuelled an obsession with solving the case that was to last the rest of his life.

7

The Detective

Stanley Swaine was an old-school police detective. At six foot two and weighing seventeen stone, he was nicknamed 'Tonner' by fellow police officers because of his size. Surviving an early brush with death, Swaine graduated from the Motor Transport Unit to Homicide, and was not afraid to throw his considerable weight or reputation around Adelaide. Six months after the disappearance of the Beaumont children from Glenelg beach, Swaine began investigating the case that had baffled the entire nation.

Swaine explored various scenarios: that the Beaumonts had been taken by a former mental patient into the Mount Lofty Ranges; that they had been handed over to a religious cult by their parents and were still alive; and that they had been abducted, murdered and buried anonymously in Brighton Cemetery. Despite these different theories over thirty years, many media outlets published Swaine's views on the case without considering the impact they had on others — especially on the parents of the three Beaumont children, Swaine's family and his own reputation.

Almost three years after Stan Swaine's death in March 2003, at age 79, his family still struggles to provide a balanced view of his legacy and his involvement in the Beaumont Case.

Swaine's former wife Pat Plummer, now in her eighties, and daughters Meg, Elizabeth and Alexandra, speak of a complex, contradictory man who became consumed with solving the Beaumont Case.

Elizabeth, the second of Stan Swaine's three daughters and one who still carries his surname, agrees with her sisters on the following issues. 'I have never dealt with my father's death or the manner of his life,' she says. 'I look upon his life with sorrow. He suffered, and lost much that he loved because of his character. His life was a tragedy [and] his obsession with the Beaumonts became worse over time and gradually overtook any [logical] consideration of the situation.'[1]

On 22 September 1952, 27-year-old Stanley Swaine was on duty as an Adelaide motor-traffic constable when he was involved in an incident that would scar the remainder of his adult life. With his partner Mick Morross at the wheel of the police utility, the pair were travelling south along West Terrace just as a motorbike sped past the Currie Street intersection doing about 130 kilometres an hour and making what Swaine later described as 'one hell of a racket'.[2] When the police vehicle drew alongside the motorbike near the intersection of Henley Beach Road and South Road, the rider of the bike suddenly stopped and hopped off. The man, who was unknown to the police officers, then stood beside the motorbike waiting for Swaine and his partner to approach him.

Because he was in the passenger seat of the police vehicle, Swaine got out first and walked towards the motorbike rider.

Unbeknown to Swaine, the rider was James William Turner, a man with a history of violent and disturbed behaviour. He had allegedly shot a police officer in the leg and had spent some time in Parkside Mental Home. Turner had maintained that he was Jesus Christ and that the police had no right to arrest the Son of God. Recently released from Parkside, Turner had deliberately removed the exhaust pipe up to the manifold of his motorbike so that the noise would attract the attention of the police. Now, as Swaine approached, Turner drew a twenty-eight-centimetre screwdriver from the long overcoat that he was wearing and lunged at the young policeman.

The screwdriver had been sharpened to a point and the metal pierced Swaine's skull above the left eye, driving past the outer layer of the frontal lobe and into the sinuses to a depth of ten centimetres. Turner immediately pulled the screwdriver out of Swaine's head and tried to stab him again (causing another minor injury to the policeman's forehead) but by that time Mick Morross had grabbed the man from behind, knocked over the motorbike and wrestled him to the ground. Swaine felt the sharp burn of pain in his head; so much blood gushed from the wound, he said, and ran down the inside of his uniform that his boots soon filled with blood.

Swaine later told a coroner's court that he didn't remember drawing his .32 Browning automatic pistol and cocking it, but that he must have done so instinctively as he watched, through blood-soaked eyes, his partner struggle with the armed man. Aiming as best he could, Swaine fatally shot

Turner through the heart. With the assailant dead, Swaine wandered the roadside, bleeding profusely, until a nurse passing by in a taxi stopped to help. Without waiting for an ambulance, the nurse put Swaine in the taxi and took him to Royal Adelaide Hospital.

Stan Swaine's wife and young family were at home when this incident happened and were listening to the radio in that pre-television era. At 10.15 am, Pat Swaine had finished the laundry and was about to listen to her favourite radio serial, *Napoleon and Josephine*, when a news item came over the air. Two motor traffic constables had been involved in a shooting incident with an unknown man and there had been a death, the report stated. The names of the two police officers were released as Mick Morross and Stan Swaine but the identity of who had actually been shot was not stated. For a moment, Pat Swaine stood staring at the radio willing the newsreader to tell her *who* had been shot dead: her husband, his partner or the unknown man?

Gathering up her young children, four-year-old Margaret (Meg) and twenty-month-old Elizabeth, Pat went to her nextdoor neighbour's house. Pat had trained as a nurse at the Royal Adelaide Hospital, and knew that her neighbour had gone through a troubled pregnancy, so she didn't want to upset her in case she had a miscarriage. But finally the silence got to her, and after Pat told her neighbour what she had heard on the radio, the pair waited for the police to contact them. When Mick Morross arrived at the Swaine residence in the Adelaide Hills, Pat believed it was her husband who had been killed. Swaine's partner told Pat the details of her husband's injuries and took her to the hospital in a police car.

Although Swaine cheated death by a matter of millimetres and fully recovered, it was clear to those closest to him that he came home from hospital a changed man. 'In a sense he never came home again,' his daughter, journalist Elizabeth Swaine, wrote in a newspaper article in 1990. 'The person who did eventually return was totally changed; he was not the father I had known but a bloodied, swollen and terrifying image who, because of his injuries, never quite looked the same again.'[3]

Before he returned to work, Swaine promptly disappeared to Melbourne with Mick Morross, leaving his young wife to look after the family. When Swaine returned to work two months after the attack, there were problems — some physical, some emotional — that were to change him as a man, a husband, a father and a police officer. The physical injuries were easy to see: a scar over the eye and a nervous tic that made his eye beat 'like a butterfly wing'.[4] The young policeman also suffered from headaches and double vision, and often had to yawn to activate a lazy tear duct. But the psychological damage, which manifested itself in bizarre mood swings, violent outbreaks against his family and obsessive behaviours, became the cross the Swaine family had to carry for the next two decades.

'Stan may have suffered from post traumatic stress syndrome,' says Pat, 'but there was no counselling in those days and I doubt he would have listened anyway. His brother [a doctor] made an appointment to see a psychologist but he didn't keep it.' Swaine always maintained that he could not trust a psychiatrist because it was a psychiatrist who had allowed James Turner to go free despite the fact that he had spoken openly about what he was going to do to the police. It would be another twenty-five years before the South Australia Police set up a counselling service with trained psychologists. There was no counselling for Swaine, his wife or their children over the years, despite Swaine maintaining that he never came to terms with the fact that he took another man's life.

Instead, Swaine turned to hypnotism. 'For five years I was very traumatised, both physically and mentally,' Swaine wrote in an unpublished memoir. 'It was common for me to feel badly every third day, sometimes feeling like throwing a typewriter through the window. However, I liked working "in the field" and persisted. I have never fully recovered.' During one long nightshift session, Swaine decided that he needed to go home. A constable on the radio desk, Col Cliffe, suggested that Swaine should allow Cliffe to hypnotise him. 'As a result, I later went home and slept for ten hours,' Swaine wrote. 'It transformed my life.'[5]

Swaine asked Cliffe to teach him how to hypnotise people. In fact, Swaine became so adept at it that he used to conduct 'hypnosis evenings' at local boy scout meetings at Norwood. 'He got so good at hypnotising people,' remembers his youngest daughter, Alexandra, 'that he was even able to do it over the phone.' In the 1960s, Stan Swaine graduated to holding public hypnosis sessions at the Arkaba Hotel on Friday nights — not unlike the hypnotists who appear on television today.

Despite his headstrong personality, Stan Swaine was undoubtedly a police officer on the way up. In 1954 he was selected to be one of the officers in charge of security for the Queen on the Royal Tour of South Australia. In the late 1950s he joined the 'larrikin squad', whose job it was to break up groups of young bodgies and widgies around Adelaide nightspots, thus preventing these 'delinquents' from causing trouble. In 1961 Swaine was seconded to the London Metropolitan Police Force to gain experience there. In a stroke of luck, the English police misunderstood his rank at the time (detective senior constable) and so he spent a stint in Scotland Yard working in the area of scientific and criminal investigation.

Stan Swaine secured his reputation in the early 1960s with the Wendy Jane Pfeiffer Case, in which a young girl was abducted from a country hamlet east of the Adelaide Hills. According to Swaine's unpublished account of the case a local clergyman confessed to the child's murder. Four hundred searchers were unable to find the little girl's body in the thick scrub, so the following morning Swaine worked with an Aboriginal tracker and followed footprints down to a river, where they heard the little girl whimpering. The father of the girl was hurriedly brought to the area to call for her, and she was ultimately found injured, but it was Swaine who carried the girl out of the scrub to the waiting press.

These experiences ultimately assisted his career (Swaine already being one of the youngest police officers in Adelaide promoted to detective at that time), and he left his family and went overseas on professional secondment for almost twelve months. With three young girls to support and a mortgage to pay, Pat Swaine had no choice but to return to work as a registered nurse. Later, her financial and professional independence from her husband would be her lifesaver.

On Australia Day 1966, Pat Swaine was on duty at Abergeldie Private Hospital when someone told her that three children had gone missing at Glenelg beach. She drove home that night never thinking that this one event would affect her family for their rest of their lives.

When the Beaumont children disappeared, Stan Swaine was not in Adelaide. Having become a detective senior sergeant in Homicide, he was prosecuting a criminal case at Quorn in the Flinders Ranges when the three children went missing from Glenelg beach. Shortly after, Swaine was made head of the Adelaide CIB Homicide Squad at the young age of forty-one. In September 1966 he investigated the 'Kaniva connection', in which a local constable overhead a telephone call from a person allegedly bringing the Beaumont children back from Hobart. However, Swaine failed to heed the advice of Melbourne detectives and believed the call to be genuine. This proved an early embarrassment for him in his career.

At a time when investigating detectives kept their own diaries of criminal investigations, and the available paperwork largely consisted of an unwieldy number of police running sheets, Swaine was asked to organise the Beaumont files for a conference of Australian and visiting New Zealand CIB detectives. However, despite having a good working knowledge of the case, he put himself at the forefront of the Beaumont investigation through one of those 'six degrees of separation' experiences that seem to be so prevalent in Adelaide. A woman living in apartments that Swaine owned in Glenelg was a Mrs Parsons — the paternal grandmother of the missing Beaumont children.

According to his family, Swaine was obsessed by money. He made a small fortune out of his Poseidon shares during the nickel boom of 1969–70, but Pat Swaine later discovered that he gambled on the stock market using funds borrowed from the police credit union in the name of his wife and children. Swaine also inherited a large sum of money from a woman whom he befriended while still in the Motor Transport Unit. With the money, Swaine was able to buy a two-storey home with an apartment upstairs in Gordon Street, Glenelg. The Adelaide detective rented the units as an investment property while the entire family chipped in to clean and renovate the property. While she was cleaning an apartment, Pat Swaine met Mrs Parsons at the Glenelg property and recognised her as someone with whom she had worked at the Royal Adelaide Hospital when training to be a nurse some twenty years before. A level of trust was quickly formed with the entire Swaine family. It seemed the Beaumonts could now count on the high-ranking, high-profile Adelaide detective to solve the mystery of this two-year-old case.

One day Swaine came home from visiting the Beaumonts and was, according to his former wife, 'all lit up'. Her husband promptly announced that he was going to solve the Beaumont Case. Mrs Parsons had told Swaine an incredible story: somehow the children were sending letters to their parents, Jim and Nancy Beaumont.

Swaine then did something equally incredible: he took his own family to the Beaumonts' home in Somerton Park one night. Even at the age of twelve, Alexandra (Alex) Swaine, who was the same age as Jane Beaumont, thought the visit was 'unnerving'. 'How must Mrs Beaumont have felt?' Alex later said. In the words of Pat Swaine, 'Stan dragged us around there [to meet the Beaumonts] and I just felt it was all wrong ... there were a lot of people there that night and there was a lot of talking going on. Mr and Mrs Beaumont had received a letter, so they said, from the children and a man was going to meet Jim Beaumont in Dandenong and hand them back ...'

Pat Swaine especially remembers the children's rooms. 'The door was open and the rooms were left the same as the day the children disappeared.' The clothing, the hats, the schoolbags, the toys were all perfectly preserved for the day when the children returned home. 'While they were all talking I kept thinking to myself ... this is all wrong. The Beaumonts were very excited, especially Jim Beaumont. When Nancy brought out other letters there was a lot of laughter in the house — almost like hysteria. There was something not quite right about everything.'

Alex recalls: 'The adults were behaving [peculiarly] that night ... I remember thinking how old the Beaumonts were ... they were both in their early forties but they had both aged.' The loss of their children had undoubtedly taken a physical and emotional toll on the pair. To secure the relationship with the Beaumonts, Swaine instructed his wife to buy a whole range of Lincot blankets from Jim Beaumont. The Swaine children referred to them as the 'Beaumont blankets' over the ensuing years.

Elizabeth Swaine also remembers her family's visit with the Beaumont family. 'With the insight of maturity, I look back and realise how inappropriate it was that, as a family, we should have become so involved with the Beaumonts,' she says.[6] According to Elizabeth, this was the first of several 'inappropriate' contacts the Swaines had with the Beaumonts.

After this first visit, Pat Swaine couldn't wait to tell her husband of her misgivings. 'I told him not to go [to Victoria]. There was something not right. How was it that Mrs Beaumont had brought out more letters while we were there that night? My gut feeling was that it was a setup. I remember saying to Stan, "You're the detective; can't you see it?" The Police Superintendent, Noel Lenton, told Stan to have nothing to do with the letters but not even he could stop him. Stan did not let Melbourne police know [about the trip to Dandenong] because the South Australia Police did not sanction it. But he wanted to do it all by himself ... he was already obsessed by it.'

It was always thought that Swaine was on 'official' police business in Dandenong but it has now been revealed that he was actually making a clandestine trip in the hope of solving the case once and for all. Swaine arranged for a man named Bill Cotton to arrive at 3 am on the morning of 26 February 1968 to secretly take Swaine and the Beaumonts to Melbourne. A businessman supplied the van in which they travelled to Dandenong, but it all went terribly wrong. Stan Swaine later wrote his own account of proceedings: 'I feel confident that this was a genuine attempt to recover the children, to let parties involved off the hook ... But we had been betrayed to the press and unknown to me we were followed by the media. When I subsequently discovered this I withdrew and returned to Adelaide. There is a whole story here as to what this betrayal cost me by way of my police career, and it was then that I became determined [to] solve the matter, and have in fact kept very interested in the matter ... during the last 35 years.'[7]

Subsequent developments, not least of which was the later revelation that the letter was sent by a Dandenong teenager as an elaborate hoax, prove that Swaine was well off the mark.

Pat Swaine was at home tending to the family horse, which was suffering from colic, when the telephone rang on the day after Stan had taken the Beaumonts to Dandenong. It was her husband. 'Stan was trapped in his room by journalists. He couldn't speak to the press because he wasn't supposed to be in Melbourne. Stan wanted me to ring Superintendent Lenton and try to get him out of there. I rang Superintendent Lenton and told him what had happened and he asked me for my phone number so that he could ring me back.' Some time later, Lenton rang Pat and told her that he had instructed Swaine, in no uncertain terms, to get back to Adelaide under his own steam. 'The police knew that the Beaumonts, in their grief, were being misled by the letters but Stan couldn't see it.'

Soon after that the phone rang again; it was the grandmother of the Beaumont children. All hell had broken loose and she too was besieged by journalists. 'I'm not staying here,' she told Pat. Soon journalists were knocking on the door of the Swaine family home. 'The phone was ringing off the hook by then and the journos were asking where Stan was,' Pat says. 'I told them I didn't know.'

Stan Swaine was not so much embarrassed as livid that someone had betrayed him and foiled his chance of solving the case. Swaine coveted media attention and was loath to criticise the press, so he turned his disgust on his own colleagues; someone in the South Australia Police must have given the media details of the secret trip. He was wrong. Swaine had made the mistake of signing the hotel registry in his own name and a suspicious hotel owner alerted police.

The Dandenong Letters did have a detrimental effect on Swaine's career, but it was more his erratic behaviour and poor judgement that precipitated his exit from the force some five years later. In an effort to redeem himself in the eyes of the South Australia Police, Swaine never stopped trying to solve the Beaumont Case. However, his relationship with the Beaumonts soured after the Dandenong fiasco.

Despite these setbacks, his eldest daughter Meg says that her father never let the case go. 'He was always talking about it and was adamant that he was going to prove one of his theories correct one day.'

'A lot of it was ego,' says Pat Swaine, who was soon to end the 27-year marriage. 'When Stan went into Homicide he said he was going to solve *all* the unsolved murders in

Adelaide. He was an excellent, analytical accident investigator but he just wasn't the right sort of person emotionally to handle homicide cases. Stan used to talk to community groups and schools about road accidents and the need to wear seatbelts.' Through intense lobbying, Swaine helped to convince the South Australian state government to be the first to introduce the mandatory wearing of seatbelts. Intelligent, well read and a good public speaker, he was also highly effective in court. But Swaine's domestic life became increasingly unpredictable.

In 1969, Swaine took his family on a six-month holiday to Europe. Meg Swaine, who was training as a nurse at the time and was aged about twenty-one, didn't go on the trip. 'It was total madness,' she says, referring to the scope and size of the tour that the family undertook. The Swaines visited many countries, including the communist USSR, where Stan Swaine asked the government tourist agency, Intourist, if he could meet with local police. Swaine was such a charming and persuasive talker that his family says he was granted an interview with the KGB.

But back in Adelaide, Swaine confided to his wife that he had 'always lived a double life'. Says Pat, 'I have always said that I was married to a man I didn't know.' Swaine took to disappearing in the middle of the night, and he beat and bullied his family. By 1973 his family had had enough. 'He was a violent man,' says his daughter Alex. 'I ended up packing his bags for him.'

After one violent episode, Pat called the police. Swaine's colleagues arrived to find him trying to break back into the house. '[The police] warned him and he went quite berserk,' Pat remembers. After issuing an order of restraint against her husband, a local police inspector warned Pat not to return to the house. When Swaine was served with divorce papers, he staked out the family home and even followed his daughter Alex to school in his patrol car. The divorce was traumatic. 'In those days you had to go and give evidence at your own divorce,' remembers Pat Swaine, who later married a former war veteran, Jim Plummer. Stan Swaine was accused of mental cruelty, which was the worst thing a serving policeman — let alone a leading Adelaide detective sergeant — could be accused of. His police career ended soon after, and he became a private investigator.

At that time, Swaine's family did not know whether his injury, the pressures of his job (including investigating the Beaumont Case), or his own personality traits were responsible for his erratic behaviour, but the last thirty years of his life certainly leave many unanswered questions. Swaine later travelled overseas and met his second wife, Treena. 'If you could get all the women he was with in one room, you'd have an interesting story,' says his daughter Meg.

Swaine lived in Melbourne for some time but returned to Adelaide when he allegedly thought that the Melbourne under-world was after him. One woman he was 'engaged' to was found murdered in the boot of a suspect's car. Swaine went on *60 Minutes* and actually got the murderer's guilty charge down-graded to assault on appeal. The promised 'reimbursement' Swaine had hoped for when the man was released from prison never eventuated. However, the Beaumont Case remained an unsolved obsession for him.

Swaine was staying with his daughter Elizabeth in Canberra in 1997 when he was told that a local woman thought she was Jane Beaumont grown to adulthood. Undergoing treatment from her therapist, the woman had a 'repressed memory' that she was Jane Beaumont and had been abducted as a child. Despite the fact that the allegations were easily disproved, the retired detective rushed into print with his newest theory. 'I believed the girl to be mentally disturbed,' Elizabeth Swaine recently told me, 'and felt that even if there was some reason to believe her, it should be the police who were notified, not my father. I said that these days a DNA test could be conducted and the matter resolved easily. He would not listen and continued to pursue the matter to an unfortunate public conclusion. Through it he looked old and foolish, and it broke my heart.'[8]

In later life, Swaine was overtaken by his obsession with money. His eldest daughter, Meg, claims that 'during his infamous stay in Melbourne, he befriended a woman who became a close friend of mine and ultimately he owed a lot of money to her. He only paid back the money after he inherited $80 000 from a distant cousin ... When she died I told him that if he didn't pay the money back that he owed, I would make his life miserable and let him never forget that he still had money that didn't belong to him.'

Elizabeth Swaine says of her father: 'He was driven to make something of his life by a sense of inferiority that afflicted him all his life. But that drive, imperfectly applied, caused him to sometimes make poor decisions and carry a large chip on his shoulder.' Stan Swaine always enjoyed the finer things in life, she says, and he then 'tried to live up to it, hence the suits, the shoes, the big cars, and an opportunistic approach to gaining money'. Even in failing health, Stan Swaine could be 'charming', 'urbane' and 'attractive to women'.[9]

Meg was in frequent contact with her father, but their relationship had its limits. 'He rode an emotional rollercoaster late in life,' says Meg. 'He would be absolutely "up" and excited about something — the Beaumont Case, some money he had come into or a business opportunity — and then it would all fall apart and he would be in a manic state. When he was down it was always someone else's fault.' Swaine would ring his daughters and tell them, sometimes weeping into the phone, that he would shoot himself if they didn't look after him. She recalls: 'He was staying with us in Adelaide in the early 1980s when he ran up a $2000 phone bill — an extraordinary amount in those days — because there was a woman in Germany whom he had convinced that he was a prophet of some sort. The stabbing that he survived in 1952 was something of a "second coming", and the group of people that she was associated with actually flew him over to Germany and hosted him for twelve months. When I confronted him with the bill, he said that I had plenty of money and could afford to pay it! I had to put an STD bar on my phone to protect us from my own father.'

In 2001, flying in the face of all the available facts, Stan Swaine stated that there was a 'strong possibility' that the

Beaumont children were still alive. However, towards the end of his life, Swaine refused to go to the police with his findings because, he said, 'the last time [I gave them information] they stuffed it up.' Instead, Swaine wanted to publish his theories in a book in order to force a judicial inquiry. He maintained that over the years the evidence he had amassed would 'hold up in court'.

On the eve of the thirty-fifth anniversary of the disappearance of the Beaumont children, Swaine again rushed into print, this time in *Who Weekly* magazine. 'For Swaine, who now walks with a stick and suffers failing sight, it has never ended,' wrote Penelope Green. 'For more than three decades, his obsession with uncovering the fate of the Beaumonts has drawn him back to Glenelg beach — most recently this Christmas Day — and he has amassed large files on the vanishing. Now he says he wants to publish. "I'm not saying it can or will solve the mystery," says Swaine warily, "but it *could*."'[10]

At the age of seventy-six, Stan Swaine was still looking for that 'lucky break' to solve the case and to publish *his* story. 'My father operated in a totally ethics- and moral-free zone when it came to the Beaumont Case,' says Meg. In his unpublished account of the case, Swaine was critical of the behaviour of both Beaumont parents on the day Jane, Arnna and Grant disappeared.

'When I first met the Beaumonts I was very sympathetic to their plight and I was determined to do everything to solve the mystery,' Swaine wrote. 'However, subsequent events eventually have driven me to other conclusions ... I have made previous submissions but I have withheld certain facts which are pertinent to the possible solving of this particular mystery.

'I did say on Television, Channel 10, at one stage that I believed that the children had been handed over by Nancy Beaumont to a cult. And there is a lot more to be said about that. The Beaumonts never objected nor made any move whatsoever to deny that what I was saying was true.'[11]

Swaine claimed that Nancy Beaumont was 'drinking with friends' on the day the children disappeared, that Jim Beaumont was 'troubled' when he returned to Adelaide that afternoon and that three weeks later the parents were in a 'happy frame of mind' when they allegedly caravanned in Victoria. He also tried to make much of a police report that the Beaumonts had not reported the children missing until '1930 hours' (7.30 pm) and that Jim Beaumont must have 'lied' about searching for the children, but Swaine was clearly wide of the mark.

While he was visiting his daughter Meg in North Queensland, Swaine heard of a scandal that hit the local Catholic Church. In the 1950s and 1960s, the stillborn of North Queensland were not recorded as registered births and therefore could not be afforded a Catholic burial. The nuns at one local hospital arranged with a local Catholic undertaker to anonymously bury the stillborn babies in the coffins of 'good' Catholic families so that they would, in essence, have a de facto Catholic burial with full funeral rites. Later, in the 1990s, when heartbroken mothers legally demanded to know where the remains of their children were buried so that they could provide them a proper burial, there were no official records of where the children's remains were. A long and protracted lawsuit ensued.

Stan Swaine, an insulin-dependent diabetic, was battling failing eyesight, poor mobility and a series of infections in the final year of his life. While staying in hospital in Adelaide, he offered the following scenario to a seemingly sympathetic hospital chaplain: had the three Beaumont children been abducted, murdered and buried anonymously in the coffins of other people in a local cemetery? A Catholic priest assigned to the hospital did not refute the story; in fact he told Swaine, possibly in order to placate him, that there may have been a bizarre burial at Brighton Cemetery around the time of the Beaumonts' disappearance. 'My father was a master storyteller,' says Meg. 'He was great at drawing people into his web of intrigue.'

The last conversation Alex had with her father was by phone from the hospital. 'This is going to be *big*,' Swaine said. 'I *will* solve it.' The urban myth surrounding the disappearance of the three Beaumont children had metamorphosed once again, ready for consumption by a new generation.

Stan Swaine died suddenly in February 2003 before he could get his final theory into print. Keen to leave hospital, Swaine had hastily married his third wife and made her the executor of his will so that she could sign him out of hospital. Soon after, Swaine's daughter Meg received a phone call from her mother at her work. Someone had told her that Swaine had passed away, his death being caused by the effects of diabetes.

The circumstances surrounding the former detective's death are full of intrigue. Swaine died on the Tuesday and was cremated on the Thursday. There was no death notice posted in the local papers until after the funeral, and the wrong date of birth was written on his death certificate: 1925 instead of 1924. His daughters were not invited to the service by Swaine's new wife because he wanted it that way, she said, telling everyone that they were estranged from him. Swaine was given a very simple funeral; he would probably have been disappointed with its lack of ceremony and the absence of the media. In fact, most of his former associates and remaining friends did not even know that he had died.

Swaine's wife did not tell his daughters the details of their father's death but later agreed to return his ashes to them. 'A year after his death to the day I rang *The Advertiser* and posted his death notice,' says Meg. 'I printed his name, correct birth date and the [year-old] date of his death and the fact that he was cremated without his family's knowledge and that his ashes were returned to his daughters for reburial. By putting it in the paper, without any fuss, people would surely know what happened. The funeral pastor was mortified when he heard that we were not informed about his death.'

Many questions about the real worth of Swaine's involvement in the case remain. 'I don't want to demonise him in death, but the truth is,' Pat confides, 'whether it was post traumatic stress syndrome or [an undiagnosed] psychosis that he had, Stan had a serious character flaw that was exacerbated by what happened to him [in 1952]. His job was to protect the public but he couldn't protect his family from himself.'

Meg is even more defiant in her belief that her father may have actually 'sidetracked' the Beaumont investigation. 'It became the defining moment of his life,' she says, 'but in the end he had no more idea what happened to those children than you or I. He took [the investigation] down dead ends where it should never have gone and he brought a lot of good, honest investigation into disrepute because he actually captured the headlines ... *he* became the story. He was an absolute master at capturing other people's grief and turning the whole situation more to his end.'

Elizabeth Swaine and her family made their peace with Stan before his death and felt that he had come to terms with not solving the Beaumont Case. 'My father was not an easy man to deal with, and his obsession with the Beaumont Case in the end made him a sad figure and, I'm sure, a frustration and irritation to the police,' she wrote to me in December 2005. 'My father had a fine mind but his emotional make-up often meant that his intellect was misapplied. But he was my father and I loved him and he is no longer here to defend himself.' [12]

Youngest daughter Alex kept her father at arm's length to protect her own family from emotional blackmail. She says, 'When I was young I always had the feeling that if [the police] found the Beaumont children, that I would get my father back. But it never happened. You just can't explain to people that it wasn't a noble thing that he was doing. In the end it was very sad.' She then contemplates the irony: 'My father spent the greater majority of his lifetime searching for the Beaumonts but lost his own children.'

Stanley Swaine did more than that. He lost his family, his career and finally himself.

8

The Adelaide Oval Case

The disappearance of the three Beaumont children from Glenelg beach has never been far from the consciousness of the Australian public. Although news of the police investigation into the unsolved mystery slowly slipped from the front pages of the nation's newspapers (except in January each year when the story was rehashed for summer holiday consumption), the events of that hot Australia Day became an integral part of Australia's urban mythology.

Then, in August 1973, two young girls were abducted from Adelaide Oval during a Saturday afternoon Australian Rules football match. Eleven-year-old Joanne Ratcliffe and four-year-old toddler Kirste Gordon did not know each other but they could easily have been mistaken for sisters. The Adelaide Oval abductions provided many parallels with the Beaumont Case seven years earlier: children taken from a public place in broad daylight during the school holidays; distraught parents making public appeals for their safe return; and a police investigation that provided few answers.

The South Australia Police used new methods to try to identify the children's abductor but the investigation into the Adelaide Oval Case produced another dead end. The questions remain: could the abductor of Joanne and Kirste also have been the same man who took Jane, Arnna and Grant Beaumont from Glenelg beach? Or were there two child abductors operating out of Adelaide — equally cold, equally calculating and supremely confident that they would get away with murder?

On Saturday 25 August 1973, Les Ratcliffe, a 38-year-old bread carter from the Adelaide suburb of Campbelltown, took his family to the Adelaide Oval in the heart of the city's parklands to watch an Aussie Rules football match. Mr Ratcliffe, a former apprentice jockey, always attended matches played by his favourite team, Norwood, which was playing North Adelaide at the hallowed oval that day. The Ratcliffes — Les's wife, Kath, their thirteen-year-old son, David, and eleven-year-old daughter, Joanne — left home at 10.30 that morning and watched the 'seconds' match in their usual spot in the Sir Edwin Smith Stand, surrounded by their friends and other Norwood supporters. By the time the first grade game started at about 1.30 pm, the crowd had swelled to over 12 000 screaming fans.

Also sitting in the grandstand that day was Mrs Rita Huckel, of Hackem, who was there with her four-year-old granddaughter, Kirste Ann Gordon. Mrs Huckel's daughter and son-in-law were away over the weekend, taking advantage of the school holidays. The Gordons planned to catch up with old friends in Renmark, on the Murray River north-west of Adelaide, where they had previously taught. They were due to return home that morning but decided to stay another day. The Ratcliffes knew Mrs Huckel but they had not met Kirste before. The little girl took an immediate liking to the Ratcliffes' daughter, Joanne, who was described by her family as a 'motherly type'.[1] When Kirste needed to go to the toilet,

Joanne offered to take her to the female toilets at the rear of the John Creswell Stand some three hundred metres away on the other side of the oval. Later, the two girls left the main group in the grandstand and went to get straws for their drinks. Then, in the third quarter of the main match, at about 3.45 or 3.50 pm, as the Ratcliffes recalled, Joanne again took Kirste to the toilet. But when they hadn't returned after ten or fifteen minutes, Mr and Mrs Ratcliffe went looking for them.

When no trace of them could be found, Joanne's parents raced to the top of the Members' Stand and Mrs Ratcliffe passed through a barricade and entered the Secretary's Office. The distraught mother asked that the Secretary of the South Australian Cricket Association, Mr Munn, broadcast an announcement that two young girls were missing. Kath Ratcliffe was told that the announcement could not be made during play because it would not be heard but she was also given the clear impression that the SACA could not make public appeals for every child who went missing at a sporting fixture. She was quietly encouraged to return to her seat and see if the girls had come back; if they did not, she was told, she should report the matter to a policeman. When she returned to where Mr Ratcliffe was waiting (the Members' Stand attendant would not let him through) the pair reluctantly returned to their seats. The announcement was made five minutes after the end of play as soon as it was requested a second time. The first report of the incident was received at Police Headquarters at 5.12 pm. By that time, the two girls had been long gone.

That night the police contacted Mr and Mrs Gordon at about 9 pm and informed them that their daughter was missing.

Kirste's parents returned to Adelaide at about midnight and Greg Gordon, a physics and maths teacher at Adelaide Boys' High, immediately went to Adelaide Oval and joined in the search. The missing children were described as follows:

Kirste Gordon

About 3 feet 4 inches tall, with blue eyes and of slim to medium build, with very fair English-type skin with faint freckles on either side of the nose. She has honey-blonde shoulder length hair with a fringe and has a slight scar above the bridge of the nose. She has a birth mark on the base of the spine and just below the hairline.

She was last seen wearing a white pleated skirt, purple jumper, and white panty hose with brown lace-up shoes.

Joanne Ratcliffe

Motherly type, about 4 feet 2 inches tall, blue eyes, medium build, with dark brown hair worn in two pigtails tied with rubber bands.

Last seen wearing a white blouse and white cardigan and mustard and black banded tank top, black jeans, white track shoes and blue stripes, a white bra and coloured panties and white socks. Also wearing a marcasite watch and imitation gold chain and gold medallion in oval shape with a two-inch purple stone hanging about the middle of the chest.[2]

The day after the disappearance, police revealed that they were investigating two persons of interest. A man dressed as a woman was seen near the women's toilets, but even he was a little too obvious a suspect. He had a protruding jaw and a large nose, and was dressed in a brown pants suit, green shirt, brown wig, silver nail polish and patent leather boots, and he carried a handbag. Police wanted to establish the identity of the man dressed as a woman seen driving a mustard-coloured Torana at about 3 pm that Saturday.

However, a second man was seen with two girls, believed to be Joanne and Kirste, at about 4 pm; the man was watching the girls as they tried to entice some kittens from underneath a car parked in a large equipment shed near the men's toilets behind the John Creswell Stand. He was later seen walking towards the southern gates with the children following him. This man was described by 61-year-old Ken Wohling, the assistant curator of the oval, as being five foot eight (173 centimetres) and wearing a brown hat with wide brim, a grey, checked sports coat and brown trousers. However, Mr Wohling only saw the suspect and the missing children from behind.

Joanne had gone to the oval to watch the football on countless occasions and was well aware of the dangers of talking to strangers. Kirste had never been to the football before. On 27 August, in the very first report of the girls' disappearance, it was mentioned that although the girls had never before met, Joanne 'would have been very keen to take care of Kirste'.[3] Joanne was a 'terror for cats and dogs,'[4] her father later told police, and it wouldn't have taken much for her to have become besotted with them.

Wohling showed the detectives who accompanied Les Ratcliffe to Adelaide Oval where the man was helping two young girls entice the kittens from under the car. He told detectives that he was in the staffroom of the shed when he heard two girls calling 'puss, puss'. He then heard a man's voice say 'I'll try and get him out for you.' Mr Wohling did not take much notice of the conversation at the time because there were many cats at Adelaide Oval and the children were always trying to play with them. 'I only saw them from behind,' Wohling said. 'I saw the man from the back walk towards the southern gate. He turned a bend and was gone.' The two girls followed the man a few yards behind. Wohling noticed that the man was stooped.

'Not long afterward the father [of Joanne] came looking in the shed,' Wohling told police reporter John Doherty. 'I assumed he was looking for the two girls. I said to him, "They're not here!"'[5] At that time, the elderly curator did not grasp the significance of Les Ratcliffe's frantic search.

On the Sunday morning after his daughter's disappearance, a heartbroken Les Ratcliffe accompanied detectives on a walk-through of his daughter's last known movements at Adelaide Oval. Several times Mr Ratcliffe broke down and cried; *The Advertiser* published a photo of the distraught father crying in the arms of Detective Inspector Col Lehmann, who was in charge of the case.

Meanwhile, police on foot and in a boat searched the Torrens River just a couple of hundred metres away. Divers began at the northern bank of the City Bridge and searched 200 metres downstream. Sheds and rubbish bins in every corner of

Adelaide Oval were searched, while other police groups searched the Festival Centre, the North Adelaide golf course and the railway yards. Roadblocks had been quickly set up and country-based police were already checking cars. Tip Top Bakery in Maylands, which employed Les Ratcliffe, took the unprecedented step of putting all their vans on the road that Sunday so that the drivers could look for any sign of the girls.

On the first day of the investigation, Superintendent Noel Lenton stated that the most important factor in the search was time. 'We need help from the public now,' Lenton told *The Advertiser*. 'Time is most important. It's no good someone ringing us with information in a week or even a few days ... if anyone has any suspicions that someone may be an active sexual deviate, we want to know about it.' He then added chillingly, 'We don't want this to become another Beaumont Case.'[6]

Lenton was just expressing what the rest of the country was thinking. Was this already another Beaumont Case? Journalists were already arriving from interstate to cover the investigation.

Police quickly dismissed the report of a transvestite near a women's toilet. A leading Adelaide psychiatrist stated that it would be 'very unlikely' that a transvestite would abduct two girls. Most child molesters were basically heterosexual and were unlikely to dress 'in drag' in public, he said. 'Public transvestites are usually homosexuals with nothing to hide,' the unnamed professional was quoted as saying in *The Advertiser*. 'General evidence is that molesters are ordinary, square-looking men who have had poor sexual adjustment and whose aim suddenly changes to a male or female child for gratification.' A recent study of child molesters in the United Kingdom, it was reported, found that all were heterosexual.[7]

Instead, police focused on the man seen leaving the equipment shed followed by the two young girls. Harry Roberts, the greenkeeper at the adjoining Adelaide Oval Bowls Club, saw a man loitering near the men's lavatory at the oval between 11 and 11.30 am. The man was described as middle-aged, about five foot eight and wearing clothes similar to those described by Ken Wohling. On the Sunday night, radio stations broadcast appeals to the public to be watchful of the man and the two young girls, even making their requests in Italian for the benefit of migrants in the city who might not have been aware of the unfolding drama because of the 'language barrier'.[8]

Adelaide had changed since the Beaumonts went missing: such public canvassing of sexual issues just would not have happened in the conservative 1960s, nor would the needs of migrants have been considered in public appeals.

Superintendent Noel Lenton also tried a new strategy: he appealed to the conscience of the girls' abductor. 'If he has any feelings at all, any human emotions, we appeal to them. We ask that he consider the welfare of the children and their parents. He may be afraid of consequences but if he has any moral courage at all, we appeal to him to release the children.'

Lenton also used knowledge of known child molesters that was now readily available to detectives. 'From our knowledge of sexual deviates and their behavioural patterns, it seems most unlikely that this is the first time this man has molested young female children,' he told the press. Lenton implored anyone who was possibly shielding the abductor — whether because of blood ties or from a misplaced sense of loyalty — to come forward. 'Whoever is withholding information has a duty to help the police in the interests of these two missing girls or other children who may be in the same position in the future.'[9]

Nothing.

On the night of Tuesday 28 August, Les Ratcliffe appealed to his missing daughter and her abductor via television. Whereas Jim Beaumont gave a brief address in 1966, Les Ratcliffe looked squarely at the camera and gave a long, personal address despite breaking down emotionally. Shown around the country by Channels Seven and Ten, Australian audiences witnessed the father baring his soul: 'Whoever is holding Joanne and Kirste, I am appealing to you personally to come forward or let them go; drop them on some main street corner. I am sure my daughter will do the right thing and go straight to the nearest person she thinks she can trust. If you have any decency in you, any respect for these two children, who are only young children, eleven and four, who have never done any harm whatsoever . . .

'If you've got them please look after them . . . Please, whatever you do, if you are sick or anything like that, I am sure if you come to the right authority they will help you . . . if there is more than one of you I would like the both of you to sit down and talk it over. I think you will find that talking will help a lot . . .'

Mr Ratcliffe then spoke directly to his daughter: 'Your first duty is to protect [Kirste] with whatever you can. Do not leave her if possible. If you do, don't go too far. Go to the first person that you think is a responsible looking person. I say this because I know you will use your head — keep your head. I have trained you what to do in a situation if these people decided to do the right thing by you . . .

'I want you and this little girl back with us . . . Sis, Sissy, if you happen to listen to this love, or you happen to get hold of the newspapers . . . while I think there is a chance that we can sort this out and get you back without any harm either way, and remember, dear, you have a young girl with you, younger than you, who doesn't understand one little iota what is going on . . .

'And please, dear, if you are locked in anywhere on your own and there is a window that you can't reach, tie your sneakers together and swing it until you break the window . . . keep trying.'[10]

Mr Ratcliffe praised the police, talked about his wife's health and reminded his daughter to dial 000 if she was near a phone. The whole thing was heartbreaking.

On the first day after the girls disappeared, police logged in 728 calls on a police running sheet that already totalled more than 40 pages. By the end of the week this number had more than doubled. Within two weeks, 3338 calls had been taken. There had to be a better way to disseminate information — and there was. The South Australia Police had a super-sleuth on the case, but it wasn't a man; it was a system.

The previous year the South Australia Police imported and installed a 'unique card index detection system'[11] developed by

Scotland Yard. The system, which was not computerised, served two main functions: first, it was a totally comprehensive catalogue of information supplied by the public; second, but more importantly, it was a system for prioritising information as it came to police. The system had been installed in Adelaide by UK detectives in response to a continuing investigation known as the Duncan Case. On the night of 10 May 1972, Dr George Duncan, a gay university lecturer, drowned after being bashed by several men and thrown into the Torrens River. Another man was also bashed and thrown into the river but was rescued by a passer-by named Bevan von Einem. The 26-year-old accountant took the injured man to the hospital, but police were not able to identify the man's attackers or those responsible for the murder of Dr Duncan.

Police used the card index system to organise thousands of snippets of information forwarded by the public about the nocturnal world of casual gay relationships on the banks of the Torrens River and the 'poofter bashings' that plagued the area. The new system uncovered a startling piece of information about the Duncan Case: it implicated a group of rogue detectives in the death of Dr Duncan. The case also introduced Bevan von Einem to the South Australia Police, but his involvement in this case appeared to be purely circumstantial.

Now, with another child abduction case on their hands, the new case management system swung into action. Whereas under the old police running-sheet procedure, calls were merely typed up and added to an ever-growing mountain of paper, information was now prioritised and allocated an action. Priority-one calls demanded immediate action; priority-two meant that work needed to be done, but not urgently; and priority-three was given to calls that did not require an action and the card was filed for future reference. At the end of two weeks, the South Australia Police had 200 priority-one calls that still required investigation.

The strength of this new system was that it was not left to just one officer to prioritise the calls. Under the police running-sheet procedure, any investigating officer could write 'AAC' ('all appeared correct') at the top of a report and that was the end of the matter. This new system used cadets, administrative staff and junior officers to type the cards and then experienced investigators to prioritise and cross-reference the new information. The Scotland Yard–designed system was considered the best in the world at the time because it allowed detectives the opportunity to rate or grade information and then allocate available resources to the investigation.

Some things, however, didn't change. The state government posted a modest reward of $5000 and within twenty-four hours a hoax caller rang one of the grieving fathers and demanded $25 000 'if he wanted to see his daughter alive'.[12] Eighty union workers employed by Babcock and Wilcox on the Torrens Island power station donated a day's pay, which added a further $2000 dollars to the award. Carpenters working on the city's Festival Hall building did the same and donated another $2000. The reward was later doubled to $10 000 by the South Australian government, which also offered a free pardon to any person who had knowledge of the crime but was not directly involved.

Public sentiment was already running hot. Jean Howard, of Walkerville, wrote the following letter to *The Advertiser*:

> Sir — if the two children apparently abducted from the Adelaide Oval on Saturday have come to any harm, I hope the Premier, himself a father, will revise his views on capital punishment ... if found guilty, any perpetrator of monstrous crimes against children should suffer the death penalty.[13]

However the Premier, Don Dunstan, rejected calls to retain the death penalty for convicted child killers. John Mathwin, the Member for Glenelg, officially asked the Premier in state parliament to reconsider plans to abolish capital punishment following the disappearance of the girls from Adelaide Oval. Rejecting the request, the Premier, a former State Attorney General, pointed out that statistics 'clearly showed that the death penalty was not a uniquely effective deterrent'.[14]

On 31 August, a new witness came forward and told the police that he saw a man in a broad-brimmed hat dragging two girls outside the southern gate of Adelaide Oval. A thirteen-year-old boy selling lollies at the ground, whose name was withheld for his own protection, told investigating detectives that he saw 'a small girl answering the description of Kirste Gordon, 4, tucked under the man's right arm.' The boy said that the man was also 'dragging a struggling, kicking girl' who fitted the description of eleven-year-old Joanne Ratcliffe, by the other arm. The older girl appeared to be trying to rescue the younger girl from the clutches of the man, the boy said.[15]

The description of the stooped, middle-aged man, wearing a brown, broad-brimmed hat, a grey, checked coat and brown trousers, was identical to that of the suspect seen with the girls retrieving kittens at Adelaide Oval. The boy said that during the last quarter of the match, as he stood beneath the archway underneath the Creswell Stand, he saw the man 'swoop'[16] on the girls from behind a pepper tree, taking Kirste under his right arm and dragging Joanne alongside him, and then walk towards the southern gateway. The older girl kicked and slapped the man as he grappled to hold the smaller girl under his arm and take them into the public car park.

'A picture is building up,' Senior Inspector Lehmann told the assembled media at a special press conference at Adelaide CIB.[17] The man in question had been seen loitering at the ground since that Saturday morning. Did he befriend the girls, using the kittens near the equipment shed as a lure, when they had left the adults in the grandstand on two previous occasions? Did the girls follow the man with the kittens and then lose sight of him or had they been lured there by the man with the promise of a kitten as a pet? When Joanne heard the siren for the start of the last quarter she might have thought that the game had finished and taken Kirste to the southern gates, which was her family's pre-determined meeting point. The man certainly chose his moment to snatch the girls: the climax of the match, when everyone's attention was focused on the result of the game. The police were able to track the man and the two girls for about 'thirty to forty yards'[18] into the public car park, but then there was no further sign of them. They now appealed for anyone who was in the car park just before the end of the match to come forward.

Detective Inspector Col Lehmann was reluctant to connect this tragedy with the unsolved Beaumont Case, lest Adelaide residents start believing that there was a maniac in their midst. When he was drawn on the comparison, all that he would concede was that 'children were missing and so far they have not been found'.[19] However, when an arts teacher at the South Australian School of Arts, Mr Waller, produced a watercolour impression of the main suspect based on Ken Wohling's description, it was hard not to notice that the man uncannily matched the published sketch of the man seen frolicking with the Beaumont children at Glenelg beach.

It was chilling. But was it a realistic connection to the Beaumont suspect or a subconscious one?

South Australia Police cadets were called into this investigation, just as they had been when they searched the Patawalonga boat haven during the Beaumont Case. Resplendent in their jackets and caps, cadets conducted a shoulder-to-shoulder search of the banks of the Torrens Lake on the southern side of the Adelaide Oval and War Memorial Drive, the main access road. The cadets searched for any evidence belonging to the girls; Joanne was wearing costume jewellery and her father Les was adamant that she was clever enough to drop something belonging to her to alert authorities. The cadets also used machetes to cut through reeds on the edge of the lake, a man-made section of the Torrens River, which was partially drained for the purposes of the search.

On 1 September the Ratcliffe and Gordon families came together for the first time when they were asked to dress store mannequins in the clothing that their respective children were wearing on the day they disappeared. Before then the couples had not met each other, but came together 'for a good talk'[20] before the mannequins were put on display in the Rundle Street Mall. Each understood the other's grief.

The grieving families presented different public faces during the same tragedy. The parents of Kirste Gordon did not want to appear 'too emotional' in public, and faced the harsh realisation that their little girl might not come home. 'We cannot help feeling that she is gone, that we will never see her again,' 28-year-old Christine Gordon told the press. 'But we dread the day that the police come to our door and tell us that the search is being toned down. We realise you can't pray for miracles but we pray that she will be found.' Mr Gordon added, 'I don't think that the full significance has really hit us yet.'[21] The couple had their youngest daughter, two-year-old Catherine, to care for.

Publicly and privately, Les Ratcliffe was unashamedly emotional, knowing in his heart that the more he talked about his missing daughter in the press the more chance the family had of resolving the mystery. Somebody must have seen or known something. Gradually, the picture of his shy, thoughtful young daughter formed in the media. Mr Ratcliffe knew that she would never have abandoned Kirste Gordon. It wasn't in her nature. And he would not abandon his daughter in her moment of need. For the next eighteen months, the Ratcliffes left Joanne's bedroom as she had left it and kept the front porch light on each night as a beacon for her to follow home.

Les Ratcliffe embraced the media, journalists, the police and anyone who could help find his daughter. Detective

Sergeant John McCall would regularly drop in on the Ratcliffe's modest housing-estate home in Campbelltown and keep the distraught parents up to date with the investigation. If Les was feeling down, McCall would take the tortured father out for a drink to get his mind off the case or just to cheer him up. They formed a very close relationship over the years. At the coronial inquest into the Adelaide Oval abduction in 1979, Les Ratcliffe told the State Coroner that he trusted McCall 'with my life'.[22]

On 7 September, a man contacted police and stated that he saw a man dragging two children matching the description of the missing girls in a street in the nearby suburb of Thebarton at about 5 pm on the Saturday the children went missing. The witness told police that he was driving along Port Road towards Hindmarsh at about 5.10 pm that Saturday when he saw a man wearing a wide-brimmed hat near the West Parklands in Thebarton. Two girls were with the man, who was described as five foot eight but athletically built and wearing a blue body shirt. The man, who also had a moustache and sideburns, did not physically match the main suspect but the witness was able to accurately describe the clothing of the girls. Had the stooped, middle-aged man changed into a disguise or did he hand the girls over to an accomplice?

Following this lead, a team of seven detectives and thirty policemen and cadets spent a week combing the streets of Thebarton, knocking on the doors of approximately 1000 homes and showing locals photos of the missing children. Several other reports appeared to confirm the sighting but an extensive search of the area, including the banks of the Torrens and Thebarton Cemetery, found no trace of the girls. An abandoned house in Thebarton, suggested by one caller as a possible hiding place for a kidnapper, was thoroughly searched and eliminated from the investigation. However, police were able at last to pinpoint the last known sightings of the missing girls:

- at Adelaide Oval between 4 and 4.30 pm, when Ken Wohling saw the girls heading towards the southern gates
- walking with a man at about 5 pm along Port Road, the main link between Adelaide and Port Adelaide a mile west of the oval
- on Port Road outside the Southwark Hotel between 5 and 5.15 pm, when a customer saw a man carrying a small girl and walking so fast that an older girl had to run to keep up
- around the corner from the hotel in Phillip Street, Thebarton — the man stopping to tie the older girl's shoelace but no longer carrying Kirste
- at North Parade, Torrensville, at about 6 pm.

If the man and the two girls were the 'Adelaide Oval' trio, they had walked about two miles (three kilometres) in an hour and a half. [23]

Despite public appeals, no-one came forward to identify themselves as having walked up Port Road with two other girls, so it was difficult for police to completely discount the Thebarton sightings.

On Saturday 16 September, Norwood played North Adelaide in the elimination semi-final of the SAFL Aussie Rules competition. It had been three weeks since Joanne and Kirste went missing from a similar match at Adelaide Oval and, although this game was being played at Norwood Oval, detectives reasoned that many of the people who had been at Adelaide Oval on 25 August would also be at this match. The mannequins of the two girls were set up at Norwood Oval in the hope that they would jog someone's memory of the day the girls were taken. Another 150 reports were indexed after the display at Norwood Oval but bit by bit the information was eliminated.

Despite the cataloguing of over 4500 pieces of information, 400 letters of correspondence and another 400 enquiries from country areas and interstate, after eight months of operation the investigation had not identified any known suspect. As the football season came around again in 1974, police hoped that this might renew people's interest in what happened at Adelaide Oval the previous August. Despite receiving 'seven or eight' calls a week about the case, the South Australia Police were at a loss to explain what happened to the girls.

Les Ratcliffe, though, would not let the investigation stall. In May 1974 he arranged for the Clifford Theatre Company to show his daughter's photo at local drive-in theatres; this image had not previously been published and in it she was wearing her hair the same way as on the day she disappeared. Every Saturday night Mr Ratcliffe, sometimes joined by his wife Kath or family friends, would walk the streets of Torrensville and Thebarton where the last known sightings of his daughter and Kirste Gordon were reported. 'Someone must know something,' he told police reporter Mike O'Reilly. 'I have met the milkmen, papermen — hundreds of people [but] sometimes we don't see a living soul in those dark streets ...'[24]

Late in 1974 both sets of parents enjoyed some emotional respite from the burden of not knowing what had happened to their lost children. On 3 August Christine Gordon gave birth to a daughter, Alisa June, in Singapore where the family had moved after her husband was granted a teaching scholarship. On 14 October Kath and Les Ratcliffe also welcomed the birth of daughter, Suzy. Although Kirste and Joanne were irreplaceable, the new babies brought some peace and joy to both families. God knows they would need it as the investigation into the disappearance of their daughters threatened to be hijacked by clairvoyants and charlatans.

In July 1974 journalist Dick Wordley, who had followed the Beaumont Case for the previous eight years, travelled to Holland once more to consult Gerard Croiset about the still unsolved case. Wordley was writing a book about the Beaumonts in which he hoped to unmask the children's killer — a 'known homosexual (now dead) who worked at the Minda Home'[25] — but he needed Croiset's input. When he arrived in Enschede, Holland, he found the ageing clairvoyant gravely ill after having had half his stomach removed due to ulcers. When Wordley also mentioned the Adelaide Oval Case that had captured the public's attention at the time, Croiset all of a sudden became very interested. 'You must see my son,' Croiset demanded fiercely. 'My son will help you now.'

Gerard Croiset Junior was 36 in 1974, 'a brilliant painter and sculptor, skilled academic and yet as earthy as home brew', as Wordley described him. He had allegedly already enjoyed success as a 'paragnost', a 'healer by touch' and a psychic detective when the Australian journalist briefed him about the

Adelaide Oval Case. Croiset Junior quickly drew a sketch of the man and the house where the children were buried and then made the startling prediction that the children's murderer would strike again 'somewhere in Australia during the current cycle of the moon'. Maybe Croiset Junior was affected by the moon because, thankfully, even allowing for the scope and size of the entire country, nothing remotely related to the Adelaide Oval Case happened.

Wordley left Holland with Croiset Senior's usual grab-bag of visions: 'a farm, a red bus, a high chimney'[26] were the only clues he gave to the whereabouts of Joanne and Kirste. It would be another four years before Gerard Croiset Junior would follow in his father's footsteps and try his luck in Adelaide.

Les Ratcliffe was not afraid to consult clairvoyants, but he drew the line at paying for their advice. 'People may think I'm a nut; I don't care,' he told the media in 1978.[27] Ratcliffe spoke to famed British spiritualist Doris Stokes and Adelaide medium Dianne Klose, and was a prime mover in bringing Gerard Croiset Junior to Australia. Stokes, who made her name in this country on the *Don Lane Show* but was exposed as a fake after her death, even gave Mr Ratcliffe the 'name' of the man who murdered his daughter and the manner in which he killed her. The grieving father admitted that talking to clairvoyants — to anyone who could help solve the mystery of his missing daughter — actually helped him become less 'uptight, aggressive and emotional'.

'It's not that we don't have any confidence in the police,' Ratcliffe told the media. 'It's just a matter of desperation,' he confessed.[28]

Gerard Croiset Junior was brought to Australia in July 1978 by the 0–10 Network, which hoped to recoup its expenses by filming a documentary about the Dutch clairvoyant's search for Joanne Ratcliffe and Kirste Gordon. Detective Sergeant John McCall had a private meeting with Croiset before he left Australia but it was more out of friendship with Les Ratcliffe than official police business. Croiset told police that he believed Joanne Ratcliffe's body was buried in a cellar in a disused house near the mid-north town of Bowmans. McCall told police reporter Rick Burnett that he had 'been given some different avenues to look at and think about' by Croiset but that 'the case is no nearer an end.'[29] Croiset Junior provided nothing of use to the investigation.

In December 1978 Les Ratcliffe called for an official inquest into the disappearance of his daughter Joanne and of Kirste Gordon from Adelaide Oval five years earlier. The previous year the Ratcliffes had shocked many in Adelaide when they sought compensation from the South Australian government over the loss of their daughter. Les Ratcliffe knew that some people would see him as a 'callous bastard' but the move to effectively sue the South Australian government was a combination of 'dissatisfaction with the government's handling of the case, the desire to bring the disappearance to public notice and a need to offset the cost of his continuing search for his daughter'.

'The money is nothing — it is the principle of the thing,' Ratcliffe told reporter Peter De Ionno. 'No amount of money could replace a hair on any of my family's heads.'[30] In an era before victims' compensation became the norm, the Ratcliffes were only able to access a paltry $6000 for what they had been through.

But now Les Ratcliffe was asking for something that the Beaumonts could not face: a public inquest into the disappearance of their child. Finally, in March 1979, State Coroner Kevin Ahern announced that he had called for all police files on the case and would conduct a public inquest into the disappearance and subsequent police investigation the following July. The inquest would last for two weeks.

The main finding of the July 1979 inquest concerned the failure of the Secretary's Office at the Adelaide Oval to broadcast the parents' appeal for the missing children. 'Any request to sound an alarm when children were missing,' Mr Ahern found, 'should be treated seriously and given immediate priority, irrespective of the place or occasion of the disappearance.'[31] The Ratcliffes had always been hurt that their request for an appeal for the missing girls had not been immediately broadcast. The then Secretary of the South Australian Cricket Association, Mr Munn (who had passed away by the time the inquest started) may simply have thought that he was being practical — the broadcast appeal may not have been heard over the crowd — but he should have tried. The coroner also criticised the fact that the Ratcliffes were advised to return to their seats and report the situation to police later, yet there was a policeman on duty in the broadcast box who had not been made aware of the situation.

Les Ratcliffe was happy that the inquest had found 'in my favour'. But it was not the end of the matter. 'I intend searching until I die or I catch the bastard, whichever comes first,' he said at the end of the inquest.[32]

Sadly, for Les Ratcliffe, it was the former. Diagnosed with cancer in 1980, the father of two dictated an open letter to the Adelaide public on 14 January 1981:

> Do not forget the Adelaide Oval abduction of August, 1973. As a parent I could not wish for anyone to live through what I have had to live through ... I do not want any sympathy. My family does not want sympathy ... the illness has caught me just when I was beginning to accept Joanne was gone forever ... despite it all, I am happy now ... The abduction has subjected [my wife and me] to a lot of rumour and innuendo. Our marriage is stronger for it.[33]

Two weeks later Les Ratcliffe died, aged 46. Neither the case nor the frustration of not knowing what happened to his daughter would beat him, but the cancer finally consumed him. Police roundsman John Doherty, who became close to the Ratcliffe family as they lived with their sorrow, wrote that Les's 'highly excited restlessness, agitation and inner despair ... drove him on and on in his attempts to find a clue to the riddle of Joanne's disappearance.'[34] Les Ratcliffe may have been a self-described 'battler' but he died an undisputed champion in the long struggle to resolve the Adelaide Oval Case.

Although the Adelaide Oval Case was never solved, police originally resisted linking it to the disappearance of the Beaumont children seven years earlier. Even today, the South

Australia Police regard the Adelaide Oval Case as the forgotten crime because it is overshadowed by the Beaumont Case.[35] Could Adelaide conceal two different child abductors who both got away with the perfect crime? Five children in seven years: the only recorded cases of multiple, unsolved abductions in Australia in the past forty years.

Unlikely.

Only in 1990 did the South Australia Police confirm that investigating police at the time had linked the Adelaide Oval abductions to the unsolved Beaumont Case.

'There is a big chance that these two crimes are linked,' Peter Alexander of the Police Association of South Australia told me. 'This type of offender, this type of killer you just can't get a handle on. Even on a worldwide basis [these are] extraordinary crimes. The psychology and supreme confidence of the guy is astounding ... one group of children taken from a crowded beach, the other from a crowded sporting field, both in broad daylight.'[36]

Who was he?

9

The Family Murders

Between 1979 and 1983, the surgically mutilated or dismembered bodies of five young men were found in various parts of Adelaide. The media dubbed the killings the 'Family Murders' when detectives revealed the existence of a small subculture of paedophilia and sexual sadism in the city's homosexual community. One of the people who belonged to that subculture was Bevan Spencer von Einem, who had once rescued a man from drowning in the Torrens River during a series of gay bashings in the early 1970s.

At first the tall, grey-haired 37-year-old accountant denied any knowledge of the unsolved murders. However, when police searched von Einem's house they discovered evidence that linked him to the 1983 abduction and murder of one of the five victims: fifteeen-year-old Richard Kelvin. Von Einem was sentenced to life imprisonment for Kelvin's murder but when he stood trial for the murders of the other victims, sensational allegations were made against him by one of the prosecution witnesses.

'Mr B' (whose identity was withheld for his own protection) told a shocked courtroom that von Einem had allegedly abducted the Beaumont children from Glenelg beach in 1966 and 'two young girls from Adelaide Oval'[1] in 1973 and that their bodies had been buried in 'Moana or Myponga', south of Adelaide. Was Bevan von Einem the monster South Australia Police had been looking for all these years?

On the night of 10 May 1972, university lecturer Dr George Duncan was bashed and thrown into the Torrens River by a group of men. The banks of the Torrens were a known haunt for homosexuals, who used the dark parklands for casual sex. Homosexuality between consenting adults was still a crime in South Australia and in every other state of Australia. A second man was also thrown into the water that night, although this was not revealed to the public at the time of the investigation into Dr Duncan's death. The man saw Dr Duncan struggling in the water but could not help him because his own leg was broken. The second man struggled to the bank of the river near Victoria Terrace and was helped by a young man who took him to the Royal Adelaide Hospital for treatment.

The rescuer's name was Bevan Spencer von Einem, a 26-year-old accountant from Campbelltown.

The Duncan Case caused a sensation in Adelaide. It was later alleged that a group of Vice Squad detectives, whose job it was to patrol the area, had bashed and thrown homosexual men into the Torrens. After a lengthy investigation that struck at the heart of police culture, two former detectives were charged with the manslaughter of Dr Duncan but were found not guilty when the trial finally concluded in the early 1980s. By that time, the South Australia Police had also become more familiar with the name Bevan von Einem.

On 24 June 1979, two bushwalkers discovered the body of a seventeen-year-old Salisbury youth, Alan Arthur Barnes, in the South Para Reservoir in the Adelaide Hills north-east of the city. Barnes's body had been dropped into the reservoir from the centre of a bridge that linked the communities of Williamstown and Kersbrook. It would have sunk below the surface of the water except that the reservoir had not yet been filled by Adelaide's winter rains. The body hit the hard mud under the bridge, breaking the victim's back, but Barnes had already died a more terrible death.

Alan Barnes died from massive blood loss caused by a shocking injury to his anus. Drugged and plied with alcohol, Barnes had been missing for a week but had died within the 48-hour period before his body was found. Pathologist Dr Colin Manock found that the youth had died after a blunt, tapered object, possibly a beer bottle, had been inserted in his anus. However, there was no blood found on the boy's clothing. Barnes had been re-dressed after his death and had obviously been kept captive by his abductor. The youth had last been seen in the early hours of Sunday 17 June hitchhiking home from the city with a friend but when the pair could not get a lift, Barnes went off by himself on Grand Junction Road. His mother reported him missing to police the next day.

When a second body, that of 25-year-old Neil Frederick Muir, was discovered on 28 August 1979, the media did not originally report the connection between the two victims. Muir's dismembered body was found floating in a plastic bag in Port River, a tidal estuary that ran into the sea at the top of the Lefevre Peninsula. The torso, from which the intestines had been removed and the dismembered legs placed inside it, also had the head tied to it with yellow cord. These had then been placed in a plastic bag and dropped from a nearby wharf at Mutton Cove. The body was not wearing any clothing, but when it was examined two things were patently evident: Muir's body had been dismembered with a saw and he had died from the effects of an anal injury similar to the type that Barnes had suffered. These facts were not released to the media.

About this time a member of the public informed police that they should investigate Bevan von Einem about the murder of Alan Barnes. Detectives first spoke to von Einem about the Barnes murder on 2 September 1979, by which time another team was investigating the murder of Neil Muir. Von Einem denied knowing Barnes but, despite the fact that the two murders had not been linked in any media report, he volunteered that he had seen Neil Muir in the city eight days before at the Duke of York Hotel. Muir, a homosexual and a drug addict, was drinking with a man of Greek or Italian appearance named 'Adam' at about 9 pm, von Einem said. When police asked if von Einem had seen Muir later that night, the mannered accountant said that Muir had wanted to go to the Lord Melbourne Hotel but he had dropped him off at the 'Buck' instead at about 10.15 pm and didn't see him after that. Von Einem then told an implausible story of later being attacked by a man with a knife in the car park of the 'Buck' and driving home by himself.

'The information was amazing,' detective turned author Bob O'Brien wrote in his book *Young Blood: The Story of the Family Murders*. 'Von Einem seems to be around every time something happens. On Sunday 2 September 1979, five days after Neil Muir was found in the river, von Einem said that he had been with Neil Muir on the Saturday night before he was killed. His story was strange. If Neil Muir wanted to go to the Lord Melbourne, why did he take him to the Buckingham Arms Hotel? He would have driven straight past the Lord Melbourne on the way. And the story about being held up with a knife — did that really happen?'[2]

The South Australia Police investigated another suspect in regard to the 1979 deaths of Alan Barnes and Neil Muir: a Mount Gambier doctor whose name had been forwarded by two drug addicts. However, the doctor, who allegedly knew Muir, was found not guilty of the crime. A psychological profile commissioned by police stated that Muir's killer was not a drug addict or a spurned lover. The killer was acting out of 'hate or fear' and that it 'may be a homosexual who had strong sexual fantasies'. In 1979 Milton Kelly, the head of the Police Psychology Unit, listed the psychopathic characteristics of the potential killer: a non-conformist who was egocentric and selfish; had no conscience, anxiety or remorse; was manipulative, impulsive, incapable of love or affection, callous, sadistic, incapable of learning from past experiences; an accomplished liar; and possibly charming and likeable.[3]

The discovery of two more bodies in 1982 would lead police back to Bevan von Einem.

On 8 March 1982, the mutilated body of nineteen-year-old Mark Langley was found in the Adelaide Hills. Two weeks earlier, Langley had left a party with two friends in the early hours of Sunday morning and drove into the city. The trio parked on the northern side of War Memorial Drive but an argument developed and Langley walked off into the darkness. His friends drove over the Albert Bridge near Adelaide Zoo, past Victoria Drive, with the University on their left, then turned back onto King William Street and headed back to where they had originally parked. There was no sign of their friend. Mark Langley was reported missing later that Sunday night by concerned family and friends.

Nine days later, Langley's body was found behind bushes on the edge of Sprigg Road, Summertown, on the northern side of Mount Lofty. No attempt had been made to hide the victim's body, which was found by a local resident who was poisoning blackberries. Langley was still in the clothes that he was wearing when he disappeared, but his satin shirt and distinctive silver chain were missing. When the body was examined, it had similar anal injuries to the previous two victims.

However, the teenager also had a 16.5-centimetre incision to the right of the middle of the abdomen. Mark Langley had been crudely operated on and then sewn up before being murdered. His abdomen had been cut with a sharp implement, stitched together with a three-ply polyester filament and taped over with a Johnson & Johnson brand surgical tape.

Detectives decided to question Bevan von Einem about the death of Mark Langley at his place of work, Pipeline Supplies, on 25 March 1982. As he had done when asked about the death of Alan Barnes, von Einem denied knowing the victim but then volunteered information that caused police to consider him more closely. Yes he was a homosexual, von Einem reiterated, and yes he went to the Torrens River to 'meet people and socialise'[4] but on the night Mark Langley disappeared, he was drinking alone at home until 11 pm. Von Einem then told the police that he left home at 11.30 pm for a drive but took the backstreets to North Adelaide to avoid random breath testing stations. After visiting the Hackney Hotel, near the Hackney Bridge across the Torrens, von Einem bought fish and chips in O'Connell Street in North Adelaide.

For a second time when questioned about a murder, von Einem concocted a story about an associate he met, someone of Lebanese appearance this time, who told him that he had been robbed at gunpoint by two men near the Torrens River on the night Mark Langley went missing. This was the second hold-up von Einem claimed to have known about on the night one of the victims went missing. The detectives, Bob O'Brien and Trevor Kipling, were amazed by von Einem's casual behaviour and his capacity to lie. Von Einem just didn't add up.

Bevan von Einem was born in 1946 and was an accountant by profession. During the 1970s, he lived alone in a unit in Campbelltown (coincidentally the same suburb as the Ratcliffe family) before moving to a house in the Adelaide suburb of Paradise with his elderly mother, Thora. Von Einem liked to be seen in public with women from his work or transsexuals he picked up in the city — allegedly so that people would not think that he was a homosexual. But von Einem, an intelligent, quietly spoken 'mother's boy', was more than that: he was a sadistic paedophile. It was later revealed that von Einem drew pleasure from picking up hitchhikers and rendering them unconscious with drugs and alcohol before sexually abusing them.

The discovery of a fourth body shocked the Adelaide public and engendered a realistic fear that the city had a serial killer in its midst. Detectives were equally concerned. The person or persons responsible were not trying to hide the bodies any more. The first two victims had been dumped in water, giving the appearance that the killer hoped they would at least sink. The last two victims, however, were left on the side of the road like bags of rubbish.

Although fourteen-year-old Peter Stogneff had disappeared on 27 August 1981, his body was not discovered until ten months later on 23 June 1982. The teenager, the youngest of the four victims, wagged school on the day he went missing after returning home to drop off his school bag. Stogneff planned to meet a friend at Rundle Mall in the city but never arrived. His parents reported him missing on the day he disappeared but, despite intensive media coverage, no information regarding the teenager was forwarded to police.

A local farmer cutting grass on the side of Middle Beach Road at Two Wells, twenty kilometres north of the Lefevre Peninsula, had earlier piled stacks of cleared foliage on the roadside so that they would dry and then be burned off in the winter months. Several days after the burn-off, the farmer was checking the remains of the fires when he stumbled across a skeleton; he had inadvertently burned the remains of a body with the grass cuttings. Although no clothing remained, dental records confirmed that it was Peter Stogneff. His body had been dismembered, like that of Neil Muir, but there was no way of determining the actual cause of death or whether there were anal injuries, because the body had been consumed by fire.

Just as a family closes ranks in a time of crisis, there was a perception that the people responsible for the murders were protecting each other. The press alleged, and sections of the conservative Adelaide community agreed with it, that a network of people bound together by homosexual, paedophile and sexually deviant relationships had long been operating in Adelaide. The network was allegedly made up of professional people — doctors, lawyers, judges and politicians — so the chance of bringing to justice those responsible for these crimes was thought to be remote. The media referred to the crimes as the Family Murders.

Then, on 5 June 1983, fifteen-year-old Richard Kelvin, the son of Channel Nine's Adelaide newsreader Robert Kelvin, went to a local bus stop 400 metres from his North Adelaide home to say goodbye to a friend and didn't return home. The bus stop was less than one kilometre from the Torrens River and less than half a kilometre from the O'Connell Street shops. Kelvin had been in high spirits. He was a keen sportsman, had a girlfriend and was doing well in school, and there was no reason for him to run away from home. The teenager had been playing with a dog collar on the day the teenager disappeared; Kelvin's friend said that the teenager was wrapping it over his knuckles and punching the air and wearing it around his neck to 'look cool'.[5] Kelvin's worried parents contacted police about an hour after their son failed to return home at the expected time of 6 pm.

Detectives later learned that a resident living fifty metres from the boy's home heard someone 'calling out'[6] and doors slamming at about 6.15 pm on the Sunday afternoon that he went missing. It was dark by then, and the street was usually deserted at that time. There was now the real possibility that Richard Kelvin had been abducted by more than one person.

Despite a widespread search, Richard Kelvin's body was not found for another seven weeks. On 24 July, a geologist collecting rocks from the scrub near an airstrip at One Tree Hill, north-east of the city, discovered the teenager's remains. The body was dressed in the clothing in which he had last been seen: a Channel Nine T-shirt and blue jeans and wearing the dog collar around his neck. He was curled up in a foetal position, which made police suspect that he may have been dumped there by only one person.

The autopsy revealed that, like three of the previous victims, Richard Kelvin had died of massive blood loss from a severe anal injury. The boy had been dead for about two weeks and the body had had been re-dressed before it was dumped. Four drugs were found in Kelvin's system, including Mandrax and Noctec, and it was clear that someone had kept the boy heavily drugged for five weeks before killing him and then dumping his body. Deep bruising on the boy's body confirmed that he had been beaten while being held captive and that the bruising was starting to clear when he was murdered. Nothing found at the scene indicated that the boy had been murdered there. Like all the others, Richard Kelvin's body had been transported to a remote area in a car and probably at night to avoid detection.

Investigating detectives linked the five crimes because of certain common elements: anal injuries (Barnes, Muir, Langley and Kelvin); dismemberment (Muir, Stogneff); abductions occurring on a Sunday (Barnes, Langley and Kelvin); and the victims having been held captive for a period of time before their bodies were dumped in or near the Adelaide Hills. But the identification of prescription drugs in Richard Kelvin's body proved the vital breakthrough in tracking those responsible for his murder.

Detectives learned that of the thousands of people prescribed Mandrax, was one 'B. von Einem', a name well known to them. Bevan von Einem was now more than just the passer-by who intervened in the Torrens River bashings a decade before; his name had been volunteered by members of the public as having been involved in the murders of Alan Barnes and Mark Langley and more recently he had been questioned over the alleged sexual assault of a young hitchhiker.

Four days after the discovery of Richard Kelvin's body, Bevan Von Einem was questioned about his Mandrax prescription at his nondescript home in the Adelaide suburb of Paradise. Armed with a search warrant to enter the premises, Detectives Kipling and O'Brien knocked on von Einem's door but when he refused to answer questions about the Mandrax prescription, this heightened their suspicions. At Adelaide Police Station later that day, in the company of his solicitor, the 36-year-old accountant claimed he had never met Richard Kelvin and knew nothing about his abduction and murder. On the night Kelvin went missing, von Einem maintained, he was in bed with the flu and had been off work for the week. This merely presented detectives with the evidence that von Einem had the opportunity to abduct the North Adelaide teenager and keep him at his home.

Under questioning, von Einem admitted that he was prescribed certain drugs because of a nervous condition which prevented him from sleeping. His prescribed medication included Serepax, Sinequan, Rohypnol and Mandrax. Von Einem allowed detectives to take hair, fingernail and blood samples while he was at the police station and then allowed the South Australia Police to search his home and car. Carpet and fibre samples were seized from the home for forensic testing and several fingerprint samples were taken from inside the house. Three empty bottles of Mandrax were found, along with other prescribed drugs. Von Einem showed detectives where he kept his Mandrax tablets and capsules hidden on a ledge behind a mirror in a cupboard in his bedroom. Although von Einem said that he had no other drugs in the home, police also found a bottle of Noctec hidden there.

Police had located two of the drugs found in three of the victims: Mandrax in Langley and Kelvin, and Noctec in Kelvin. Surveillance of von Einem's Paradise home on the day it was searched confirmed his close association with another known male person who visited the suspect and stayed the night.

During August and September 1983, von Einem went overseas and visited the Soviet Union and United Kingdom. While he was away, the South Australia Police continued to gather evidence that would possibly link him not only to the murder of Richard Kelvin, but to the other victims found mutilated and dismembered in the Adelaide Hills. Five raids, conducted on 12 October 1983 after von Einem returned to Adelaide, focused on the suspect's associates and on gathering further evidence from his Paradise home.

The committal trial to determine whether there was enough evidence to prosecute von Einem for the murder of Richard Kelvin began on 20 February 1984. Presented with irrefutable evidence that Kelvin had been in von Einem's company before the teenager died, von Einem changed his alibi and admitted that he had met Kelvin on Sunday 5 June 1983. Von Einem now stated that he was driving along O'Connell Street in North Adelaide looking for a spot to park near some shops when he almost hit the boy as Kelvin jogged into the side of his car. The two began talking, von Einem now maintained, and the conversation turned to problems Kelvin had been having at home and at school. Kelvin willingly got into the car and they drove to von Einem's home, the accused now said, to show the boy his harp.[7] The fifteen-year-old stayed at the Paradise home for only two hours before von Einem drove the boy into the Adelaide CBD, dropped him off beside a hospital and gave him $20 to catch a taxi home.

At Bevan von Einem's subsequent trial in October 1984, it was revealed that of 525 fibres found on Richard Kelvin's body, 196 came from the accused's home or clothing. Five of von Einem's head hairs were found inside the boy's jeans and the dye that von Einem used to mask his greyness was traced to those hairs. On 2 November 1984, Von Einem was found guilty of the abduction and murder of Richard Kelvin. Von Einem was sentenced to life imprisonment, which meant only twenty-five years with a non-parole period of eighteen years. On appeal, this was doubled to a non-parole period of thirty-six years. Held in B Division of Yatala Labour Prison, von

Einem now faced more charges as detectives built a case to link him to other unsolved murders, but it would take time. Six years in fact.

On Friday 2 February 1990, eight divers from the Underwater Recovery Squad began a search of the Myponga Reservoir, fifty-five kilometres south of Adelaide. Police refused to confirm what exactly they were looking for but a source close to the search said that they a looking for 'a safe' but did not say why. A report about the five-day search in *The Advertiser* on 8 February prompted the police to confirm that they were in fact looking for a body but that the squad had been conducting a 'black water' training course (in which a safe had been found) but had now been diverted and were searching for human remains.[8] The divers resumed their search on Monday 19 February at the base of the reservoir wall, and again on Saturday 3 March in deeper sections of the reservoir, by which time the full significance of the search was about to be revealed in the media.

On Monday 5 March 1990, committal proceedings began against Bevan von Einem for the murders of Alan Barnes in 1979 and Mark Langley in 1982. However, it was not until 17 March that interim suppression orders preventing the media from releasing dramatic evidence were lifted, 'thrusting the case into nationwide prominence'.[9] A witness, who was an associate of Bevan von Einem known only as 'Mr B', said that von Einem had killed at least ten young people between 1966 and 1983, including the three Beaumont children, the two girls who disappeared from Adelaide Oval and all five youths found murdered between 1979 and 1983.

During four days of testimony, Mr B described how he and von Einem would pick up hitchhikers, drug them and then sexually abuse them. Von Einem would offer the youths a combination of alcohol and the sedative Rohypnol, which rendered the victims unconscious and at the paedophile's mercy. This had happened about a dozen times and Mr B had been with von Einem when the convicted murderer picked up Alan Barnes in June 1979, although he said he did not play any part in the murder of the teenager or the disposal of his body. Mr B said that he disapproved of von Einem's methods, despite the fact that he had joined in one of the rapes, and was sickened by the fact that von Einem used surgical implements in his attacks.

Then, *The Advertiser* observed, 'dressed casually in an open-necked shirt and check trousers' and in an equally casual, matter-of-fact manner, Mr B told a packed court that von Einem had taken the Beaumont children from Glenelg beach in January 1966. Von Einem used to go to Glenelg beach in summer to 'perv' on people in the public showers, Mr B said under cross-examination. Mr B said that von Einem had performed some 'brilliant surgery' and 'connected them together' but one of the Beaumont children had died and he had dumped the body in 'Moana or Myponga'.[10]

Mr B also said that von Einem had told him he had abducted two girls from Adelaide Oval. Mr B later identified the two girls as Joanne Ratcliffe and Kirste Gordon. When asked if he thought that Von Einem was responsible for the deaths of all five young men found between 1979 and 1983, Mr B said 'Yes'.[11]

On the night Alan Barnes died, Mr B and von Einem picked up the victim from 'Number One' police beat near Jolly's Boat House on the Torrens River. Mr B and von Einem, whom he had met only two weeks earlier, drove around the area between Parliament House and the Main North Road in Nailsworth looking for a hitchhiker to drug and rape. They saw Alan Barnes walking in the parklands and offered him a lift to Salisbury.

Barnes was offered marijuana, some drinks and tablets, which Mr B told the teenager were Rohypnol, and by the time von Einem stopped in O'Connell Street to have something to eat, Barnes was falling in and out of consciousness. Von Einem allegedly phoned another man to join the group and told Mr B that they were going to rape Barnes, 'video the murder' and then 'dump the body off a bridge'. When Mr B was asked, 'Do you want to come with us and do some surgery on this guy?' he declined to go with von Einem.[12]

A few days later Mr B saw von Einem, who told him that the youth had died from massive blood loss during the rape. The third man who had joined the group was concerned that Mr B had been part of the 'pick up', and von Einem warned Mr B that if he told anyone what he knew about the rape, he would be implicated in Alan Barnes's murder. When Barnes's body was discovered, Mr B went to the police and told a Detective Sergeant Kappe what he knew. Mr B again met von Einem, who threw him up against a wall and told him that someone had been talking to the police about 'drugging hitch-hikers'[13] and warned him again to keep his mouth shut. Mr B did not speak to von Einem again.

Mr B told the court that he had spoken to detectives in 1979, 1983, 1989 and finally 1990, when he was granted immunity from prosecution. Under cross-examination, Mr B said that he was not with von Einem and the other man when Barnes was actually killed and that he was in fear of his life from this other man, who was sitting in court that day. (The court suppressed the man's identity.) Mr B's sister, who had been seventeen in 1979, proved to be a surprise witness for the defence when she said that her brother came home 'thrilled' all those years ago because he had witnessed a murder. When she asked how the man was killed, her brother said, 'They shoved something up his arse and he bled to death.' Mr B did not say who 'they' were, she remembered, but she didn't believe him because he was 'such a liar'.[14]

Mr B hardly presented as a reliable witness. Von Einem's counsel, Marie Shaw, described Mr B as a drug abuser with a selective memory, who was only interested in the reward on offer for the crimes now referred to in the media as the Family Murders. It was far too easy, she continued, to point out inconsistencies in his accounts and she was critical of the manner in which he had 'slowly leaked details' to the police in the eleven years since Alan Barnes's body had been found. Having been told of von Einem's alleged connection to the Beaumont and Adelaide Oval cases, many openly questioned Mr B's motives. In lifting suppression orders against the publication of these allegations, Magistrate David Gurry was even more scathing: 'It is directed towards highlighting the inconsistencies, the piecemeal and selective nature of his [Mr B's] disclosures to the police and to the court. As I sit here I still have, ringing in my ears, Mr B's admission in court in terms of his obligations in this matter "the court comes last" and the fact that much of what he says may be inherently improbable given normal expectations of human behaviour.'[15]

Mr B stated that the relatives of all ten victims 'deserved to know what really happened' to their loved ones and that he deserved the total $500 000 reward on offer for the unsolved crimes. 'The mental torture I am going through, not being able to sleep right, getting two or three hours sleep at night ... it's been like this for me for eleven years ... You have no idea what I have been going through.'[16] He had not revealed his allegations earlier because he did not trust the police and he feared associates of von Einem.

However, a third witness, identified only as 'Mr C', told the court that he was a school friend of Alan Barnes and that in 1979 Barnes introduced him to Bevan von Einem at the Gateway Hotel. Barnes left with von Einem and some other people to attend a party but Mr C did not go with them. Barnes later told his friend that he could get 'anything he wanted', which meant drugs, as long as he did 'certain things', meaning sexual favours. At another meeting at the Gateway Hotel, von Einem said to Mr C that he too could get 'anything he wanted, including drugs' as long as he brought other 'young lads, his own age' and engaged in sexual acts. Mr C excused himself to go to the toilet and left the hotel immediately.

On the day that Barnes's body was discovered, Mr C started receiving phone calls from a man with a 'muffled voice' who threatened him to 'keep your mouth shut or you're going to get it'. That night he received another twenty nuisance calls before he took the phone off the hook. He received more threatening phone calls when Barnes was buried; when von Einem was arrested for the Kelvin murder a week and a half earlier; and before the start of the committal hearing, when his wife and child were also threatened. This was a total of more than 200 calls. Mr C did not contact police until 1990 because he was afraid of 'the power of the Family then'.[17]

The prosecution strategy consisted of two categories of evidence: the first, to establish 'similar fact evidence' between the circumstances of Richard Kelvin's death, for which Bevan von Einem was found guilty, and the deaths of Alan Barnes and Mark Langley. Brian Martin QC, for the Crown, stated that the three crimes were so 'strikingly similar' as to indicate the same person was responsible. The second category concerned von Einem's pattern of behaviour, including Mr B's assertion that the convicted murderer picked up, drugged and raped hitchhikers. Brian Martin called thirty-two witnesses — hitchhikers and associates of von Einem's alike — to establish the pattern of von Einem's behaviour.[18]

Three transsexuals, referred to by the pseudonyms 'Ms F', 'Ms H' and 'Ms S', told the court that Bevan von Einem was obsessed with hitchhikers but preferred to pick up young males — 'rough trade' he called them — between the ages of fourteen and nineteen. It was his 'hobby', they said. Von Einem would offer hitchhikers a lift 'anywhere they were going' and then invite them to a party. He would offer the youths 'no-doze' tablets, telling them that the drugs would keep them awake all night; in fact they had the opposite effect. Von Einem would take his victims back to flats owned by friends and then sexually abuse the youths. It took one young man two days to wake up, they said.[19]

However, the only thing remotely related to the Beaumont or the Adelaide Oval cases was a comment that Ms H made. Von Einem, she said, had once 'saved her' when someone tried to force her into a car near the Adelaide Oval during the 1970s. Von Einem had also allegedly told her that he wasn't interested in 'girls'. He preferred young men older than thirteen because younger children, he added sinisterly, were 'too small'.[20] This did not sound like someone who had abducted five young children, four of them girls, and there was no reason to question Ms H because she had been called as a prosecution witness against von Einem. But, just as importantly, it suggests that the area near Adelaide Oval, close to the notorious 'Number One beat', was a haunt for sexual predators.

On 12 May, despite real misgivings that Bevan von Einem had either been bragging about his predatory exploits and threw in the name 'Beaumont' to shock his associates, or that Mr B was lying under oath, the South Australia Police confirmed Adelaide's worse kept secret: that they had been searching the Myponga Reservoir for the bodies of the three Beaumont children. The extensive search of the reservoir had been triggered by Mr B's revelations during Bevan von Einem's committal hearing. Now that von Einem had been committed to trial on charges of murdering Alan Barnes and Mark Langley, there was hope that the fate of the Beaumont children and of Joanne Ratcliffe and Kirste Gordon might finally be revealed. As it stood, after the failure once again to locate any remains relating to the unsolved cases, there were only Mr B's allegations. There was no physical or factual evidence and it was highly unlikely that von Einem would allow himself to be cross-examined.

The tenuous connection between von Einem, the four other Family Murders, the Beaumont children and the Adelaide Oval abductions — a connection based on the hearsay evidence of a discredited witness — was in danger of collapsing like a house of cards. And that's exactly what happened.

In June, lawyers acting for von Einem filed an application seeking the 'quashing, dismissing or permanent staying of the charges on the ground that the proceedings were an abuse of process ... the application was based mainly on the assertion that von Einem could not be guaranteed a fair trial, as a result of the media publicity of a prejudicial nature.'[21]

While Supreme Court judge Justice Kevin Duggan dismissed the application, he criticised the judgement (but not the motives) of the South Australia Police officers in the murder case again von Einem. Justice Duggan ruled that, while police should not have been able to inform the public via the media, there was 'no doubt' that police had promoted the view that 'the murders of five youths were linked and that they were connected with a large number of sexual offences against young men'.[22] Justice Duggan also criticised the decision to lift suppression orders on the reporting of Mr B's allegations about von Einem and hitchhikers, the Beaumont children and the Adelaide Oval case.

'In addition to the responsible reporting, there were many examples of sensational and misleading articles and programs,'

Justice Duggan said. 'Some of the "reporting" was no more than groundless speculation.' He found, however, that such conduct fell short of the abuse of process that von Einem's defence team was looking for, and he remained confident of 'the modern jury's ability to assess evidence critically and to comprehend and act upon directions to reach conclusions upon the evidence alone'.[23]

However, in December 1990 the Attorney General advised the Crown prosecutors to enter a motion of *nolle prosequi* in the charges against von Einem relating to the murder of Mark Langley (meaning that the charge would not proceed) because of lack of evidence. The prosecution could not use the Kelvin conviction, the evidence from von Einem's associates or the testimony of Mr B in the Langley murder case. The prosecution still had von Einem on record as lying about Alan Barnes and was keen to continue, but on 1 February 1991, the Barnes murder charge was also dropped for the same reasons.

Did Bevan von Einem murder all five young males in the crimes known as the Family Murders? The police think so, but von Einem continues to plead his innocence of the Kelvin murder and has twice failed to have his case reopened. Was he the 'bogyman' Adelaide had been searching for all the years — the person responsible for the abduction of the Beaumonts and the girls at Adelaide Oval? Trevor Kipling, one of the detectives who brought von Einem to justice, certainly thought he was capable of it. 'You know, I think that he has done the lot,' he told former colleague Bob O'Brien, 'the Beaumonts and Ratcliffe and Gordon as well.'[24]

But huge inconsistencies remain. Why would a killer change from picking up little girls under the age of thirteen to young boys aged over thirteen? Von Einem was twenty when the Beaumonts went missing in 1966 and twenty-seven when the girls were abducted from Adelaide Oval. He was known to have dyed his hair from a young age because of premature greying, and may conceivably have dyed his dark hair light brown in January 1966, but he was still much younger than the suspects seen at Glenelg (aged thirty-five to forty) and Adelaide Oval (aged forty-five) in 1973. Even if a case can be made for von Einem sexually 'experimenting' in his younger years before transferring his attentions to young men as he got older, one unmistakeable issue remains: Why didn't von Einem hide the body of Richard Kelvin (whose murder he *was* found guilty of) with the bodies of the three Beaumont children or the Adelaide Oval victims?

The bodies of the five Family Murder victims remained hidden for a period of one week to ten months. The bodies of the Beaumont children have remained hidden for forty years.

Even if Bevan von Einem's sexual behaviour and *modus operandi* rule him out as a suspect in the Beaumont Case, does The Family exist? Even if the network of paedophiles in Adelaide is overstated, there are still many today who believe that it does exist in some form. As recently as 2001, a former South Australian magistrate was jailed for 25 years for offences against children aged from eight to ten in the mid-1980s. Peter Michael Liddy, one of the state's longest serving judicial officers, 'exploited his position of high trust when he took the children away on surf club trips,' wrote *The Advertiser*.[25]

Liddy, who was arrested in 1999, is the first Australian judicial officer ever to be convicted of child sex offences.

Was there a paedophile network in existence in the mid-1960s and early 1970s, silently working within child-based organisations such as schools, welfare groups or sporting clubs with apparent immunity? Or did the man who abducted the Beaumont children from Glenelg beach in 1966 just get lucky and, having realised how easy it was to get away with murder, commit an indescribable crime a second time in 1973?

10
The Legacy

In the forty years following the disappearance of Jane, Arnna and Grant Beaumont from Glenelg beach, the fate of the three children cast a giant shadow over the entire country. Many of the people touched by the tragic event — the detectives, the media, the people of Adelaide — would never be the same. In the ensuing decades, Jim and Nancy Beaumont waited in Glenelg for news of their children, who would never return.

Every Australia Day, the story of the missing Beaumont children is repeated in the media and reinterpreted by subsequent generations of people too young to remember the events of January 1966. Many theories became urban myths and took on a life of their own. Different ideas about the possible whereabouts of the children were promoted within the media for a variety of reasons — some honourable, some newsworthy — but often for financial or personal gain.

The tragedy of the missing Beaumont children became part of Australian folklore — a perpetual nightmare for parents who continue to warn their children of the dangers of talking to strangers. Many people of that generation have not been able to move beyond the reality of what happened to the Beaumont children at the beach that day. Some still cling to the hope that the children are alive; living somewhere under assumed names. To entertain the alternative is to consider a fate too terrible to imagine.

On the first anniversary of her children's disappearance from Glenelg beach, Nancy Beaumont dreamed for the first time since she could remember. 'I don't usually dream,' she told journalist Ian Mackay. 'In fact this is the first real dream I've had since the children went.'

'But last night I dreamt I heard a knock on the back door. It was the children. They said "Hello Mum". The only thing I said was "Where have you been?" They were standing there in the back lobby [of the house]. I cried, and felt them all over.'[1]

Nancy Beaumont had changed since her children were first taken from her. Back in 1966 she was fatalistic, believing that the children were dead, but a year later she was clinging to the hope that they were still alive. It was the only thing she and her husband had left.

'Jim and I are both convinced the children are alive,' she said in 1967. 'I know I said I believed they had been murdered the week they disappeared but I was sick then. The doctor had kept me asleep. But if the children had been murdered, their bodies would have been found. You couldn't hide three bodies and who would murder three children?'[2]

The Beaumonts steeled themselves against reality; as long as their children's bodies weren't found, there was a possibility that the children were still alive. They knew that the children weren't buried under the floor of the Paringa Park warehouse because their children were still *alive*. 'I'm convinced the children are alive — I know it,' Nancy said. 'Of course I can't possibly think for a moment that they are dead. You can't say these things ... I know that there is a possibility, but I can't say it to myself, can I?'[3]

'Who can imagine what the last year has been like,' Jim Beaumont said at the time. He then added: 'If you knew our children, you would know that nobody could do anything to hurt them. They were so ... well, understanding.' Jim carried with him, wherever he went, a package of twenty photos of his children — Jane, Arnna and Grant playing in the family's backyard and pictures taken at the zoo and on holidays.

'Our children are alive,' Jim said. 'Nance and I would go mad if we couldn't believe that.'[4]

During that first year Jim and Nancy Beaumont saw the children's birthdays come and go — Grant's on 12 July, Jane's on 10 September, and Arnna's on 11 November — but it was the first Christmas alone that they dreaded. 'These have been terrible days for us. Empty,' said Nancy. 'Christmas was the worst time. All those toys. Other kids riding about on new bikes — you can imagine how empty our house was.'[5]

'Nance and I decided to get out [of Adelaide],' Jim Beaumont told journalist Tom Prior. 'We couldn't stand the house with the empty rooms. We started driving to Sydney but we only got as far as Mildura. Christmas Day was terribly hot and we just couldn't stay in the caravan looking at each other ... we got in the car and we were home by Boxing Day. But there was nothing at home.'[6]

The Beaumonts went on a short caravan holiday north of Adelaide as the first anniversary of the children's disappearance approached, but the journalists still found them. Jim and Nancy also found it impossible to escape the public glare and the speculation. 'So many things remind us of what happened,' Jim told journalist Ian Mackay. 'I read the paper. I see a photograph of a child, or a television commercial and see children — it's with us all the time. Even when I go out on business. I talk to customers, and they know what has happened. There's not much they can say, but they feel they have to say something. I appreciate their thoughts and their prayers.

'But people can be vicious. There have been all kinds of rumours — for instance, that I am a member of the Plymouth Brethren, or that I was the taxi driver said to have picked up the children from the beach — and some even more unpleasant.'[7]

Some even said that Jim wasn't the children's father, because he looked older than he actually was, and that he and Nancy were not married — a social taboo at that time. The discovery of secret cults living in communes in the Melbourne hills during the 1983 Ash Wednesday bushfires continued to fuel the myth that Jim and Nancy had either handed their children over to a religious cult or that the children had been stolen by people that the family knew and hidden in a commune, possibly interstate.

It needs to be clearly stated for all time: in the first month of the investigation, the South Australia Police cleared Jim and Nancy Beaumont of having any part in the disappearance of their children. Nothing in their behaviour, or in any information supplied by the public, has changed that stance in the ensuing forty years.

But the speculation gnawed away at them, especially Nancy Beaumont, who blamed herself; why had she let her children go to the beach unattended? 'All I can say is that the beach was the same distance away [1.5 kilometres] as school,' she said in 1967, 'and they went to school every day by themselves. The only thing I can think is that they accepted a lift from the beach because they had missed the 12 o'clock bus. I told them not to get into a car with anybody they didn't know, but if they had missed their bus they might have accepted an offer of a lift home.'[8]

For many years afterwards, the Beaumonts were implored by family and friends to move away from Glenelg and to make a fresh start but they refused. 'I can't in case the kiddies come home,' Nancy rationalised. 'You see, I'm waiting for them to come back here. I never know. Perhaps someone could drop them at the front gate. Wouldn't it be dreadful if I wasn't here?'[9]

But the Beaumonts finally did move — first to a two-storey apartment in Somerton Park in the mid-1970s — before making the difficult decision to separate. No-one can appreciate what Jim and Nancy had to go through in the years after their children disappeared but the fact that they remained good friends and stayed physically close to each other speaks volumes of their relationship. Jim Beaumont reverted to his Christian name, Grant, and Nancy formed a new relationship. The Beaumonts also retained their dignity in refusing to be interviewed after they separated.

During the 1980s, news reports concerning the Beaumont investigation were rare but still elicited great interest. In December 1981, almost seventeen years after the children went missing from Glenelg beach, a woman contacted the Channel Seven current affairs program *State Affair* and said that she had played with the Beaumont children that Australia Day morning and knew why they left the beach that day. Channel Seven asked Stan Swaine, who was then working as a private detective, to investigate the claims, but when the matter was referred to the South Australia Police all that could be substantiated was that the Beaumont children had been seen at the beach — which they already knew.

'So once again the parents of the three missing Beaumont children have been subjected to the agony of further hope, doubt and despair by thoughtless journalists,' wrote Banksia Park resident Ward McNally to *The Advertiser*. 'It seems to me that the simple application of even the lowest standards of decency would have demanded respect for the suffering of two fellow human beings, and dictated that those responsible for the latest assault upon the emotions of Mr and Mrs Beaumont secretly test their so-called "new evidence" before giving it the widespread publicity it received.'[10]

In January 1985 a Perth woman told *The West Australian* she believed that the Beaumont children were alive and living in Kalgoorlie. In the late 1960s, the 56-year-old woman said, she had lived in a railway camp called Reid near the South Australian border in the Nullarbor Desert. Three children who answered the general description of the Beaumont children moved into the camp with their elderly parents in 1966 before moving to the Western Australian gold town of Kalgoorlie. Perth CIB detectives interviewed the woman, her husband and her son and were able to track down the family described by them in Geraldton, Western Australia. Their name was Kilowsky and they definitely were not Jane, Arnna and Grant Beaumont.[11]

Arguably the most bizarre development to date in the Beaumont investigation occurred in March 1986 with the discovery of a suitcase of newspaper clippings at a suburban rubbish tip. Workmen at the West Torrens dump stumbled across a 'comprehensive file of annotated newspapers and newspaper clippings'[12] relating to the Beaumont Case over the past twenty years. The clippings were underlined in red pen with comments scrawled in the margins: 'not in sand hills, in sewerage drain', 'she used to comb my hair', 'I understand', 'lies, all bluff' and 'no, no, no'. Were these clipping from the person who took the children or who knew what happened to them? Police investigations quickly established that the clippings had been dumped by the family of an 'eccentric' old woman who spent years collecting news stories on the Beaumont Case. When the elderly woman died, her relatives had taken the file and some of her personal belongings to the local rubbish tip.

As the twentieth anniversary of the children's disappearance passed, the South Australia Police were forced to admit that a deathbed confession was probably the only hope the case now had of ever being solved. Despite 'thousands' of leads, Detective Superintendent Rob Lean, who was then in charge of the case, stated that 'we are probably no closer to finding the offender, if there was one, than we were 20 years ago.'[13] Lean's comment is interesting: *if there was one*. Two decades after the children went missing from Glenelg beach, the police could not even rule out that the children had died from misadventure.

Another interesting comment Rob Lean made at the time was regarding the number of people who still volunteered new information every January on the anniversary of the children's disappearance. 'They say they haven't told anyone before because they didn't think they wanted to get involved,' the detective superintendent told journalist Greg Hurnell. 'Now they think they better tell someone.'[14] If only these people had come forward in 1966, Lean lamented, when the children had first disappeared.

And still the parents of the missing children had no peace. In February 1990, Jim Beaumont was 'conned' by a News Limited journalist into granting an interview for the first time in 22 years. Doctors had to treat the 64-year-old for a stress-related illness when the article was published. The journalist had not identified himself when soliciting remarks regarding the Family Murders, and Mr Beaumont reiterated his stance in *The Advertiser* the following month: 'I don't know what to believe [about the children's disappearance], I don't know any more than you.'[15]

In May 1990 *The News* published digitally enhanced photos of what the three Beaumont children might have looked like if they were alive in 1990. *The News* trumpeted: 'The world leader in photographic identification, Bette Clarke, told today how she "aged" the photographs of the Beaumont children who disappeared 24 years ago ... while she uses a computer to complete the process [in Toronto, Canada], Mrs Clarke says most of the work comes from her portraiture and anatomy skills.'

'"Except for the hair,' Mrs Clarke stated, 'I am confident that all three children would look today almost exactly as I have shown them."'[16]

The News commissioned the Toronto Police Department to undertake the imaging and then published the photos around

Australia, just in case the children were still alive and living under assumed names. The South Australia Police prepared the elderly parents for the distress these photos would undoubtedly cause by making them available to Jim and Nancy Beaumont before they were published (Nancy refused to look at them, Jim just looked and handed them back), and the pictures caused 'a huge backlash of public sympathy' for them from the Adelaide community.

But many in the media just couldn't let go of the case. The pressures of the unsolved investigation broke Brian Taylor, the ADS7 newsreader who had helped Jim and Nancy Beaumont in their time of grief. The newsman became too close to the case, liaising with Gerard Croiset, leading searches and conducting investigations on his own. Taylor's marriage suffered and, when his television career in Adelaide ended, he moved to Western Australia and lived in anonymity.

Dick Wordley, former crime reporter for *The News* and *The Herald*, twice travelled to Holland to speak with Gerard Croiset and remained convinced, as the case entered its third decade, that the children were still alive. Wordley became an advocate for the missing children of Adelaide and, rightly or wrongly, regularly used his connections to keep cases such as that of the missing Beaumont children in the public arena. However, Wordley made the mistake of latching onto the Dandenong Letters, sent to the children's parents in 1968, as evidence that the three siblings were possibly alive and living in a commune, most likely in Victoria. In a 1990 article, Wordley demanded to know why the police had not fully investigated the letters, why Detective Sergeant Stan Swaine went to Dandenong, and what convinced the parents that the letters were genuine. He expected that the case of the missing Beaumont children would 'torment' him the rest of his life.

'I've had a lot to do with sects and abducted children,' Wordley told fellow journalist Deborah Tideman, 'and it's amazing the way people can be controlled: once they believe, they believe entirely.'[17]

The same could be said of urban myths.

In 1990 former Homicide Squad detective Jack Zeunert confirmed that Adelaide detectives had investigated the existence of a US-based religious sect in the Adelaide Hills during the late 1960s and early 1970s. 'It was his belief for many years,' Deborah Tideman wrote, 'that the children were taken by someone they knew, and were still alive.' Zeunert said that police had traced the sect to a home in Alberton, but had lost track of it in Western Australia. Zeunert believed that the involvement of a sect 'carried some weight'[18] because the Beaumont Case did not 'follow the usual pattern of sex killings', presumably because there was no known suspect or any discovery of the victims' bodies.

Finally, in May 1992, advancements in fingerprint technology solved the mystery of the Dandenong Letters once and for all. Major Crime Task Force detectives questioned a 41-year-old Melbourne man about the letters sent to Jim and Nancy Beaumont in February 1968. High-tech analysis was able to extract fingerprints from the letters and then directly link them to a man who had been seventeen at the time the letters were sent. Major Crime Task Force detectives took pains to emphasise that 'the interview [of the Melbourne man] and evidence was peripheral to the Beaumont investigation. It was tied up with the investigation, but we would not expect it to solve the mystery completely on its own. The man was not interviewed previously and was only approached after the re-examination of the evidence.'[19]

Originally the Melbourne man refused to admit to his part in the writing of the letters. A senior detective who questioned the man was able to obtain an example of his handwriting and compare it to two anonymous letters sent to Mr and Mrs Beaumont in 1968. However, after several days of 'intense negotiation' between Adelaide detectives and the Melbourne man and his solicitor, the 41-year-old confessed to sending the letters as a hoax and then phoning the Dandenong Post Office to ensure that Jim Beaumont had taken the bait. Detective Superintendent Jim Litster stated that, 'We are able to confirm the letters were in fact written by the male person [but] were no way connected with the disappearance of the three children.' Then he added, 'I understand the person involved is extremely remorseful and it would seem that an act that he had carried out as an immature youth has come back to haunt him ... Owing to the [statute of limitations], no charges will be preferred.'[20] Maybe in the interests of restorative justice the man could have been given some time with the aged Jim and Nancy Beaumont to explain what he had been thinking at the time he wrote the letters.

A routine police matter, using new technology to re-examine old evidence, was enough to finally settle one piece of the Beaumont jigsaw that never really fitted the puzzle.

The revelation that the Dandenong Letters were a hoax should have been enough to silence the ubiquitous Stan Swaine forever. However, in 1997, the former Adelaide detective again put his reputation on the line when he declared that he had 'found Jane Beaumont' living in Canberra. Three years earlier, a 41-year-old woman who allegedly shared the same birthday as the eldest Beaumont girl (10 September 1956) and had 'some of the same [physical] characteristics' as the missing girl, had volunteered to medical authorities that she was 'Jane'. Swaine, who was staying in the nation's capital with his daughter Libby at the time, came into contact with the woman and rushed into print with his new theory when she declined to go public with her claims.

'As I understand it,' Swaine told *The Advertiser*, 'She [the Canberra woman] has been traumatised and has suffered amnesia.' He then added, 'I can't prove any of these facts.'[21]

Swaine wanted the woman to provide a fingerprint sample and then match it against Jane Beaumont's schoolbooks, which he knew were still in the possession of the South Australia Police. The woman declined, and applied to have a restraining order served on Swaine and her former therapist. She then went into hiding. The South Australia Police quickly dismissed Swaine's claims after they checked official records in Canberra; tracked down her parents, who supplied a copy of their daughter's birth certificate; and then learned that Swaine had based his allegations on information supplied to him by *Woman's Day* magazine.

With the Beaumont investigation now in its third decade, South Australia Police became increasingly impatient with Stan

Swaine. They had always treated Swaine with cautious respect, listening to his theories and even discussing his knowledge of the early years of the case, but by the late 1990s their patience was wearing thin. Swaine had 'investigated' or provided police with a number of 'leads' over the years but many had proved to be nothing more than red herrings. With Swaine threatening to publish a tell-all book rather than trust his former colleagues again, Detective Superintendent Paul Schramm stated that if the former detective was 'not prepared to provide factual information to police then I'm disappointed in that.'[22]

In the following years, many of the detectives who originally worked on the case died, taking with them many of the facts about the original investigation. In 1966, Ron 'Wings' Blight had been a 42-year-old detective whose smoking habit grew from twenty cigarettes a day to fifty when he took on the Beaumont Case. When Blight spoke to journalist Tom Prior in 1993, he said that 10 000 leads had been logged during the past twenty-five years, and every one of them had been followed.

'Neighbours would put in someone living up the street and you had to go and interview them,' Blight said. 'You knew it was a lost cause but you knew you just had to do it.' Blight summed up the case fairly quickly, though. 'Once we started to make full inquiries, I was convinced those children had been taken, probably murdered, on the day they were last seen. They were probably murdered within, say, twenty-four hours and probably a long way from Adelaide. He [the abductor] probably said [to the children], "I'll give you a ride home in the car instead of getting the bus" and, once he had them in the car — gone.'[23]

The cold hard truth is that the children were most likely taken so that they could be sexually assaulted, not so that they could be secretly integrated into a religious sect. Blight felt Jane, the eldest, was possibly the target, the others merely brought along because they were with her, and then all three murdered.

'I've had various awards and citations in my time,' Blight told journalist Penelope Debelle in 1995. 'I'd trade them all in to have got the answers to this one because it was such a human thing,' he said.[24] 'You felt as though you got to know the children that well. They were an attached family, very attached.'[25] Cigarettes, however, would catch up with him, and Blight never did get the answers he was looking for.

In May 1996 the family of the late Geoffrey Leane, the former Deputy Commissioner of Police, showed their father's diaries to *The Advertiser*. Leane, a former Rat of Tobruk, who died in September 1990, believed that the children's bodies were in a shipping container lying unclaimed in a foreign port. Because of the sensitivity of the case, and in deference to the feelings of the parents, Leane did not go public with his beliefs although he did brief the Premier at the time, Frank Walsh. An unsubstantiated 'newscast'[26] in the late 1980s apparently supported Leane's theory, but the former Deputy Commissioner's assertions were quickly dismissed; no skeletons had been found in a shipping container and no foreign port had reported such a find.

Millionaire developer Con Polites went to his grave believing that the bodies of the three children were still buried in the Paringa Park warehouse in Wilton Road that Dutch clairvoyant

Gerard Croiset had identified. As early as 1978, Polites was agitating for further excavation of the site. The Greek property developer was in regular contact with clairvoyant Gerard Croiset (via journalist Dick Wordley) and neither Polites nor the Dutch clairvoyant had ever wavered from the belief that the remains of the three Beaumont children rested there. Croiset reiterated his claim that the children had been 'smothered' by a cave-in of 'old underground brick kilns'. Of course, no such kilns ever existed. Polites stated that the original excavation did not go deep enough and that he 'felt so sad we got so far [in 1967] and couldn't achieve what we set out to do.'[27]

However, the owners of the warehouse remained adamant: they would not sanction another excavation and go through another fiasco like the one in March 1967 unless there was a court order instructing them to do so. It was not until 1996 that Polites could organise another dig, after first advocating in 1995 that sophisticated sonar equipment should be used to explore under the floor of the warehouse. The South Australia Police resisted sanctioning a new dig at the site. 'If there was some evidence to strongly suggest [the children's remains] are there, well, of course we'd be interested,' said Detective Sergeant Brian Swan, who was now in charge of the investigation. 'But at this stage the warehouse [theory] is not based on any factual evidence at all.'[28]

Not that this stopped Con Polites. In April 1996, he entered negotiations with the new owner of the warehouse, Mr David Woolaway, who had leased the building to a bathroom renovation company. However, Polites still needed confirmation from a reliable source about where the 'tunnels' to the brick kiln were situated under the concrete. After soliciting advice from Brisbane CSIRO and Scotland Yard in the UK, Polites abandoned the idea of bringing in sonar equipment, relying instead on the recollections of a 38-year-old local man who said that he used to play with the Beaumonts at the site some thirty years before.

Almost three decades after Dutch clairvoyant Gerard Croiset identified the Paringa Park warehouse as the resting place of the missing Beaumont children, Con Polites financed a second excavation of the warehouse's concrete floor. In the absence of any clear knowledge of where the old brick pits lay, Polites' team — a forensic archaeologist (Geraldine Hodgson), a private detective (Frank Church), an architect (Stephen Tiong), soil engineers, security men and even an artist (Lorraine Wyndham-Miller) — first planned to drill holes in the concrete and analyse the soil content. Digging began at seven o'clock in the morning of 1 May and by 11 am nine holes had been dug. By 3 pm, the digging had stopped and the team had packed up.

Although the core samples proved that there were sandpits under the concrete, nothing of the children was found.

Despite this, Polites continued with the partial excavation through June and July. Two specially trained Weimaraner sniffer dogs were used to explore the 'tunnels' formed from the excavation of rubble. A newspaper from 1958, a piece of clothing and a man's footprint preserved in sand were found but no evidence of the Beaumont children. Still, the real estate millionaire would not be deterred. 'I've had a gut feeling since that day [Croiset] told me [the children's remains] were there,' he told *The Sunday Mail*'s Shane

Maguire. 'I grew to admire Mr Croiset and like him. I had a lot of respect for him and so I believed I would be letting him down if I didn't pursue what he wanted. The old brick kilns were a well-known playing spot for kiddies all those years ago and I believe the Beaumont children were playing in a pit, it collapsed and buried them.

'I became so frustrated with not being able to do anything that I often said to my wife that if I could one day buy the building, I will pull it down and search properly ... I have three children of my own and I know I would be devastated if one morning I woke up and found they had gone forever. Any person with compassion would have to want to know what happened to Jane, Grant and Arnna ...

'All those years ago, Mr Croiset told me the children weren't the victims of a crime, just a terrible accident. I asked him how much I could pay him ... he said through an interpreter, "You have insulted me. I don't want any money. I've come out here to find the children."

'Now, how can you not like a man like that?'[29]

Excavation at the Paringa Park warehouse ended in September 1996 with nothing to show for it except a thirteen-centimetre bone, which was analysed and found to belong to an animal. Con Polites passed away in 2003 still believing in Gerard Croiset.

But the rest of Australia had lost its fascination with the Dutch clairvoyant. After Croiset died in 1980, other psychics took up the Beaumont Case. In March 1990, 51-year-old Adelaide woman June Cox informed Major Crime Squad detectives that the missing Beaumont children, and Joanne

Ratcliffe and Kirste Gordon, were 'calling her' from where their bodies were buried in a paddock near Myponga Reservoir. The children had been speaking to her for the past eleven years but only recently had she been able to pinpoint exactly where their remains were.

As it happens, the media had just reported that Adelaide detectives were searching the Myponga Reservoir in light of the 'Mr B' revelations at the committal hearing of Bevan von Einem in the Family Murders Case. Investigating detectives politely listened to Mrs Cox and then put her assertions at the bottom of a very long list of priorities as they followed yet another bizarre twist in the long history of the Beaumont Case.

In an article published in *Woman's Day* in January 2005, former Adelaide-based clairvoyant Scott Russell Hill revealed that he had been a friend of the Beaumont family and a playmate of the missing children through a mutual friend he named as 'Tracy'. Journalist Jenny Brown wrote that 'because of his connection to the Beaumont family, Scott's been working away on the case for years, sifting clues both actual and supernatural.' Described by Brown as 'the breakout star of Network Ten's *Sensing Murder*', Russell Hill was also a contributor to *Woman's Day* magazine, in which he commented on a range of topics from true crime to whether Judge Judy and her husband really are soul mates.

The media clairvoyant had been able to solve many of the riddles to the Beaumont mystery because the children had guided him 'from the other side', the article maintained. Allegedly, he first 'saw' the children at age 16 when he visited

Mr and Mrs Beaumont with 'Tracy' at the family home: 'During the afternoon,' Russell Hill said, 'we talked, played music and took photos. But I was distracted — because right there, standing in the corner of the Beaumonts' lounge room, was the ghost of little Grant, shimmering with blue spirit energy and wearing his blue bathers ... That was my first encounter with the children in spirit. There have been many more.'[30]

The only problem is that Grant Beaumont was wearing green and white striped bathers under green shorts when he disappeared. Russell Hill could possibly explain this away by saying that because the spirit of the little boy was bathed in 'blue light' his bathers merely looked blue. Russell Hill does not mention whether he alerted Jim and Nancy Beaumont to the fact that their son's ghost was in the room with them, although he has no problem talking about it in the media some twenty-five years later. And because the Beaumonts have remained silent for so long, it cannot be verified whether either of them or their children knew Scott Russell Hill or his friend Tracy.

I wanted to discuss these points with the celebrity seer, but when I contacted Scott Russell Hill for an interview via his website I received a polite response from his personal assistant saying that, as Scott was contracted for a television special the following year, he would not be available for an interview. Surely Scott Russell Hill has gone to the police with his information and an arrest would be imminent? Being truly clairvoyant, he would easily provide the South Australia Police with the name of the children's abductor, the anonymous man's present address, a current description in case he is not home when they call, and the final resting place of little Jane, Arnna and Grant?

'He still feel's the children's energy in the Glenelg area,' writes Brown, 'persuading him that one or all of them are buried there.'

Scott Russell Hill believes he knows the identity of two key suspects — someone known to Jane, he says. 'Jane would never have gone with somebody she didn't know ... So I'm not off in some astral, airy-fairy world. I'm confident I can bring the Beaumont mystery to some form of closure.'[31]

If anything, people like Scott Russell Hill prove that the spirit of Gerard Croiset is alive and well.

The Beaumont children have long had a unique social, cultural and historical significance. Several authors, starting with Adelaide writer Wally Watkins in the late 1960s, attempted to write a book on the Beaumont Case but it was just too difficult to marry the facts of the case, jealously guarded by the South Australia Police, with the urban myths explored in the media. Some didn't even try. In 1993, publishers Stuart Coupe and Julie Ogden commissioned eleven Australian crime writers to create solutions for a list of famous, unsolved crimes, including the Beaumont mystery. Author Jean Bedford wrote about the Beaumont children in her chapter of the anthology called *Case Reopened.*[32] Taking her cue from Detective Superintendent Rob Lean, Bedford writes of a deathbed 'confession' of sorts: the body of man found with a self-inflicted gunshot wound to the head in a deserted shed near Coober Pedy. A suitcase full of newspaper clippings — an echo from the actual Beaumont investigation — incriminates the man in a number of infamous child abductions.

But this was fiction, and the Beaumont mystery cannot be so easily explained.

Adelaide journalist Tom Prior, who had followed the case from its infancy and who interviewed the couple early in 1966, admitted in his book *The Sinners' Club* that 'If a reporter can afford to be obsessed with one story, I became obsessed with the Beaumont case.' Prior, though, made some insightful observations: 'Jim and Nancy Beaumont were loving parents and built their lives around Jane, Arnna and Grant. There were rotten things said at the time the children disappeared but, as I wrote then, not many parents would survive scrutiny as well as the Beaumonts, not many couples thrown suddenly into a blinding spotlight would prove to have as few things to hide.

'The Beaumonts were, and are, good people who made one tragic mistake. They thought they still lived in a decent world where it was safe to let children go to the beach alone. No responsible parent would dare do that now, least of all in SA. Adelaide is one of the reasons I gave up crime reporting. I kept seeing the faces of my children among the photographs of the missing and the dead.'[33]

Of the Beaumont Case, Walkley Award–winning journalist Andrew Rule wrote that for forty years all of Australia has been 'mesmerised by a story as mysterious as Picnic at Hanging Rock, and as sinister as Silence of the Lambs'.

'It has been burned into the national psyche, transcending time and place in a way other crimes have not. It marks, perhaps, an end of innocence for an old Australia, when doors are left unlocked and kids went to the beach alone. The Beaumont children are as much a part of popular culture as Ned Kelly and Don Bradman ... names that echo down the years and have become part of our mythology.'[34]

There have been other abductions in Adelaide since the Beaumonts, but none — not even the Adelaide Oval case — has had a similar impact. On 4 January 1983, ten-year-old Louise Bell was snatched from her Hackham West home by an intruder who is believed to have cut through a window flyscreen. The Bells, heartbroken at their loss, shut themselves away from the media. Almost a decade later, on 7 October 1992, twelve-year-old Rhianna Barreau left her Morphett Vale home and walked to the nearby Reynella shopping centre. Police believe she was abducted and murdered although, like Louise Bell, her body has never been found. Rewards have been posted for these cases but they remain unsolved to this day.

In 1995, country singer Beccy Cole even recorded a song, entitled *Lost Souls*, about the number of high-profile missing children cases in Adelaide. One of the verses was about the Beaumont children. The song was the brainchild of *Advertiser* photographer Barry O'Brien, who wrote the lyrics, with the newspaper paying for the cost of the CD's production. The 'song from the heart', which it was hoped would unlock the mystery of several missing children cases, allegedly had the endorsement of the children's parents — the Beaumont, Ratcliffe, Gordon and Barreau families — and the South Australia Police. 'In what police describe as a world first initiative,' wrote *Advertiser* journalist Peter Morgan, 'a compact disc will be launched today aimed at drawing information on cases that have frustrated detectives for decades.'[35]

As worthwhile as the motives were, the CD shone no new light on any investigation. Similarly, a Perth punk band called The Beaumont Children — named in the same provocative vein as San Francisco's The Dead Kennedys — had no measurable success in the late 1970s.

In 1997 writer Beth Spencer best summed up the place the Beaumont children now hold in the Australian psyche: 'The Beaumonts are the lost children who never grow up: disappearing off the map one day, into a kind of Neverland. Still (presumably) within Australia but unable to be located by the usual means — by parents, police, journalists; even the clairvoyants couldn't find them. So now they are permanently locked in a kind of Louisa May Alcott world of notes left on kitchen tables, playing forever in the shadows at the back of old amusement park rides; trapped in a nation's memory vault and desire for an innocent past.'[36]

That may just be the major legacy of the disappearance of the three Beaumont children in 1966.

*From left: Grant, Arnna and Jane Beaumont in the backyard of
their Somerton Park home*   Newspix

*G. A. (Jim) Beaumont and his wife, Nancy, pictured in 1966 after
their children went missing from Glenelg Beach*   Newspix

Police photo of where the children came up from the beach —
Colley Reserve, Glenelg Beach

Colley Reserve, where the children were last seen playing under
sprinklers

MISSING
BEAUMONT CHILDREN
SOUTH AUSTRALIA

At 10.00 a.m. on Wednesday, 26th January, 1966 the undermentioned children left their home at 109 Harding Street, SOMERTON PARK to go to the beach at GLENELG (a distance of about two miles). They have not been heard of since despite extensive Police enquiries.

1. **Jane Nartare BEAUMONT, 9 years** – 4 ft. 6 in. tall. Hair: fair, ear length, s u n bleached, pushed back with a fringe in front. Two front teeth prominent. Well spoken but stutters when excited.

2. **Arnna Kathleen BEAUMONT, 7 years** – 4 ft. tall, dark brown hair with a fringe, suntanned complexion. Dark brown eyes, plump build.

3. **Grant Ellis BEAUMONT, 4 years** – 3 ft. tall, brown hair with a fringe, brown eyes, olive complexion.

SUSPICION IS ATTACHED TO AN UNKNOWN MAN,

DESCRIPTION

Male, late 30's or early 40's, 6 ft. to 6 ft. 1 in., light brown hair long at the back with a part on the side, slim build and thinfaced, fair complexion.

Any person who can give any information relating to this matter is asked to contact their nearest Police Station

URGENTLY

Issued by the South Australian Police Dept.

Poster, released by Detective Sergeant Stan Swaine in 1967, seeking information about the missing Beaumont children   Courtesy of SAPOL

The former home of the Beaumont children (right) in Somerton Park, Glenelg

© Alan J. Whiticker

The cake shop in Moseley Street, Glenelg, where the Beaumont children were last seen on the day they disappeared

© Alan J. Whiticker

24-1-66

Dear Mum and Dad,
I am just about to go
to bed and the time is 9:00. I have put Grant's
nappy on as there is no need to worry about
him while getting into sheets Grant wanted to
sleep in his own bed, and so one of you
will have to sleep with Anne.
Although our rooms are not in very good condition
I hope you will find them as comfortable as we do.

Goodnight to you both,

Jane xxx

P.S. I hope you had a very nice time wherever
you went.

P.S.S. I hope you don't mind me taking your
radio into my room, Daddy.

(ABOVE)
The letter written by Jane Beaumont to her parents after babysitting her siblings two days before they disappeared

(LEFT)
Police cadets searching Patawalonga boat haven Newspix

Dear Mum and Dad. We had a really beautiful lunch today. We had some turky, and a lot of vegetables. They tasted really nice. The man is feeding us really well. The man took us to see the Sound of Music yesterday. Little Grant fell asleep in it though. He could not understand it. The man was very disappointed that you brought all those policemen with you. He knew all the time that they were there, he says that is why he sent the message to go across the street so that it would disturb the positions of the policemen. The man said that I had better stop now, so I will.
Grant and Arnna send you their love.
        Love Jane, Arnna and Grant
xx xyxxxx xxxxxxxxxxxxxxxxxxxx xxx

(ABOVE)
Former Detective
Sergeant Stan Swaine,
pictured in 1981,
became obsessed with
the Beaumont Case.

Newspix

(LEFT)
An artist's impression of
the man suspected of
abducting the
Beaumont children

Newspix

This Paringa Park warehouse was excavated in 1967 and 1996 after clairvoyant Gerard Croiset claimed the children were buried there.

Myponga Reservoir, south of Adelaide, which was searched by police in 1990. No trace of the Beaumont children was found.

11

The Case Today

Today, the unsolved Beaumont and Adelaide Oval cases each carry a reward of $100 000. The only case with a higher reward, one of $500 000, is the 1994 National Crime Authority bombing that killed Detective Sergeant Geoffrey Bowen and seriously injured lawyer Peter Wallis. 'Not a lot of people take up the option of providing information for a reward,' Superintendent Peter Woite said in a 2005 media release. 'No doubt a lot of people have information which could be useful to us, but for various reasons are not prepared to provide it.'[1]

Modern technology in policing methods, which provided the breakthrough in the Dandenong Letters in 1992, has not made any further advances in the forty-year-old Beaumont Case. However, this does not mean that the South Australia Police and other interstate crime authorities have not investigated certain 'persons of interest' who have come to their attention.

The City of Adelaide is still sensitive about the Beaumont name. Many people did not want to be interviewed out of deference to the health and well-being of Jim and Nancy Beaumont, and the Major Crime Investigation Branch declined to comment directly on the continuing investigation. The parents of Jane, Arnna and Grant Beaumont will take no comfort from this, but forty years later no-one is any closer to solving the mystery than they were on the day the children went missing from Glenelg beach.

In January 1966, Brian Swan was a seventeen-year-old police cadet at the Largs North Police Academy when he was called in to help search for three children who had gone missing from Glenelg beach on Australia Day. On 3 February 1966, Swan joined a group of serving policemen and other cadets in the search of the Patawalonga boat haven, which had been drained earlier that morning. Swan trudged through the black ooze from Kings Bridge to the lock, prodding for any sign of the missing children, and he also spent time searching the sandhills at Glenelg North before joining a dozen cadets on a three-day search of Marion Council rubbish dump. Nothing related to the missing children was found.

Detective Sergeant Brian Swan, now in his late fifties, has been in charge of the Beaumont Case since 1988.

In the late 1960s, police cadet Peter Woite was a budding Aussie Rules junior at the Port Adelaide club. After representing South Australia in 1970, the centre-half forward resisted the temptation to join the Victorian Football League, and went on to be part of the premiership-winning Port Adelaide team in 1977. Woite later joined the team defeated by Port in that grand final — Glenelg — and played in twenty matches during 1979–80, taking his career total to over 200 games. At the beginning of the new millennium, by which time he had been named in the greatest Port Adelaide team of the twentieth century, Superintendent Peter Woite was Officer in Charge of the Major Crime Investigation Branch of the South Australia Police.

As the Beaumont Case reached its fortieth year, the legacy of the unsolved investigation has passed on to Peter Woite and Brian Swan.

Detective Sergeant Brian Swan first 'picked up' the Beaumont file in 1988 and from that day he's 'worn it' like an extra suit.[2] In person, Swan is blunt and to the point but he is also a pragmatist, and is in no way obsessed with the Beaumont Case or deluded that he will one day solve it. While dealing with the countless leads provided by the public about the fate of the missing Beaumont children, Swan also played a major role in the five-year investigation into the Snowtown Murders during the 1990s; the capture and extradition of the chief suspect in the 2001 murder of British tourist Peter Falconio; and, more recently, the disappearance and possible murder of bikie leader Steve Williams. But the Beaumont Case is special.

'It is hard for any investigator to pick up a case this old and get a feel for it,' Swan said in a 1995 interview. 'When you can go and speak to someone from day one, you get a feel for them: you know if they're edgy. Here, all you can do is read cold statements.'[3]

There is an old saying among detectives: 'A case can die with the detective who investigates it.' In the 1960s and 1970s, detectives were allowed to keep their own diaries of investigations while others refused to commit information to paper for confidentiality reasons, preferring to carry the facts of a case in their head. Many of the detectives who worked on the Beaumont Case have died, taking with them the peripheral facts of the original investigation, and the files have had to be organised and transferred onto computer. Today, the Beaumont files are kept in a dozen large boxes in the bowels of the Major Crime Investigation Branch. All the information on hard copy has been transferred onto the police computer system, which has a search engine and a greater capacity for cross-referencing information.

Swan continually investigates leads from the public both in Australia and overseas; about ten to fifteen come through each year. In his eighteen years in charge of the Beaumont file, he has supervised excavations, carried out background checks and travelled interstate. 'Everyone has a theory,' he says. A person will ring the Major Crime Investigation Branch in Wakefield Street with a new 'lead' — for example, the name of a man selling ice-creams and drinks on the beach that day forty years ago — and no matter how remote the link to the Beaumont children, he will investigate it. 'I'll contact the person who forwarded it and take it from there,' he says, knowing that he will also do most of the legwork himself.[4]

Do the South Australia Police believe that the Beaumont children are still alive? 'You can't say there's no hope,' Swan told journalist Penelope Debelle a decade ago. 'If you're asking me what my personal belief is, I find it very, very hard to believe three children could still be alive today, with all the publicity this case has received over thirty years, and for them not to know their biological parents.'[5]

But if the children are dead, where do you begin to search? Glenelg alone has many old homes that have not been renovated since the 1960s and whose backyards have not been disturbed in all that time. Sandhills ring South Australia's beaches: which one do you search? Beyond the Adelaide Hills, ridges are dotted with old mineshafts: where do you start? You need to be practical, Swan says. Technology such as sonar equipment, heat-sensing radar and even cadaver dogs can only stretch so far and, logistically, thousands of square kilometres would need to be searched. 'Bodies can stay hidden forever,' Swan said. 'But I think anybody, whether police or not, would love to find those children for the sake of the parents' peace of mind.'[6]

'There have been a number of locations that warranted digging up,' Swan told journalists in December 1995. 'I've personally been involved in [searching] two cellars, three dams, a drain ...'[7] One of the first reports Brian Swan was able to dismiss concerned a young man whose name was forwarded by a member of the public for investigation. The man wasn't even born when the Beaumont children disappeared.

After the Myponga Reservoir search in 1990, bones found in a Glenelg car yard in Brighton Road in 1990 were originally thought to belong to 'an Aboriginal male buried on the site'[8] but were later identified by a pathologist as animal bones. Then in 1992, Swan investigated claims that the Beaumont children's bodies were buried in a dam in Second Valley. The reports had first been checked out in the late 1980s after no fewer than five different sources had volunteered information that the bodies of the Beaumont children may have been dumped there. The South Australia Police confirmed that local farmers used the dam to dispose of the carcasses of dead sheep and that no evidence relating to the Beaumont Case was found. Bones found at Glenelg South in 1997, including part of a spinal cord, were also identified as animal remains.

In November 2000, sales consultant Trevor Terrell lifted loose floorboards in his 1910 cottage in the Adelaide suburb of Queenstown and found the skulls of three small children and dozens of small bones on the soil below. Terrell thought that he may have solved the mystery of the missing Beaumont children but forensic tests showed that the remains belonged to three unidentified premature or stillborn babies. Despite this, many people were convinced the bones belonged to the missing children and contacted the police with their theories about the case.

Many people have had hunches about the case over the years, but they invariably rush to the print media first. The South Australia Police then have to respond to allegations and misinformation that is already in the public arena. For example, as recently as April 2004, a casual remark made by a man in New Zealand sparked a media frenzy on both sides of the Tasman Sea.

A man waiting to be served in a butcher shop in the North Island coastal town of New Plymouth was talking to a sales-woman when he recognised her Australian accent. Unsolicited, he told the woman that when he was a child growing up in the South Island city of Dunedin, his mother believed they were living next door to the missing Beaumont children. A shop assistant who overheard the conversation then reported it to the local police sergeant. With nothing more to go on than a throwaway comment, the sergeant made the mistake of appealing to the media for assistance.

From there, the comment jumped the Tasman. Although the South Australian Major Crime Investigation Branch told the Australian media that it had fully investigated many calls of a similar nature over the years and could not act until briefed by New Zealand Police, the media quickly grabbed hold of the issue.

On 15 May the sister of the man who made the remark in the butcher shop went to the New Plymouth police station. Her brother, realising the storm that he had unleashed, did not want to be interviewed but she confirmed his story. The following day, journalists from *The Advertiser* in Adelaide arrived in New Zealand and showed the woman photos of the three Beaumont children. The New Zealand woman said that Arnna looked 'like one of the girls'[9] she played with in 1966. She then gave police the name of the girl who lived next door to her in the late 1960s so that police could investigate the claims.

Within days, the woman identified, 47-year-old Judith Hewitt (née Larson), was found living in a Dunedin boarding house. Even the woman was confused: 'As far as I know I was born here [in New Zealand] and I've never left,' Ms Hewitt told reporter Miles Kemp. 'It was all those years ago. I can't say for sure, and I'm not saying until the DNA test is done. It could be me . . . I just don't know and it is up to the police.'[10]

Judith Hewitt volunteered information about her childhood, as well as the possibility of a DNA sample, and the matter was quickly cleared up. The fact that Ms Hewitt attended kindergarten in Dunedin before 1966 should have been enough for the media, but a simple birth certificate quickly confirmed that she was the biological daughter of her parents (her father, a Korean War veteran named Doug Larson, was deceased and his body buried in Oamaru Soldiers' Cemetery). While the whole affair may have been a welcome diversion for New Plymouth police, whose largest active file was marked 'Stolen bikes,' Detective Sergeant Jennifer Glover echoed the feelings of most people when she said, 'I feel very sorry for the Beaumont family, and very sorry we couldn't help.'[11]

It seems incredible that people living on the other side of the Tasman could believe for four decades, without ever having seen photos of the three Beaumont children, that their neighbours could be the missing Australian children. It is just as inconceivable that Jane, Arnna and Grant Beaumont could have been kidnapped from Glenelg beach in 1966 and then somehow taken out of the country without passports. That people believed such things *were* possible simply indicates the strength of the urban myths that surrounded the case.

In July 2005, the South Australia Police provided me with the two-page, hand-typed résumé of the unsolved case that it gives to all media organisations. The résumé, which appears not to have been updated for some time, provides the briefest overview of what is known to have happened at Glenelg that day over forty years ago.

Résumé of the investigation into the abduction of three BEAUMONT children missing from Glenelg Beach, South Australia, since the 26th of January, 1966

On Wednesday the 26th of January 1966, three children, Jane BEAUMONT aged 9 years, Arnna BEAUMONT aged 7 years, and Grant BEAUMONT aged 4 years, disappeared from the Glenelg foreshore Adelaide, South Australia. Despite extensive Police enquiries, they have not been seen or heard of since.

BACKGROUND

The BEAUMONT family consisted of Mr. Beaumont, who at the time of the disappearance was a middle-aged travelling salesman, ex-taxi driver, Mrs. Beaumont also middle aged, who performed home duties, and their three children. The two eldest children attended a local primary school. It was apparently common for Mrs. Beaumont to allow the three children to go to the beach together. The eldest child Jane was apparently very 'grown-up' and 'motherly' towards the two younger children. The children were apparently generally well behaved, had been instructed not to speak to strangers, and got along well with each other. The Beaumont family lived in a typical suburban home less than three kilometres from the beach.

EVENTS OF 26/1/66.

The 26th of January is Australia Day, usually associated with a public holiday. The 26th of January 1966 however fell on a Wednesday, therefore the holiday was taken at a later time. At this time of the year however all schools in South Australia were on school holidays. January is also mid-summer in Australia, and on the 26th of Jan. '66 the weather in Adelaide was hot, clear, with a light breeze. High tide was around 12.30 p.m.

It has been established that the events of this day leading up to the disappearance of the three children were as follows:

0945 hrs — Mrs. Beaumont allows the three children to walk the short distance to the bus stop.

She understood that they were going to the Glenelg beach for the day, and would return home on the bus at about noon.

1000 hrs — Bus driver recalls collecting the three children. Although he cannot recall them getting off the bus, He [sic] round finished in Moseley St. Glenelg, a short distance from the beach. Another passenger also recalls seeing the children on the bus.

1015 hrs — The children are seen by the local postman walking along Jetty Road Glenelg towards the beach.

1100 hrs — The children are seen sitting on a section of lawn alongside the Holdfast Bay sailing club overlooking the beach, by a school friend of Jane. This person does not speak to Jane.

1200 hrs — Between 1100 hrs and 1200 hrs, several persons recall seeing the children on this same section of lawn. They also recall seeing the suspect either talking or playing with the children. At 1145 hrs the children are known to have attended at a local cake shop and purchased food, including extra food other than what they would have eaten. The children paid for this food using money other than what their mother had provided them with. It would appear that the children also purchased food for the suspect, using money provided by him.

The children were last seen at about 1200 hours on that day. It is believed that the male person seen talking and playing with the children between 1100 hours and 1200 hours, may be responsible for their disappearance. No mode of travel is known for this person.

The three missing children are described as follows:

Jane Nararlie [sic] BEAUMONT: born 10/9/56. 4'6" tall, with fair ear-length sun-bleached hair with a pushed-back fringe at the front. She may have been wearing a tortoise shell hair band with a yellow ribbon in her hair. She had hazel eyes, a thin face, thin build, and had freckles. At the time of her disappearance she was wearing light green shorts, canvas tartan pattern sandshoes with white soles. She was carrying an airways type bag (possibly blue) containing three towels, a book titled 'Little Women', and a white money purse containing eight shillings and sixpence. She was well-spoken, but stuttered when excited. Her two front teeth were prominent.

Arnna Kathleen BEAUMONT: born 11/11/58, 4' tall, with dark brown hair with a fringe. She had dark brown eyes, suntanned complexion, and plump build. She was wearing tan shorts over red and white striped bathers. She was also wearing tan coloured sandals.

Grant Ellis BEAUMONT: born 12/7/61, 3' tall, with short brown hair with a fringe. He had brown eyes, olive complexion, very suntanned, thin build. He was wearing green swimming trunks with vertical white stripes, under green cotton shorts. He was also wearing red leather type sandals.

The male person seen talking and playing with the Beaumont children immediately prior to their disappearance is described as follows:

Male, mid to late 30's, about 6' tall, thin to athletic build, with light brown short hair swept back and parted on the left side, clean-shaven, suntanned complexion, with a thin face. Australian accent. Wearing blue bathers with a single white stripe down the outside of each leg.[12]

The résumé does produce a number of interesting insights. Firstly, a minor one: Jane Beaumont's middle name is incorrectly listed as 'Nararlie'. The carry bag the children took to the beach is described as being 'possibly blue' not green, as stated in earlier reports. More importantly the South Australia Police place postman Tom Patterson's sighting of the children at 10.15 in the morning, not the afternoon as was reported in the media. When Mr Patterson was interviewed by the South Australia Police in February 1988, he again stated that he saw the children at 2.55 pm. However, there is no corroborated sighting of the Beaumont children after they left Wenzel's Cakes at midday. Lastly, the description of the man differs from original media reports: he has 'light brown short hair' as opposed to 'blond' and 'in need of cutting', as was reported in *The Advertiser* on 29 January 1966; and the description of the bathers he was wearing differs from eyewitness accounts, having one extra detail that cannot be found in any other media report of the time. According to the résumé, the man's bathers were blue 'with a white stripe down the outside of each leg'.

In 1966 these were the colours of the Henley Beach Surf Lifesaving Club, north of Glenelg. Were the children befriended by a surf-lifesaver, or a person posing as one, in previous trips to the beach that summer? Although the South Australia Police declined to be quoted on the continuing investigation, the question needs to be asked: did the South Australia Police investigate the names of those surf-lifesavers who patrolled local beaches at Henley, Glenelg, Brighton and Seacliff at the time the children disappeared? Even if 'The Family' network of paedophiles is an exaggeration, paedophiles have been known to infiltrate sporting clubs, such as surf lifesaving clubs, because of the easy access to children.

Peter Woite and Brian Swan physically bristle at the mention of the word 'suspect' in relation to the Beaumont Case. As far as they're concerned, there is only one suspect and that is the man seen with the children on the day they disappeared. Any person who is investigated regarding the events of Australia Day 1966 is termed a 'person of interest'[13] until the police have enough corroborated evidence to 'suspect' them of being involved in the crime. After forty years of investigation, the South Australia Police have no known suspect in regard to the disappearance of the Beaumont children. However, this has not stopped the Major Crime Investigation Branch in South Australia, and similar authorities around the country, from investigating several 'persons of interest'.

In 1998 an 86-year-old Queensland man, Arthur Stanley Brown, was charged with the rape and murder of sisters Judith and Susan Mackay in Townsville. The bodies of the sisters, aged seven and five, had been found in a dry creek bed on 26 August 1970. At that time, Brown was working as a maintenance man with the Queensland Public Works Department, and was aged fifty-eight. He pleaded not guilty to the charges. The elderly man was later released when the jury in his 1999 trial could not reach a decision and authorities declined to proceed with another trial because of Brown's age and alleged dementia.

When Arthur Brown's photo was published around the country, people in Adelaide couldn't believe the similarity between the man's long, gaunt face and the sketches of the Beaumont and Adelaide Oval suspects. Major Crime Superintendent Paul Schramm was forced to comment on the growing media speculation about Brown's possible involvement in the unsolved Adelaide crimes. 'I agree there is some similarity,' Schramm told John Merriman in *The Advertiser*, 'but I would stress that at this stage that is purely coincidental and in itself doesn't amount to any evidence that Mr Brown has had anything to do with the matters in SA.'[14]

Brown was born in the small town of Merinda, near Bowen in North Queensland, in 1912. A meatworker in Townsville during World War II, he was later employed as a roving maintenance man until his retirement in 1977. Brown worked on government buildings, including Aitkenville State School where the Mackay sisters attended. In the early days of the investigation, Brown's name had been forwarded to

Townsville detectives as a suspect in the brutal double murder but it was not until twenty-eight years later, after his own family went to police about his sexual deviance, that he was arrested by police.

A former Adelaide woman, who was now living in Victoria, saw Brown's photo in the newspaper alongside the sketches of the Beaumont and Adelaide Oval suspects. Although she did not come forward in 1973 when Joanne Ratcliffe and Kirste Gordon were abducted, the woman told the media that it was Arthur Brown she saw struggling with two young girls as she walked with her family from Adelaide Zoo all those years ago. However, the South Australia Police could not rely on the woman's identification of Brown because his photo had been published in the media beside the sketches of the suspects and had not been selected from a traditional photo 'line-up'.

Arthur Brown was officially eliminated as a suspect in both the Beaumont and Adelaide Oval cases in 2001. During its investigation into Brown's movements, Queensland Police could find no evidence that Brown was in Adelaide in 1966 or 1973 or that he had ever visited South Australia. Brown certainly fitted the description of the Adelaide Oval suspect but he hardly matched the 'sun-tanned surfie' seen on the beach with the Beaumont children in 1966: he would have been fifty-three that year. Brown passed away in 2002 without facing any of the charges brought against him, including murder, rape, sodomy, deprivation of liberty and administration of drugs.

In 2004 the Victorian Police confirmed that they were launching a fresh inquiry into the movements of sadistic paedophile Derek Ernest Percy, who had been jailed for the murder of a twelve-year-old girl in 1969. Percy, a 21-year-old naval rating stationed at HMAS Cerberus in Melbourne at the time, was charged with the mutilation murder of Yvonne Tuohy at the Westernport Bay fishing village of Warneet in Victoria but was found not guilty by reason of insanity. Instead, Percy was 'confined to safe custody at the Governor's pleasure' which is for a nominal period of twenty-five years. However, in 1998 Justice Geoff Eames ruled that Percy's 'safety or that of members of the public would be seriously endangered if he were released on a non-custodial supervision order.'[15] Justice Eames declined to set a minimum term and Derek Percy remains the only Victorian offender found mentally unfit to plead who is still in jail.

In July 1969, Yvonne Elizabeth Tuohy and her friend Shane Spiller, aged eleven, were walking to the beach for a picnic when Percy tried to abduct the pair. While Shane escaped and was able to give a detailed description of the man and the car, the disembowelled body of Yvonne Tuohy was found gagged, bound and with her throat cut about ten kilometres away at Devon Meadows. Thanks largely to Shane Spiller's keen observation, Victorian police were able to quickly apprehend Percy that night at Cerberus Naval Base, take him to Frankston police station and charge him with murder. Percy was questioned about other unsolved child murders in the 1960s and police believe his diaries, written both before and after his capture, give the best indication of his possible involvement in other crimes.

'His writings described ways of abducting, murdering and mutilating children and were found in his locker at HMAS Cerberus and in a search of his cell after he was sentenced,' wrote Justice Eames in 1998. 'A psychiatrist who assessed Percy for the defence after his arrest for the Yvonne Tuohy murder concluded, from things he had written, that he had many psycho-sexual abnormalities and was highly likely to have killed other children.'[16]

In February 2005 Percy was questioned by Victorian, New South Wales and South Australia Police and Australian Federal Police concerning the disappearance of the three Beaumont children and several other unsolved crimes:

- The rape and murder of Christine Sharrock and Marianne Schmidt at Wanda beach on 11 January 1965. The fifteen-year-old Sydney schoolgirls had gone to nearby Cronulla beach with Marianne's four younger siblings but headed off into the Wanda dunes by themselves in the early afternoon. Their bodies were found buried in sand dunes the following day, stabbed to death and violated.
- The strangulation murder of six-year-old Canberra schoolboy Alan Redston on 27 September 1966. The little boy's body was found beside a creek in a polythene bag, 'hogtied' with a length of rope, his hands tied behind his back with tape and his ankles bound to a rope around his neck. The little boy had not been sexually assaulted and had not been killed where his body was found.
- The strangulation and mutilation murder of three-year-old Simon Brook on 18 May 1968 in the inner suburb of Glebe in Sydney. The little boy had wandered away from

his home, and his body was found the next day several streets away on a vacant block. The boy had been strangled before his genitals were mutilated with a razor blade.

- The disappearance and possible murder of seven-year-old Linda Stilwell from the Melbourne beachside suburb of St Kilda in August 1968. Linda disappeared on her way home from an amusement park named Little Luna Park near the esplanade at St Kilda beach. She was last seen laughing and walking beside an unknown man at about 6 pm.[17]

Percy was first questioned about these crimes on 5 May 1970, when he admitted to Detective Sergeant K. S. Robertson of the Victorian Police that 'whilst on beaches in New South Wales, he had sordid thoughts towards children, and his agreement that he might have committed other offences had not the children been in the company of their parents.'[18] If Derek Percy were responsible for the above murders — and this is only conjecture — then he might well be the most prolific child killer in Australian history. But was Percy responsible for the disappearance of the Beaumont children?

The theory that serial killers have a psychological 'calling card' is a relatively modern concept that would not have been known to police in the 1960s. Looking at the crime for which Derek Percy was jailed, three characteristics stand out that may be applied to other unsolved crimes: children, the water and sadism. All the victims were under the age of fifteen. Percy had a fascination for water that extended beyond his becoming a naval rating. Christine Sharrock and Marianne Schmidt were murdered on the beach at Wanda, the Beaumonts went missing

from Glenelg beach, Linda Stilwell was abducted from St Kilda
Esplanade and Alan Redston's body was dumped near a creek.
In regard to the third issue, the Wanda beach victims and
Simon Brook were mutilated, and Alan Redston was slowly
strangled. The body of Linda Stilwell, like the Beaumonts, was
never found.

Derek Percy is known to have been in New South Wales in
1965 (Wanda beach) and 1968 (Simon Brook), and in
Melbourne in 1968 (Linda Stilwell) and 1969 (Yvonne Tuohy).
However, it is not known whether he visited Adelaide or
Canberra in 1966; Percy would have been too young to drive.
There is a suspicion that he was on holiday with his parents in
Adelaide in January 1966, but where does a seventeen-year-old
hide the bodies of three small children, especially when he is on
holiday with his parents and does not know the lie of the land?
Percy was a teenager in 1966 and does not fit the description of
the man in his mid to late thirties seen frolicking with the
Beaumont children on Glenelg beach.

The other major problem is that Derek Percy was in custody
when Joanne Ratcliffe and Kirste Gordon were abducted from
Adelaide Oval. It is largely because of this fact that Percy is
unlikely to have been responsible for the disappearance of the
Beaumont children.

However, Percy may one day be held to account for another
death. In 2001, 43-year-old Shane Spiller disappeared from his
home on the south coast of New South Wales. Fearing for his
life as Percy applied for parole in Victoria, it is believed that
Spiller took his own life, although his body has never been found.

On 26 January 2005 — not surprisingly, the thirty-ninth anniversary of the disappearance of the Beaumont children — Superintendent Peter Woite released a statement refuting claims from interstate police about another 'person of interest' in the Beaumont Case. Claims by no less than the Tasmanian Commissioner of Police, Richard McCreadie, that convicted child killer James O'Neill 'could be responsible' for the abduction of the three Beaumont children were quickly dismissed by Woite. McCreadie was the arresting officer in 1975 when O'Neill was charged with the murder of nine-year-old Ricky John Smith and sentenced to life imprisonment. O'Neill, who had travelled extensively throughout Australia before murdering in Tasmania, later confessed to the murder of Bruce Colin Wilson. O'Neill was also investigated over the abduction and sexual assault of four boys in Victoria in the early 1970s. Why not the Beaumonts then?

'Until [the South Australia Police] find another murderer or until they discover what happened to the Beaumont children, then you can't discount [O'Neill's involvement],' McCreadie said at the time. However, Detective Superintendent Woite told the media that James O'Neill had recently been interviewed by the South Australia Police while in jail in Tasmania and had been 'discounted from our inquiries'.[19]

The physical constraints of the Beaumont Case (as well as the Adelaide Oval Case) have always remained: no physical evidence belonging to the missing children has ever been retrieved; no actual murder scene has been identified; and because the children's remains have not been recovered, there is no hope that any forensic evidence or a suspect's DNA could ever be identified. Forty years on, the only description of a suspect that police have is that of the man seen playing with the children on the morning they disappeared, and there is nothing tangible to link that man to the children's disappearance other than the fact that he never came forward to identify himself.

This is not said to be critical of the South Australia Police. It is just a realistic assessment of what they have to work with.

In 1998 the South Australia Police published a profile of a typical child molester or abductor. Created by criminal profiler Sergeant Robyn Filmer, the profile was established in response to the seven unsolved child abductions in Adelaide stretching back to the Beaumont children in 1966. By researching those offenders who had been identified and found guilty of their crimes, the South Australia Police attempted to describe the type of person who preyed on children. While Filmer stated that it was impossible to 'categorise human behaviour into specific classifications that will be applicable to all situations,'[20] it was possible to analyse the behaviour of offenders and identify the *type* of person who committed the crime.

The 'average' child molester is over twenty-five years of age, Filmer stated, and is male, single and lives alone or with parents. The person associates mainly with young people and has hobbies or interests that appeal to children. The offender is highly skilled in identifying children who are 'vulnerable' for attack. This, in itself, is a very broad classification. However, if a child molester is also a serial murderer, as is likely in the Beaumont and Adelaide Oval cases, then the profile can be even further refined.

Former FBI agent Robert K. Ressler is the world's leading authority on serial killers. Ressler invented the term 'serial killer' to describe the phenomenon of repeat murderers in America in the 1970s. In his book *Whoever Fights Monsters*, Ressler identifies several characteristics that are common in most serial killers:

- Most are white males under the age of thirty-five.
- They are the products of dysfunctional families — typically unloving mothers and absent fathers.
- They are intelligent but employed in menial occupations.
- Many suffer from a physical ailment or disability.
- The initial impulse to murder comes during a period of personal stress, such as a death in the family, the break-up of a relationship or even the loss of a job.[21]

Is this the type of person the South Australia Police should be looking for? Does it describe someone already known to them — someone jailed perhaps for another crime? If it doesn't, then all that the South Australia Police, the children's parents and the rest of us can do is to wait for that cosmic roll of the dice: the deathbed confession.

'Someone could ring up,' Brian Swan once hypothesised, 'and say, "My husband [did it] . . . I've held this secret for so many years." That person may be on her own deathbed, and just wants to relieve herself of this secret.'[22] However, even if someone presented themselves to police and confessed, the confession would have to be accompanied by corroborating evidence, such as the burial site of the children or possession of an item belonging to them.

But time is working against solving the Beaumont Case. Many of the original witnesses — the 74-year-old woman who saw the children frolicking with 'the man', the elderly couple who spoke to the man, and the postman who waved to the children in Jetty Road — have passed away. There is a distinct possibility that even the person responsible, described as being in his mid to late thirties in 1966, is also long dead. Maybe all these years we have been searching for a phantom: someone who no longer exists.

One of the idiosyncrasies of the Beaumont Case is that there has never been a public inquest into the events of 26 January 1966 because, according to the South Australia Police, the parents never requested one. A coroner's inquest that tabled the known facts would have been difficult for Jim and Nancy Beaumont, but it may have spared them a lifetime of public scrutiny, innuendo and myth-making. An inquest would only be held today if new evidence came to light, but the more time passes the less likely it is that this will happen.

Detective Sergeant Brian Swan's continued hope is that the mystery of the disappearance of the three Beaumont children will be solved while their parents are still alive. Swan wants what we all want — resolution: 'for [the children's] remains to be found so that the Beaumonts can bury their children properly ... and know where they are.'[23]

Forty years later, we are all still waiting.

Glenelg, the unique Adelaide beach suburb with the palindromic name, has changed in the forty years since the three Beaumont children disappeared from Colley Reserve.

Twenty years after the original jetty was destroyed, a new jetty was built in 1969 at a cost of $127 000, although some remarked that it did not compare 'with the size and magnificence of its predecessor'.[24] In the same year, an extensive amusement park development was finally finished at Colley Reserve. Some time later the old yacht club on the corner of Moseley Square was converted into a museum and information centre to promote tourism.

If you walk past the shops in Jetty Road and into Moseley Square, the drive-through roundabout that was in operation during the 1960s is now closed off to traffic and is a paved mall. The tramlines are still there, but even they were being renovated when I visited in July 2005. Looking south from the jetty, one is struck by the flat, grey, saucer-like surface of the ocean. Past the horizon there is nothing for 3300 kilometres until you reach George V Land, the Australian sector of Antarctica. It's hard to believe that a place as peaceful as Glenelg could even conjure a storm, let alone wash away a jetty.

Colley Reserve is almost gone now, engulfed by development. Where Jane, Arnna and Grant Beaumont played under sprinklers, Stage 2B of the Holdfast Shores development is being built. This entertainment precinct and plaza will replace the tin sheds of sideshow alley and the garish Magic Mountain waterslides from the 1980s, taking its place among the multi-storey resorts that currently overlook the beach. Soon there will be little left of the original grassed foreshore — nothing the Beaumont children would remember — except for the rotunda where the Salvation Army Band used to play on still summer nights not that long ago.

In July 2005, contractors were planning to tear down the warehouse in Somerton Park (formerly Paringa Park) where the remains of the three Beaumont children were thought to lie. A workman showed me the scarred concrete floor where well-meaning but misguided citizens searched for evidence of the children in 1967 and 1996. When the warehouse was finally demolished in December 2005, the South Australia Police were at last able to complete an exhaustive search of the excavated site. No evidence of the children was found, and claims that the Beaumonts may have been accidentally buried there now seem foolish and parochial.

There is a monument in the middle of Moseley Square, a striking stone obelisk dedicated to the pioneers and founders of the colony. Metallic letters spell out the names of Flinders, Sturt, Light, Wakefield and Torrens beneath a brass replica of a ship facing Holdfast Bay. Even poor foot constable Albert King, shot and killed by a drunk almost a century ago, has his own plaque in Moseley Square. But there is nothing for the Beaumont children.

But what words could the people of Adelaide write on a monument for three young children now missing for forty years? What words could possibly comfort Jim and Nancy Beaumont for what they have been through?

When Her Majesty Queen Elizabeth II unveiled a memorial at Runnymede in October 1954 for all those who gave their lives in the Battle of Britain and have no known graves over Europe, she read a passage from Psalm 139. On 10 December 1955, when the burghers of Glenelg marked their centenary as a council and unveiled their honour roll for

those who lost their lives in the war, they quoted the same
passage. Maybe those same five lines from King David would
be a fitting tribute to Jane, Arnna and Grant Beaumont:

> If I ascend into heaven thou art there;
>
> If I descend into hell thou art present.
>
> If I take my wings early in the morning,
>
> and remain in the uttermost parts of the sea,
>
> Even there also shall thy hand lead me,
>
> And thy right hand shall hold me.[25]

But building a monument to the Beaumont children is
unlikely to happen.

Let the truth, then, be their memorial.

Endnotes

Chapter 1

1. Geoffrey Dutton, *Founder of a City: The Story of Colonel Light*, Rigby, Adelaide 1960.
2. *Australia Information Guide: South Australia*, www.australian1.com
3. Max Lamshed, *Adelaide Sketchbook*, Rigby, Adelaide, 1967.
4. Max Lamshed, *Adelaide Sketchbook*, Rigby, Adelaide, 1967.
5. D. Whitelock, *Adelaide: A History of Difference 1836–1976*, University of Queensland Press, St Lucia, 1977.
6. D. Whitelock, *Adelaide: A History of Difference 1836–1976*, University of Queensland Press, St Lucia, 1977.
7. *Daily Telegraph*, 18 June 1999.
8. ABC AM Online, 3 April 2001.
9. Malcolm Brown, *Sydney Morning Herald*, 25 May 1999.
10. *The Advertiser*, 17 March 1990.
11. Alan Sharpe, *Crimes That Shocked Australia*, Atrand, Sydney, 1982.
12. Peter Hoystead and Paul B. Kidd, *Shallow Graves: The Concealments of Killers*, Five Mile Press, Melbourne, 2002.
13. Susan Mitchell, *All Things Bright and Beautiful: Murder in the City of Light*, Pan Macmillan, 2004.
14. Kerry-Anne Walsh, *The Sun Herald*, 8 August 2004.
15. Geoffrey Dutton, *Founder of a City: The Story of Colonel Light*, Rigby, Adelaide, 1960.

16. Geoffrey Dutton, *Founder of a City: The Story of Colonel Light,* Rigby, Adelaide, 1960.

17. Geoffrey Dutton, *Founder of a City: The Story of Colonel Light,* Rigby, Adelaide, 1960.

18. Susan Mitchell, *All Things Bright and Beautiful: Murder in the City of Light*, Pan Macmillan, 2004.

19. Kerry-Anne Walsh, *Sun Herald*, 8 August 2004.

20. Kerry-Anne Walsh, *Sun Herald*, 8 August 2004.

21. Peter Pierce, *The Country of Lost Children: An Australian Anxiety*, Cambridge University Press, 1999.

Chapter 2

1. Australian Bureau of Statistics, 1966 Census figures (Cat. No. 3105.0.65.001, Table 79).

2. *The Advertiser*, 26 January 1966.

3. Author's interview with Peter Alexander, Head of the SA Police Association, July 2005.

4. Kerry-Anne Walsh, *The Sun Herald*, 8 August 2004.

5. *The Advertiser*, 3 February 1965.

6. *The Advertiser*, 21 January 1965.

7. *Australia Through Time: 2002 Edition*, Random House, Sydney, 2002.

8. *Chronicle of the 20th Century*, Viking, Melbourne, 1999.

9. *The Advertiser*, 29 September 1965.

10. Tom Brown, *Glenelg: 1836–1972*, Strehlow, Adelaide, 1973.

11. *The Herald*, 4 February 1966.

12. W. H. Jeanes, *Historic Glenelg: Birthplace of South Australia*, Glenelg Council, 1979.

13. W. H. Jeanes, *Historic Glenelg: Birthplace of South Australia*, Glenelg Council, 1979.
14. W. H. Jeanes, *Historic Glenelg: Birthplace of South Australia*, Glenelg Council, 1979.
15. Moseley Square Memorial, Glenelg.
16. Tom Brown, *Glenelg: 1836–1972*, Strehlow, Adelaide, 1973.
17. Ken Anderson, Doug Easom and Brian Francis, 'The Beaumont Disclosures' in *The News*, 22 February 1968.
18. Ken Anderson, Doug Easom and Brian Francis, 'The Beaumont Disclosures' in *The News*, 22 February 1968.
19. Ken Anderson, Doug Easom and Brian Francis, 'The Beaumont Disclosures' in *The News*, 22 February 1968.
20. Alan Dower, *Deadline*, Hutchinson, Victoria, 1979.
21. Ken Anderson, Doug Easom and Brian Francis, 'The Beaumont Disclosures' in *The News*, 22 February 1968.

Chapter 3

1. All quotes attributed directly to Jim and Nancy Beaumont are taken from 'The Beaumont Disclosures' by reporters Ken Anderson, Doug Easom and Brian Francis, first published in *The News* on 21–22 February 1968, unless otherwise indicated.
2. *The Advertiser*, 29 January 1966.
3. *The Sunday Mail*, 29 January 1966.
4. *The Advertiser*, 28 January 1966.
5. *The Advertiser*, 3 February 1966.
6. *The Advertiser*, 29 January 1966.
7. Official police résumé of the case, 1966.
8. *The News*, 22 February 1968.

9. *The Advertiser*, 28 January 1966.

10. *The Advertiser*, 30 January 1966.

11. *The Sunday Mail*, 29 January 1966.

12. *The Sunday Mail*, 29 January 1966.

13. *The Sun News-Pictorial*, 31 January 1966.

14. *The News*, 3 February 1966.

15. *The News*, 4 February 1966.

Chapter 4

1. *The Advertiser*, 27 January 1966.

2. *The News*, 27 January 1966.

3. *The News*, 27 January 1966.

4. *The Advertiser*, 31 January 1966.

5. *The Advertiser*, 28 January 1966.

6. *The Advertiser*, 29 January 1966.

7. *The Advertiser*, 31 January 1966.

8. *The Sunday Mail*, 29 January 1966.

9. *The Advertiser*, 10 February 1966.

10. *The Advertiser*, 31 January 1966.

11. *The Advertiser*, 29 January 1966.

12. *The Advertiser*, 27 January 1966.

13. *The News*, 10 February 1966.

14. *The Advertiser*, 16 July 1966.

15. *The Herald*, 15 July 1966.

16. *The Advertiser*, 7, 8, 9 February 1966.

17. *Where Were You When: The News That Stopped a Nation*, News Custom Publishing, Victoria, 2003.

18. Author's interview with Jan Van Schie, July 2005.

19. *The Advertiser*, 3 August 1966.

20. *The Advertiser*, 3 August 1966.

21. *The News*, 3 August 1966.
22. *The Advertiser*, 3 August 1966.
23. Leigh Bottrell, *The Herald and Weekly Times*, 8 August 1966.
24. Author's interview with Leigh Bottrell, September 2005.
25. *The Advertiser*, 9 August 1966.
26. *The Advertiser*, 12 September 1966.
27. *The Advertiser*, 12 September 1966.
28. *The Advertiser*, 17 October 1966.
29. Alan Dower, *Deadline*, Hutchinson, Victoria, 1979.
30. *The Advertiser*, 20 September 1966.
31. *The Advertiser*, 30 September 1966.
32. *The Advertiser*, 8 October 1966.
33. *The Advertiser*, 10 October 1966.
34. *The Advertiser*, 10 October 1966.
35. *The Advertiser*, 9 November 1966.
36. *The Advertiser*, 9 November 1966.
37. *The News*, 9 November 1966.
38. *The Advertiser*, 9 November 1966.
39. Jack Harrison Pollard, *Croiset the Clairvoyant: The Story of the Amazing Dutchman*, Doubleday, New York, 1964.

Chapter 5

1. Jack Harrison Pollard, *Croiset the Clairvoyant: The Story of the Amazing Dutchman*, Doubleday, New York, 1964.
2. Jack Harrison Pollard, *Croiset the Clairvoyant: The Story of the Amazing Dutchman*, Doubleday, New York, 1964.
3. Jack Harrison Pollard, *Croiset the Clairvoyant: The Story of the Amazing Dutchman*, Doubleday, New York, 1964.

4. Jack Harrison Pollard, *Croiset the Clairvoyant: The Story of the Amazing Dutchman*, Doubleday, New York, 1964.
5. Jack Harrison Pollard, *Croiset the Clairvoyant: The Story of the Amazing Dutchman*, Doubleday, New York, 1964.
6. Jack Harrison Pollard, *Croiset the Clairvoyant: The Story of the Amazing Dutchman*, Doubleday, New York, 1964.
7. Jack Harrison Pollard, *Croiset the Clairvoyant: The Story of the Amazing Dutchman*, Doubleday, New York, 1964.
8. Jack Harrison Pollard, *Croiset the Clairvoyant: The Story of the Amazing Dutchman*, Doubleday, New York, 1964.
9. *The Advertiser*, 3 August 1966.
10. *The Sun*, 7 November 1966.
11. *The Sun*, 7 November 1966.
12. *The Sun*, 7 November 1966.
13. *The Advertiser*, 10 November 1966.
14. *The Advertiser*, 11 November 1966.
15. *The Advertiser*, 12 November 1966.
16. *The Advertiser*, 12 November 1966.
17. *The Advertiser*, 12 November 1966.
18. *The Advertiser*, 12 November 1966.
19. *The Advertiser*, 13 November 1966.
20. Ryutaro Minakami, *Fabulous Adventures of Gerard Croiset in Japan*, <http://homepage3.nifty.com/kadzuwo/japan/croiset.htm>, viewed October 2005.
21. Willem Tanhaeff, *About Gerard Croiset*, Esotera Magazine, Berlin, September 1980.
22. C. E. M. Hansel, *ESP: A Scientific Evaluation*, Prometheus, Buffalo, 1989.
23. Harry Edwards, *A Sceptic's Guide to the New Age*, Newport, NSW, 2004.

Chapter 6

1. Ken Anderson, Doug Easom and Brian Francis, 'The Beaumont Disclosures' in *The News*, 22 February 1968.
2. Ken Anderson, Doug Easom and Brian Francis, 'The Beaumont Disclosures' in *The News*, 22 February 1968.
3. Ken Anderson, Doug Easom and Brian Francis, 'The Beaumont Disclosures' in *The News*, 22 February 1968.
4. Ken Anderson, Doug Easom and Brian Francis, 'The Beaumont Disclosures' in *The News*, 22 February 1968.
5. Ken Anderson, Doug Easom and Brian Francis, 'The Beaumont Disclosures' in *The News*, 22 February 1968.
6. Ken Anderson, Doug Easom and Brian Francis, 'The Beaumont Disclosures' in *The News*, 22 February 1968.
7. Ken Anderson, Doug Easom and Brian Francis, 'The Beaumont Disclosures' in *The News*, 22 February 1968.
8. *The Advertiser*, 15 November 1966.
9. *The Advertiser*, 16 November 1966.
10. *The Advertiser*, 18 November 1966.
11. *The Advertiser*, 16 November 1966.
12. *The Advertiser*, 27 January 1967.
13. *The Advertiser*, 11 March 1967.
14. *The Advertiser*, 14 March 1967.
15. Alan Dower, *Deadline*, Hutchinson, Victoria, 1979.
16. *The Herald*, 29 February 1968.
17. *The Advertiser*, 29 February 1968.
18. Alan Dower, *Deadline*, Hutchinson, Victoria, 1979.
19. Ken Anderson, Doug Easom and Brian Francis, 'The Beaumont Disclosures' in *The News*, 22 February 1968.
20. Alan Dower, *Deadline*, Hutchinson, Victoria, 1979.
21. Alan Dower, *Deadline*, Hutchinson, Victoria, 1979.

22. Author's interview with Doug Easom, October 2005.
23. Alan Dower, *Deadline*, Hutchinson, Victoria, 1979.
24. Stan Swaine, unpublished writings courtesy of the Swaine family.
25. Alan Dower, *Deadline*, Hutchinson, Victoria, 1979.
26. Alan Dower, *Deadline*, Hutchinson, Victoria, 1979.
27. Alan Dower, *Deadline*, Hutchinson, Victoria, 1979.

Chapter 7
1. Elizabeth Swaine's correspondence with the author, December 2005.
2. *The Advertiser*, 2 August 1990.
3. *The Advertiser*, August 1990.
4. All other quotes from other members of the Swaine family are from the author's interviews in Adelaide in July 2005.
5. *The Advertiser*, 2 August 1990.
6. Elizabeth Swaine's correspondence with the author, December 2005.
7. Stan Swaine, unpublished writings courtesy of the Swaine family.
8. Elizabeth Swaine's correspondence with the author, December 2005.
9. Elizabeth Swaine's correspondence with the author, December 2005.
10. Penelope Green, 'Vanished', *Who Weekly*, 22 January 2001.
11. Stan Swaine, unpublished writings courtesy of the Swaine family.
12. Elizabeth Swaine's correspondence with the author, December 2005.

Chapter 8

1. *The Advertiser*, 27 August 1973.
2. *The Advertiser*, 27 August 1973.
3. *The Advertiser*, 28 August 1973.
4. *The Advertiser*, 28 August 1973.
5. *The Advertiser*, 28 August 1973.
6. *The Advertiser*, 28 August 1973.
7. *The Advertiser*, 27 August 1973.
8. *The Advertiser*, 28 August 1973.
9. *The Advertiser*, 28 August 1973.
10. *The Advertiser*, 29 August 1973.
11. *The Advertiser*, 7 September 1973.
12. *The Advertiser*, 28 August 1973.
13. *The Advertiser*, 28 August 1973.
14. *The Advertiser*, 28 August 1973.
15. *The Advertiser*, 31 August 1973.
16. *The Advertiser*, 31 August 1973.
17. *The Advertiser*, 31 August 1973.
18. *The Advertiser*, 31 August 1973.
19. *The Advertiser*, 28 August 1973.
20. *The Advertiser*, 1 September 1973.
21. *The Advertiser*, 30 August 1973.
22. *The Advertiser*, 10 July, 1979.
23. Timothy Hall, *Wanted: A Casebook of Unsolved Crimes of Violence in Australia*, Angus & Robertson, Sydney, 1976.
24. *The Advertiser*, 2 May 1974.
25. *The Advertiser*, 6 July 1974.
26. *The Advertiser*, 6 July 1974.
27. *The Advertiser*, 26 July 1978.
28. *The Advertiser*, 26 July 1978.

29. *The Advertiser*, 7 August, 1978.
30. *The Advertiser*, 13 October 1977.
31. *The Advertiser*, 25 July 1979.
32. *The Advertiser*, 25 July 1979.
33. *The Advertiser*, 6 February, 1981.
34. *The Advertiser*, 6 February, 1981.
35. Author's interview with Brian Swan, July 2005.
36. Author's interview with Peter Alexander, July 2005.

Chapter 9

1. *The Advertiser*, 17 March 1990
2. Bob O'Brien, *Young Blood: The Story of the Family Murders*, HarperCollins, Sydney, 2002.
3. Bob O'Brien, *Young Blood: The Story of the Family Murder*, HarperCollins, Sydney, 2002.
4. Bob O'Brien, *Young Blood: The Story of the Family Murders*, HarperCollins, Sydney, 2002.
5. *The Advertiser*, 11 May 1990.
6. Bob O'Brien, *Young Blood: The Story of the Family Murders*, HarperCollins, Sydney, 2002.
7. Bob O'Brien, *Young Blood: The Story of the Family Murders*, HarperCollins, Sydney, 2002.
8. *The Advertiser*, 8 February 1990.
9. *The Advertiser*, 17 March 1990.
10. *The Advertiser*, 17 March 1990.
11. *The Advertiser*, 17 March 1990.
12. *The Advertiser*, 17 March 1990.
13. *The Advertiser*, 11 May 1990.
14. *The Advertiser*, 11 May 1990.
15. *The Advertiser*, 11 May 1990.

16. *The Advertiser,* 17 March 1990.
17. *The Advertiser,* 11 May 1990.
18. *The Advertiser,* 11 May 1990.
19. *The Advertiser,* 11 May 1990.
20. *The Advertiser,* 11 May 1990.
21. *The Advertiser,* 19 June 1990.
22. *The Advertiser,* 3 December 1990.
23. *The Advertiser,* 3 December 1990.
24. Bob O'Brien, *Young Blood: The Story of the Family Murders,* HarperCollins, Sydney, 2002.
25. *The Advertiser,* 8 September 2001.

Chapter 10

1. Ian Mackay, 'Beaumonts Keep Their Optimism', *The Advertiser,* 26 January 1967.
2. Ian Mackay, 'Beaumonts Keep Their Optimism', *The Advertiser,* 26 January 1967.
3. Ian Mackay, 'Beaumonts Keep Their Optimism', *The Advertiser,* 26 January 1967.
4. Ian Mackay, 'Beaumonts Keep Their Optimism', *The Advertiser,* 26 January 1967.
5. Ian Mackay, 'Beaumonts Keep Their Optimism', *The Advertiser,* 26 January 1967.
6. Tom Prior, *The Sinners' Club,* Penguin, Melbourne, 1993.
7. Ian Mackay, 'Beaumonts Keep Their Optimism', *The Advertiser,* 26 January 1967.
8. Ian Mackay, 'Beaumonts Keep Their Optimism', *The Advertiser,* 26 January 1967.
9. John Pinkney, *Great Australian Mysteries,* Five Mile Press, Melbourne, 2003.

10. Letters to the Editor, *The Advertiser*, 9 December 1981.

11. *The Advertiser*, 15 January 1985.

12. *The Advertiser*, 12 March 1986.

13. *The Advertiser*, 23 January 1986.

14. *The Advertiser*, 23 January 1986.

15. *The Advertiser*, 15 March 1990.

16. *The Advertiser*, 28 May 1990.

17. Deborah Tideman, 'Are the Beaumonts Still Alive?', *The Advertiser*, 23 February 1990.

18. *The Advertiser*, 24 February 1990.

19. *The Advertiser*, 1 June 1992.

20. *The Advertiser*, 6 June 1992.

21. *The Advertiser*, 6 August 1997.

22. Penelope Green, 'Vanished', *Who Weekly*, 22 January 2001.

23. Tom Prior, *The Sinners' Club*, Penguin, Melbourne, 1993.

24. Penelope Debelle, 'The Beaumonts 30 Years On', *The Advertiser*, 16 December 1995.

25. Tom Prior, *The Sinners' Club*, Penguin, Melbourne, 1993.

26. *The Advertiser*, 26 May 1996.

27. *The Advertiser*, 28 January 1978.

28. *The Advertiser*, 16 December 1995.

29. Shane Maguire, 'The Hunt for a Tragic Answer', *The Sunday Mail*, 30 June 1996.

30. Jenny Brown, 'Solving the Beaumont Mystery', *Woman's Day*, 31 January 2005.

31. Jenny Brown, 'Solving the Beaumont Mystery,' *Woman's Day*, 31 January 2005.

32. Stuart Coupe and Julie Ogden, *Case Reopened*, Allen & Unwin, Sydney, 1993.

33. Tom Prior, *The Sinners' Club,* Penguin, Melbourne, 1993.
34. Andrew Rule, *Where Were You When*, News Custom Publishing, Melbourne, 2003.
35. *The Advertiser,* 28 June 1995
36. Beth Spencer, '101 Degrees', ABC Radio National's *Radio Eye*, 1997.

Chapter 11

1. *The Sunday Mail,* 24 October 2005.
2. Margaret Parker and Tim Parker, 'Unsolved Murders', *Who Weekly,* 11 December 1995.
3. Penelope Debelle, 'Case Not Closed', *The Advertiser,* 18 December 1995.
4. Margaret Parker and Tim Parker, 'Unsolved Murders', *Who Weekly,* 11 December 1995.
5. Penelope Debelle, 'Case Not Closed', *The Advertiser,* 18 December 1995.
6. Margaret Parker and Tim Parker, 'Unsolved Murders', *Who Weekly,* 11 December 1995
7. Margaret Parker and Tim Parker, 'Unsolved Murders', *Who Weekly,* 11 December 1995.
8. *The Sunday Mail,* 9 February 1997.
9. *The Advertiser,* 18 May 2004.
10. *The Advertiser,* 23 May 2004.
11. *The Advertiser,* 20 May 2004.
12. Official résumé of the Beaumont Case, courtesy of the South Australia Police.
13. Author's interview with Peter Woite and Brian Swan, July 2005.

14. *The Advertiser*, 5 December 1998.

15. Unreported Judgements: *The Herald & Weekly Times Ltd v The Attorney General (Victoria)*, 20–21 June 2000 and 7 September 2001, www.butterworthsonline.com

16. Unreported Judgements: *The Herald & Weekly Times Ltd v The Attorney General (Victoria)*, 20–21 June 2000 and 7 September 2001, www.butterworthsonline.com

17. Timothy Hall, *Wanted: A Casebook of Unsolved Crimes of Violence in Australia*, Angus & Robertson, Sydney, 1976.

18. Unreported Judgements: *The Herald & Weekly Times Ltd v The Attorney General (Victoria)*, 20–21 June 2000 and 7 September 2001, www.butterworthsonline.com

19. *The Advertiser*, 26 January 2005.

20. *The Advertiser*, 12 November 1998.

21. Robert Ressler and Thomas Schachtman, *Whoever Fights Monsters*, St Martin's Paperbacks, New York, 1993.

22. Margaret Parker and Tim Parker, 'Unsolved Murders', *Who Weekly*, 11 December 1995.

23. Margaret Parker and Tim Parker, 'Unsolved Murders', *Who Weekly*, 11 December 1995.

24. W. H. Jeanes, *Historic Glenelg: Birthplace of South Australia*, Glenelg Council, 1979.

25. Psalm 139:8–10, The Bible.

Appendix

The Beaumont children mystery — a timeline of events (1956–2006)

1956

10 September   Jane Nartare Beaumont, the eldest daughter of Jim and Nancy Beaumont, is born.

1958

11 November   Arnna Kathleen Beaumont is born.

1961

12 July   Grant Ellis Beaumont is born.

1966

26 January   Jane, Arnna and Grant Beaumont travel to Glenelg beach, southwest of Adelaide, at 10 am. They are reported missing by their parents that evening.

27 January   Police begin searching Glenelg and Brighton beaches and the surrounding esplanade. ADS7 sets up a mobile broadcast studio to transmit updates of the search.

28 January	First descriptions of the children are published: their clothing, ages and final movements.
29 January	A £500 reward is posted by the South Australian government. First clue is provided by a 74-year-old woman, who saw the children playing under the sprinklers with a tall, thirty-year-old man.
31 January	Adelaide *Advertiser* artist Peter von Czarnecki provides first sketch of the main suspect.
2 February	Police conduct a house-to-house search for the missing children. An elderly couple tell police they had a conversation with the man seen with the Beaumonts at Glenelg.
3 February	Patawalonga boat haven is drained and searched for the bodies of the missing children.
4 February	Two men are prosecuted for false reports regarding the whereabouts of the missing children.
11 February	Retired Sydney detective Ray Kelly arrives in Adelaide to help the Beaumont investigation. He leaves after just one day.
16 February	The Suburban Taxi Service announces the foundation of a public fund to support the Beaumont family.

18 February	Hobart police launch a search for a man in the Sandy Bay area who fits the description of the Beaumont suspect.
23 February	Twelve police cadets search Marion Council dump after a man reports he has found a 'shallow grave'. Nothing is found during a three-day search.
12 March	Life-size models of the three missing children in the clothes they wore to Glenelg beach are exhibited at the Sydney Easter Show.
14 March	For the first time, police acknowledge the theory that the children knew their abductor.
19 April	Scotland Yard contact South Australian detectives working on the Beaumont Case to obtain assistance in their investigation into the murders of two children in Staffordshire.
15 July	The total reward for information regarding the missing children is raised to $10 100 after Adelaide businessman Barry Blackwell donates $2000.
1 August	Dutch clairvoyant Gerard Croiset is consulted for the first time and says the children are 'buried in a cave'. He asks for film and photographs of Glenelg to be sent to him in Holland.

7 August	Croiset states that the children 'lie buried in sand two kilometres from where they were seen near a merry-go-round at Glenelg beach'.
9 August	Civilian volunteers resume searching the Glenelg and Brighton areas following the revelations by Gerard Croiset.
25 September	Dr D. B. Hendrickson contacts Croiset and informs the clairvoyant of diggings he has carried out on the grounds of the Minda Home at Brighton. Croiset tells Hendrickson that he is 'close'.
28 September	Kaniva policeman Senior Constable Bob Grose overhears a telephone conversation in which the Beaumont children are said to be returning from Hobart.
10 October	After South Australia Police say that the reference to the Beaumonts in the Kaniva phone call was not a hoax, Jim Beaumont and Brian Taylor travel to Kaniva to investigate.
10 October	The grounds of the Minda Home in Brighton are nominated as the children's burial site by alleged clairvoyant Gerard Croiset.
12 October	Two South Australian women come forward and prove the 'Kaniva' connection was misinterpreted. They were in fact talking about family friends.

8 November	Dutch clairvoyant Gerard Croiset arrives in Adelaide. He begins retracing the children's final steps through Glenelg the following day.
10 November	Croiset investigates the Minda Home for clues of the children's whereabouts but fails to nominate any one spot.
11 November	Croiset announces that the remains of children are buried under the floor of a warehouse in the Adelaide suburb of Paringa Park. He flies out of the country that day.
15 November	South Australian Premier Frank Walsh announces that his government will not subsidise the excavation of the Paringa Park warehouse.

1967

26 January	On the first anniversary of the children's disappearance, a citizen's action committee announces plans to raise funds to excavate the Paringa Park warehouse.
1 March	Excavation begins on the floor of the Paringa Park warehouse.
8 March	Rubbish found in one of the cavities under the floor of the warehouse is ruled out of having anything to do with the missing children.

10 March	Excavation of the floor of the warehouse finishes, with no signs of the Beaumont children.
7 September	Adelaide detectives deny that they are investigating a former mental patient from Glenside Hospital in relation to the whereabouts of the missing children.

1968

5 January	Surplus money raised to excavate the Paringa Park warehouse by a citizens action committee is donated to charity.
26 February	Detective Sergeant Stan Swaine accompanies Jim and Nancy Beaumont to Dandenong in order to meet a man who says he is going to return their children. Nothing happens.
18 March	Police abandon a search on Mud Island in Port Phillip Bay, eighty kilometres south of Melbourne, after investigating an anonymous letter.
3 April	Police search a scout camp at Anglesea, near Geelong, Victoria, after a woman reports a possible gravesite. It turns out to be a mound of rubbish.
20 September	The crew of the Australian freighter *Devon* are questioned in Auckland, New Zealand.

The ship was docked in Adelaide when the Beaumont children went missing, and later in Melbourne when a young girl disappeared.

1970

12 April   Melbourne police question a convicted murderer, 21-year-old Derek Percy, about the Wanda Beach Murders (1965) and the disappearance of the Beaumont children.

1971

30 January   South Australia Police search vacant land at O'Halloran Hill after a tip-off about the Beaumont children.

1972

10 May   Dr George Duncan, a gay university lecturer, drowns after being bashed and thrown into the Torrens by several men. Another man is rescued by a passer-by: 26-year-old accountant Bevan von Einem.

1973

25 August   Eleven-year-old Joanne Ratcliffe and four-year-old Kirste Gordon are abducted from Adelaide Oval by an unknown man during an Australian Rules match.

28 August	First report links the disappearance of two young girls from Adelaide Oval to the Beaumont Case seven years before.
1 September	An artist's sketch of the man seen walking from Adelaide Oval with the two missing girls bears an uncanny resemblance to the suspect seen with the three Beaumont children at Glenelg beach in 1966.

1974

6 July	Gerard Croiset Junior, the son of the Dutch clairvoyant who came to Adelaide to search for the Beaumont children in 1966, predicts that the man who abducted the two girls from Adelaide Oval will strike again 'within 16 days'. He is wrong.

1978

28 January	Following the twelfth anniversary of the Beaumont children's disappearance, real estate millionaire Con Polites advocates the further excavation of the Paringa Park warehouse.
26 July	After speaking to British spiritualist Doris Stokes, Les Ratcliffe believes he knows the name of the man who took his daughter and where her remains are buried.

31 July	Gerard Croiset Junior visits Adelaide and vows to solve the five-year-old Ratcliffe–Gordon disappearance from Adelaide Oval.

1979

10 July	A coronial inquest hears that Adelaide Oval officials refused to broadcast that the two girls were missing during an Australian Rules match in 1973.

1980

14 December	In an interview with journalist Dick Wordley, Les Ratcliffe reveals that he is dying of cancer and asks his daughter's abductor to contact him. He hears nothing.

1981

1 February	Les Ratcliffe, the father of one of the girls abducted from Adelaide Oval in 1973, dies of cancer. Before his death he pens an open letter to the people of Adelaide not to forget its missing children.
2 December	Police investigate reports by a woman claiming that she played with the three Beaumont children on the day they disappeared and knows why they left the beach. No new evidence is uncovered.

7 December	South Australian detectives allow forensic examination of the Dandenong Letters, allegedly written by Jane Beaumont to her parents in 1968.

1983

4 January	Ten-year-old Louise Bell is abducted from her Hackham West home in Adelaide. No trace of the child is found, despite an extensive search.
24 July	The body of fifteen-year-old Richard Kelvin is found seven weeks after he went missing from a public bus stop in Adelaide. Kelvin had been dead only two weeks and had obviously been kept alive by his abductor.
3 November	Bevan Spencer von Einem is arrested for the murder of Richard Kelvin and is suspected of being involved in the deaths of four other young men since 1979.

1985

12 January	A Western Australian woman claims that three children living in Kalgoorlie in the late 1960s were the missing Beaumonts. Police rule out the claim after they identify the people, now living in Geraldton, Western Australia.

1986

12 March	Council workers find a file of newspaper clippings related to the Beaumont Case. Police investigate when annotations on the clippings comment where the children's bodies may be buried.
13 March	An Adelaide family comes forward and says that they dumped the annotated news clippings. They belonged to a woman who was obsessed by the case.

1990

2 February	Major Crime Squad detectives and members of the Underwater Recovery Unit search the Myponga Reservoir but refuse to confirm or deny that they are looking for the remains of the Beaumont children.
23 February	Journalist Dick Wordley says that the postal worker who spoke to Jim Beaumont in Dandenong in 1968 may hold the key to the mystery of the fate of the three children.
24 February	Former homicide detective Jack Zeunert states that a religious sect operated in the Adelaide Hills in the 1970s and it was not unreasonable to suggest that children could have been kidnapped or handed over to it.

17 March	Suppression orders are lifted during the trial of Bevan von Einem stating that he was responsible for as many as ten murders, including the Beaumont and the Adelaide Oval victims, and that their bodies were dumped at Myponga Reservoir.
27 March	Adelaide clairvoyant June Cox says she knows the burial place of the Beaumont children as well as Joanne Ratcliffe and Kirste Gordon. Although she tells police the 'children were calling her', nothing is found.
28 May	*The News* computer artist Bette Clarke digitally ages photos of the three Beaumont children in order to determine what they would look like if they were still alive.

1992

| 6 June | A Melbourne man, who was seventeen in 1968, admits that he sent the Dandenong Letters to Jim and Nancy Beaumont. Advances in fingerprint technology had identified the man. |
| 7 October | Rhianna Barreau, aged twelve, is taken from her Morphett Vale, Adelaide, home. |

1995

16 December	Adelaide millionaire Con Polites advocates the use of sonar equipment to solve the mystery of the Paringa Park warehouse once and for all.

1996

26 January	Dame Idina Probyn uses the thirtieth anniversary of the children's disappearance to appeal for further excavation of the warehouse. She believes the children went there 'for a picnic' and were accidentally buried.
1 May	Workmen begin drilling the cement floor of the Paringa Park warehouse searching for signs of the Beaumont children. The dig lasts almost five months but no new evidence is found.
26 May	Former South Australian Deputy Commissioner Geoffrey Leane, who died in 1990, revealed to his family that the Beaumont children were abducted and their remains discovered in an abandoned shipping container in an overseas port. South Australia Police dismiss the claims.

1997

2 February	Bones found behind a Glenelg service station in Brighton Road are proven to be animal bones.

6 August   Ex-detective Stan Swaine declares that
                        the Beaumont children were handed
                        over to a cult and that he has found Jane
                        living in Canberra. The woman later takes
                        out an AVO against the Adelaide
                        investigator.

1998

5 December   An 86-year-old Queensland man, Arthur
                        Brown, is charged with the murders of
                        Judith and Susan Mackay in Townsville in
                        1970. Brown resembles the suspects in the
                        Beaumont (1966) and Adelaide Oval
                        (1973) cases but all charges are dropped
                        against him because of his age.

2000

8 November   Sales consultant Trevor Terrell discovers
                        the bones of three small children under
                        floorboards in his 1910 cottage in the
                        Adelaide suburb of Queenstown. They are
                        found to be the remains of premature
                        babies.

2004

12 May   Police in New Zealand investigate a man's
                        claims that the Beaumont children were
                        kidnapped and raised in Dunedin. The
                        Australian media latches onto the story.

14 May	Victorian police confirm that they are reinvestigating the movements of murderer Derek Percy, jailed in 1970, in regard to several unsolved crimes, including the Beaumont children. Percy was only aged sixteen in 1966 and cannot be placed at Glenelg.
23 May	New Zealand Police rule out any suggestion that locals Judith Hewitt and Albert Larson are the missing Beaumont children. Both have New Zealand birth certificates.

2005

December	The Paringa Park warehouse is demolished and further excavation is carried out. No evidence of the Beaumont children is found.

2006

26 January	The fortieth anniversary of the disappearance of the three Beaumont children from Glenelg beach.

Index

Made in the USA
Monee, IL
30 April 2021

67320050R00181